RECORDS FROM UR AND LARSA DATED IN THE LARSA DYNASTY

BY

ETTALENE MEARS GRICE, Ph.D.

MEMBER OF THE YALE BABYLONIAN SEMINARY

WIPF & STOCK · Eugene, Oregon

Wipf and Stock Publishers
199 W 8th Ave, Suite 3
Eugene, OR 97401

Records from Ur and Larsa Dated in the Larsa Dynasty
By Grice, Ettalene Mears
ISBN 13: 978-1-55635-951-4
Publication date 4/11/2008
Previously published by Yale University Press, 1919

To My Teacher

PROFESSOR ALBERT T. CLAY, Ph.D., LL.D., Litt.D.

in

Grateful Appreciation

PREFACE.

The Yale Babylonian Collection contains at the present time about ten thousand tablets, about half of them belonging to the period usually referred to as that of the First Dynasty of Babylon, in the latter part of the third millennium B. C. A large number of the Yale texts are dated in the Larsa Dynasty, whose power in Babylonia was brought to an end by Ḫammurabi's conquest of this kingdom. The kings of Larsa and the length of their reigns are known from the dynastic tablet published in 1915 in *Miscellaneous Inscriptions in the Yale Babylonian Collection* (Yale Oriental Series, Babylonian Texts, Vol. I).

In this large collection of texts of this period there is a group of one hundred and thirty-six which were found at Mugheir, or Muqayyar, on the site of the ancient city of Ur. The first one hundred and ten texts in the present volume have been selected from this group, and form the first considerable number of texts to be published from this site.

The remaining one hundred and forty-three texts have been selected from the large number of tablets in the Yale Babylonian Collection coming from Senkereh, the site of the ancient city of Larsa (the Biblical Ellasar of Gen. 14:1). The texts in this second group have been chosen with the purpose of collecting the data offered by the Yale tablets for a study of the Dynasty of Larsa, which covers a period of more than two hundred and fifty years in the latter part of the third millennium B. C., and which was for a time the ruling power in southern Babylonia, until its sovereignty was brought to an end by the rise of Babylon and the conquest of Larsa by Ḫammurabi, the great king and lawgiver of Babylon (called in Gen. 14:1 Amraphel, king of Shinar).

An attempt has been made to include most of the valuable texts in the Yale Collection which are dated in the reigns of the Larsa kings previous to the beginning of the reign of Rîm-Sin, the last king of the dynasty (who is regarded by some as Arioch, king of Ellasar, mentioned in Gen. 14:1). To these have been added one text of each of the first thirty years of Rîm-Sin's reign, and a few texts containing representative date formulæ of the last thirty-one years of his reign, a period which was known as the Isin era because the dates refer to the number of years after the fall of the city of Isin, an event which marked the rise of Larsa to the suzerainty of southern Babylonia. In some cases where no complete or unmutilated date could be found, it has been necessary to copy more than one text of a given year of Rîm-Sin. In a few cases, where tablets were badly injured, or where they were so large that they would have required too much space, only the date formulæ have been copied. There have also been included a larger number of texts of four of the years of Rîm-Sin, probably the fifth year to the eighth year inclusive, two of which are designated by formulæ which have hitherto been regarded as of Sin-idinnam.

I desire to express my gratitude and appreciation to Professor Albert T. Clay, under whose direction I have been permitted to study, for his unfailing kindness and generosity in making my work possible. I take this opportunity of expressing my thanks also to Professor Charles C. Torrey, Professor George A. Barton, Dr. James B. Nies, and Dr. Clarence E. Keiser, a member of the Yale Babylonian Seminary, for valuable help and suggestions. It gives me pleasure to thank also in this way my friend Deaconess Ethel Percy, who has devoted much time and labor to assisting me with tedious details in connection with my manuscript, as well as Miss Lucile Graham, who kindly assisted in arranging the catalogue of the texts.

ETTALENE M. GRICE.

NEW HAVEN, JUNE, 1918.

CONTENTS.

RECORDS FROM UR AND LARSA DATED IN THE LARSA DYNASTY

INTRODUCTION.

There are two kinds of business documents in this volume, Nos. 106–149, 242, and 253 being legal contracts, the rest being temple records of various kinds, from brief notes to elaborate inventories.

The contracts include deeds for lands or houses; promissory notes for grain, oil, or silver; partition contracts; and agreements regarding the sale or hire of slaves;—No. 135 even recording the purchase of the right to serve as priest for five days. (For a full description of the contents, see the Catalogue.)

The temple records cover a great variety of subjects, including inventories of the large flocks of sheep which belonged to the temples, and records concerning receipts at the temple or payments from the temple property, referring to gold, silver, dates, wool, grain, bitumen, etc. Hardly any two of them are of exactly the same nature.

Nearly all the texts in the volume are written in Sumerian, or in a mixture of Sumerian and Semitic in which Sumerian predominates. Yet there are a few exceptions to the rule, Nos. 90, 108, 110, 179, 224 (?), 231, 234, and 239, for example, being Semitic except for the date formulæ.

It is interesting to note that some of the numerals were probably called by their Semitic names. For in the texts from Ur the scribes occasionally wrote in full the Semitic loan-words for 1000, *li-im* (Nos. 19:30; 30:39); 100, *me-at* or *me-a-at* (Nos. 5 VII:17; 19:32, 33; 30:39); and 60, *šú-ši* (5:8, 32; 7:9; 101:1). In the Larsa tablets the totals are occasionally named in a similar way, though for 1000 the sign *li* is used, for 100 the sign *me*. (See Nos. 196:9; 208 III:13, 19; IV:2; 212:69, etc.)

The texts from Ur are nearly all official records from the principal temple of the city, *Ê-nun-maḫ*, the temple of the moon-god Nannar or Sin and his consort Ningal. But there are five contracts, Nos. 106–110, which are similar to the contracts from Larsa. No. 98 is possibly an exercise tablet. On any other hypothesis it would be difficult to understand the large number of erasures and the fact that the salutation of a letter appears on one side of a tablet the other side of which contains a list of women's names. This text, together with No. 105, an exercise tablet containing names of places, suggests that there was probably a temple school at Ur like the one at Nippur. The many exercise tablets among the large collection of tablets from Larsa in the Yale Babylonian Collection proves the existence of such a school at Larsa. It seems likely that there were schools in connection with all the principal temples in Babylonia. The Larsa texts are similar in general character to those from Ur, though somewhat more varied in form and subject matter.

Several different standard weights are mentioned among the texts. In the Larsa texts are used the standard of the merchants (No. 154:2, 6, 8, 11) and the standard of the temple of Nannar (No. 122:11). In No. 15 I:3, from Ur, the standard shekel is that of the god Nannar, in No. 69:3, that of the sun-god Babbar or Shamash, the patron god of Larsa. The use in Ur of the standard weight of Shamash and of the date formulæ of the Larsa Dynasty is due to the fact that the documents were written at a period when Ur was not independent, but was subject to its neighboring city of Larsa.

Seven texts, Nos. 33, 46, 47, 50–53, record the delivery of sheep to ^{lu}*SA-GAZ*, the ideogram used in the Amarna letters for the Ḫabiri. Perhaps the *SA-GAZ* of these texts may have been mercenary soldiers, according to the suggestion of Scheil in the *Revue d'Assyriologie* XII, pp. 114, 115.

The purpose of the series being mainly the presentation of the texts that they may be accessible to scholars, a full discussion of the texts, transliterations, and translations are omitted. Nevertheless certain points of unusual interest may be briefly mentioned.

A list of gods, including also some epithets, is included for the convenience of those who are interested in the study of the gods of the period. In any effort to use the texts in the present volume to determine the gods most venerated in southern Babylonia during the latter part of the Larsa Dynasty, it should be remembered that Texts 1–110 are from Ur, according to both the testimony of those from whom they were bought, and the contents of the texts themselves; while Nos. 111–253 are for the most part from Larsa. It is noteworthy that the personal names contain West-Semitic gods. These gods, and other Amorite elements in the personal names, show that there were at this time many Western Semites in southern Babylonia, as well as in Babylon and other cities farther north. Still more interesting is the fact that the god Marduk, who a few years later was made by Ḫammurabi the head of the Babylonian pantheon, is not once mentioned in these texts. In spite of the fact, shown by the variety of gods in the names, that the people of Ur and Larsa had wide intercourse with other cities and countries, they had not yet felt the quietly growing power of Babylon, which within a few years was raised by its great king Ḫammurabi to a position of such importance that its name was given to the entire land.

It has been very difficult to identify with any of the signs which were commonly used to describe lambs, the sign , found after *sal-síl* and *síl* in most of the lists of sheep. On account of the frequency with which the sign appears (*sal-síl* and *síl* are, next to *ganam* and *udu-nita,* by far the most numerous kinds of sheep in the lists), it must refer to some very common variety of sheep. The form, together with the facts that *nu-ŭr,* a term which appears constantly in the lists of flocks of the period of the Ur Dynasty, is not found in these Larsa Dynasty lists, and that *sal-síl* and *síl-* are mentioned in the lists between the full-grown animals, *ganam* and *udu-nita,* and the sucklings, *sal-síl-ga* and *síl-ga,* leads us to conjecture that this sign is a ligature for *nu-ŭr,* and means "sterile" or "immature." As evidence that ligatures for familiar phrases were actually in use, we may refer to the expression *lal-ni,* "balance," which is always written as a ligature. See Nos. 13:1, 23; 58:7; 168:12; 209:4; etc.

The writing of *guškin,* "gold," in these texts, varies. More commonly than the ordinary *AZAG-GI* is used *AZAG-ZI.* (See Nos. 41:11; 45:7; 140:24; 168:22; *et multa.* Compare in these texts the forms of *GI* and *ZI* used in other connections.) Occasionally we have instead *AZAG-MU.* (Nos. 114:17; 124:26.) The variation may have arisen from the general similarity of the three signs *GI, ZI,* and *MU,* or it may be that we have here variants of the *GI* sign. An analogous example of the wide latitude regarding the making of signs in this period is seen in the sign registered as *LAGAB+KUL* in the ideogram for bitumen (Brünnow 11673, 11674). See Nos. 90:2, 4; 231:1, 2, etc.; 234:1, 6, etc.; 239:1, 2.

The sign *e* has the value *rabû,* "to be great." In such passages as Nos. 13:18; 15 I:5; 193:8; 207:7; etc., it must mean "be as great as," "be worth."

The fact that occasionally the names of certain kinds of sheep are included in the inventories of flocks, with blanks before these names indicating that there were no sheep of these kinds in the flocks there listed (see Nos. 5 II:2, 4, 20, 22; IV:2, 4; V:2, 4; 6 II:21, 22) leads us to believe that the scribe copied a regular form, as was done in the Cassite Period. (See Clay, *Bab. Exp.* XV, pp. 96, 111.)

The diagonal marks in No. 15 were not for the purpose of cancellation, because the text is beautifully preserved, and was found in the archives. Perhaps they take the place of check marks,[1] such as those marking separate items in YBC 7260, etc. The marks on Nos. 31, 32, etc., were probably caused by their being tied to objects.

Because of the number and the character of the many Yale texts from Larsa which refer to a certain Balmunamḫe, we are led to believe that he was a prominent business man of the city whose private archive has been unearthed. This seems to be indicated by the Yale texts in the present volume, in twenty-five of which he

[1] See Clay, *Bab. Exp.* XIV, p. 16.

appears, not as a witness, but as an active party to the transactions.[1] Ten of these texts record his purchase or exchange of lands or houses; in six he appears as the purchaser or owner of slaves; in four he lends grain or silver; in two he is mentioned as the official in charge; in three he is represented as the owner of property, one of these texts (No. 132) being a tax receipt. It is to be noted that in Nos. 122 and 181 he is mentioned with his father, Sin-nûr-matim. The documents recording all these transactions are such as a business man would keep among his own records, while those recording his selling property or borrowing money would have been kept by the other party to the contract. His activity was continued during a long period, for his name occurs on Yale documents from the reign of Warad-Sin and throughout the reign of Rîm-Sin, the latest which has been observed (YBC 6756) being dated in the forty-second year of Ḫammurabi.

A very common form of the oath formula in contracts from Ur and Larsa of the Larsa Dynasty is like that of the contracts from Nippur of the same period (see Chiera, *Legal Documents from Nippur*, p. 18), *mu lugal-bi*. Yet there is some variation in the Ur and Larsa contracts. Of the contracts among the present texts, sixteen have no oath formula, thirteen have *mu lugal-bi*, six have *mu ^{d}Nannar ^{d}Babbar ù* (the name of the king) *lugal*. Two case tablets, Nos. 121, 125, have *mu Warad-^{d}Sín lugal* on the case and *mu lugal-bi* on the tablet, while a third case tablet has *mu lugal-bi* in both places. No. 130 has *mu Warad-^{d}Sín lugal*, No. 124 has the oath by two kings, Warad-Sin of Larsa and Sin-iribam of Erech,[2] while in No. 127 the oath is by Warad-Sin and his father, Kudur-Mabuk. With the data at hand it is possible to come to no conclusion other than that at Ur and Larsa there was no adherence to a single stereotyped form of oath.

THE DATE FORMULÆ.

The chief importance of the texts assigned for publication here lies in the historical data furnished by the date formulæ. The full discussion of the chronological material of these and other texts of the Larsa Dynasty is to be found in the monograph entitled "Chronology of the Larsa Dynasty" (*Yale Oriental Series, Researches*, Vol. IV, Part 1); it seems appropriate, however, to mention here a few facts concerning the new chronological material of this volume. For the names of the kings and the length of their reigns, see the dynastic tablet published in Clay, *Miscellaneous Inscriptions*, p. 30 f.

[1] See List of Personal Names for references.

[2] This new king of Erech, who bears the same name as one of the kings of Larsa, is of especial interest.

All the texts in the volume which can be placed with certainty are from the time of seven rulers of the Larsa Dynasty, from Nûr-IM to Rîm-Sin. About twenty of the date formulæ have not appeared before, others enable us to expand or correct the readings of formulæ which have been previously published.

In the first number of the *Revue d'Assyriologie* for 1918, Thureau-Dangin will publish the inscription of a four-sided prism which if uninjured would have given a complete scheme of the Larsa Dynasty. In its perfect form, it gave for the first four rulers only the length of their reigns; beginning with the fifth king, it gave the formula for each year, to the end of Rîm-Sin's reign. The lengths of the reigns of the first four kings, which are broken from the prism, can be supplied from the Yale dynastic list, mentioned above. Unfortunately the second face of the prism is entirely destroyed, and the inscription is otherwise considerably injured. An advance copy of most of the text, which has been kindly sent by Thureau-Dangin, shows that there are preserved more or less complete formulæ for the years from the beginning of Gungunu through the twenty-fifth year of Sumu-ilu, and from the seventh[1] year of Rîm-Sin to the close of his reign. In contrast to most date-lists, the prism gives full formulæ, several of those of Rîm-Sin occupying six or seven lines each. There is thus one gap of about fifty-four years, which together with the many fragmentary formulæ of the prism, must be supplied, as far as possible, from dated documents of the period.

Of the fifty-four years which are missing from the Louvre prism, twenty-nine have been restored, some of them tentatively, from published texts or new formulæ from Yale tablets. Several unidentified formulæ of the Larsa Dynasty probably belong also in this gap, but cannot be definitely placed until more evidence is discovered. (See Catalogue.)

Though according to the dynastic list published by Professor Clay, Ṣili-IM reigned only one year, two date formulæ mention him. Besides the usual formula for his first year (see No. 117), eight texts[2] are dated *mu Ṣi-lí-*^{d}*IM nam-lugal-ta sír-ra.* Since *sír* has the value *nasâḫu,* "to wrench out," the meaning is probably "The year when Ṣili-IM was deposed from the kingship." Since all the texts which bear this year-name are dated in the twelfth month, while the one which refers to Ṣili-IM's first year was dated in the ninth month, it seems reasonable to suppose,

[1] Since the total number of years in the reign is given by the prism as sixty, whereas the Yale dynastic list gives sixty-one, the testimony of the prism would be that the first formula on the fourth face of the prism is that of the sixth year. However, since there are two formulæ of Rîm-Sin for which there is no place in his reign except the fifth and sixth years, it seems best to regard the number of years given by the Yale tablet as correct.

[2] Nos. 8–11, 54–57.

accordingly, that Kudur-Mabuk conquered Larsa and placed his son Warad-Sin on the throne during the last four months of the year; and that he preferred not to change the year-name entirely, but allowed it still to contain the name of Ṣili-IM, stating that he was no longer king. In this case "The year when Ṣili-IM was deposed from the kingship" might be called the accession year of Warad-Sin, as distinguished from his first (complete) year, a terminology used in the Neo-Babylonian Period.

A new formula, found on twenty-two Yale texts, reads more or less fully "The year when he built the lofty platform for the temple of Shamash in Larsa." This is proved to be of Warad-Sin, not in the usual way by the mention of the king in the date or the oath formula, but by the seal impression. No. 165 states that it is sealed with the seal of the king. The seal impression has slight traces of a standing figure, and a clear inscription: "Warad-Sin, king of Larsa, son of Kudur-Mabuk." From this no conclusion can be drawn other than that the new formula is of Warad-Sin.

The greatest single contribution furnished by the temple records to our knowledge of the chronology of the dynasty is given by Nos. 202 and 207, which give us the order of the formulæ for the last five years of Warad-Sin and the first four of Rîm-Sin, his brother and successor. Since in each text the date formulæ occur twice in the same order, and since we know independently of these texts, from oath or date formulæ which mention the name of the king, that the second, third, fourth, and fifth belong to the reign of Warad-Sin (although the order was not known), and that the sixth is the first year of Rîm-Sin, it is possible to conclude that we have here the date formulæ for nine consecutive years, beginning with the eighth year of Warad-Sin, and ending with the fourth of Rîm-Sin. The contribution of these two texts is especially important because they give nine years which have been broken from the Louvre prism, which contains no formulæ of Warad-Sin's reign, but begins, after the missing second face, with a badly mutilated formula for the seventh year of Rîm-Sin.

For the reign of Rîm-Sin the Louvre date-list and the dated business documents of the period furnish abundant material. For the order of the formulæ from the seventh to the thirtieth years of Rîm-Sin we must depend on the date-list; from published texts and the dated tablets of the Yale Collection, which furnish many examples of the formulæ of Rîm-Sin, with many variants, it is possible to restore most of the fragmentary formulæ of the prism, about one third of the formulæ appearing here for the first time. Unfortunately in one or two instances the same part of the formula is injured on the tablets as in the prism, while in three cases the mutilated form of the prism suggests a fuller form than has yet been found on a dated tablet.

A number of conclusions concerning the dates of Rîm-Sin's reign which had been reached before the contents of Thureau-Dangin's prism were known, are confirmed by the prism.

For example, it had been concluded from evidence such as is offered by a text which contains records for three years; by the names of persons mentioned in the texts, especially shepherds and a certain Balmunamḫe,[1] whose private archive seems to have been unearthed by the Arabs; as well as from the general appearance of the tablets, that two date formulæ which have hitherto been regarded as of Sin-idinnam, record achievements of Rîm-Sin instead.[2] The new date-list of Thureau-Dangin confirms this conclusion, showing them to be the formulæ for the seventh and the eighth years of his reign.

Another fact of more general interest can be learned from the two texts which record formulæ for nine and five years respectively., It has been questioned by scholars when the date formula for a year was determined. Now text No. 207, dated in the first month of the fourth year of Rîm-Sin, carries the record as far as the year then beginning; while No. 202, dated in the twelfth month of the third year, refers to grain for the succeeding year, using the date formula for the fourth year. Hence it is shown conclusively that at some time during the twelfth month (the exact day is not mentioned), the date formula for the succeeding year had been determined and announced, so that it was used by the scribe. How much earlier the date formula for the following year may have been fixed can be determined only by the discovery of new data.

The Yale texts furnish three synchronisms between kings of Larsa and those of other dynasties. The oath formula of No. 124 mentions a hitherto unknown king of Erech[3] as a contemporary of Warad-Sin. The formula for the fifteenth year

[1] See above.

[2] The formulæ are:

*mu ê ᵈBàr-ul-e-gar-ra šàg Adab*ᵏⁱ *mu-un-dú-a*

*ù alam guškin ᵈSín-i-din-nam lugal Ararma*ᵏⁱ*(-ma) mu-un-dìm-ma*

The year when he built the temple of Bar-ul-e-gar-ra, in Adab, and finished a golden statue of Sin-idinnam, king of Larsa;

and *mu ká-gal a-a-a-bi Maš-gan-šabra*ᵏⁱ *mu-un-dú-a*

ù e a-šàg šàg-tum-ma 4 kaskal-gid mu-un-si-ig-ga

The year when he built the city gate and its adornment in Mashganshabra, and enlarged the canal of field and meadow for four double leagues.

They have been regarded as belonging to the reign of Sin-idinnam, as stated; the former because of the reference to his statue, the latter because it has been regarded as a variant of the formula

*mu ᵈSín-i-din-nam bád-gal Maš-gan-šabra*ᵏⁱ *ba-dú*

The year when Sin-idinnam built the great wall of Mashganshabra.

[3] See above.

of Rîm-Sin (see Nos. 141, 147) celebrates his victory over the armies of Erech, Isin, Babylon, Rabiqum, Sutium, and Warad-NE-NE, king of Erech. Though this formula is badly mutilated in Thureau-Dangin's prism, the full form is found on several Yale documents. Accordingly we have the relative position of Sin-iribam, a contemporary of Warad-Sin, and Warad-NE-NE, who was reigning in the fifteenth year of Rîm-Sin, welcome new material for the Dynasty of Erech, which like the Larsa Dynasty, was unfortunately broken from the king-list found at Nippur.

Another new date formula (see Text No. 3), which cannot yet be placed, reads: *mu ugnim Nim^{ki}-ma ù Za-am-bi-ia lugal I-si-in^{ki} ^{giš}tukul ba-an-sìg.*

The year when with his weapon he smote the army of Elam and Zambia, king of Isin.

When it is learned to what reign this formula belongs, we can determine positively the question of the overlapping of the dynasties of Larsa and Isin, and calculate accurately the chronology as far back as the beginning of the Ur Dynasty. It is possible that this formula belongs to the reign of Sin-idinnam.

As stated above, in the monograph *Chronology of the Larsa Dynasty* the reasons for some of these and other conclusions will be given more fully, and there will be a more complete discussion of the materials for reconstructing the history of the dynasty.

NAME INDICES.

The following abbreviations are used: b., brother; d., daughter; f., father; gf., grandfather; gs., grandson; h., husband; m., mother; p.n., (?) perhaps not a personal name; w., wife; YBC, Yale Babylonian Collection. ^{f} is written before some feminine names: other names which are probably feminine are given without being so indicated.

Personal Names.

A-bu-ṭa-bu-um, 46:5.
A-bu-ú-a-tum, YBC 7260 III:40.
A-bu-wa-qar
1. s. of *I-din-Ìr-ra, dam-qar*, 141:26.
2. *dam-qar*, 203:3.
3. 23:4 / 138:3, 6 / 147:4 / 194:8 / 221:9 / 224:14, 30, 32 / 236:2 / YBC 4748 I:8.

A-da-a-a, 148:51.
A-da-làl, 130:3, 5, 11.
A-dan-ni-iš-ì-lí, A-dan-ni-iš-ili, A-a-dan-ni-iš-ì-lí
1. f. of *I-bí-dNin-šubur*, 4 V:17.
2. *na-kid*, 1 IV:9.
3. 2 IV:12.

Ad-da-ilu, 40:6.
Ad-da-kal-la, s. of *dDa-mu-lù-ti*, 141:29.
A-da-a-a-tum
1. *lusimug*, 119:26.
2. 253:21.

A-di-ma-ti-ili, Ad-ma-ti-ì-lí, 138:4, 5 / 140:8.
A-du-ki-šá, 114:11.
A-gu-ú-a
1. s. of *Bi-in-Na-ru-um, na-kid*, 1 II:31.
2. s. of *I-di-ia, na-kid*, 2 IV:4 / 5 II:31 / 6 II:8.
3. s. of *Ka-na-a-a*, b. of *A-at-ta-a*, 4 V:39, 46.
4. s. of *Ka-na-a, na-kid*, 15 IV:10.
5. s. of *Pi-i-ir-Na-ru-um*, 5 II:12.
6. *dìm*, YBC 6278 Case:16.
7. 16 II:12.

A-ḫa-mar-ši
1. f. of *Ṣi-lí-dBa-ú*, 141:25 / 147:16.
2. *arad*, 40:3.
3. YBC 4748 II:21; VII:7.

A-ḫa-tum, fA-ḫa-a-tum
1. w. of *Šú-ub-na-AN*, 110:3, Seal.
2. *nin-dingir*, YBC 7260 III:23.
3. *šú-gé*, YBC 4726:15.

A-ḫa-tu(?)-(?), 87:8.
A-ḫi-a-a-am-ši, 34:5 / 131:29.
A-ḫi-Ê-a, 68:2.
A-ḫi-el-li-ka-am, gìr, 205:5.
A-ḫi-ma-a-a, 20:15 / 21:2 / 24:6 / 32:4 / 42:12 / 66:4 / 82:4.
A-ḫi-šá-gi-iš
1. f. of *A-bil-dAmurru*, 106:Seal.
2. b. of *dSín-šar-ri*, YBC 4726:4.
3. *na-kid*, 6 I:15 / 30:15.
4. 2 II:14 / 4 IV:23 / YBC 4750 V:13.

A-ḫi-šá-ilu, YBC 7260 III:29.
A-ḫu-ú-a-tum, YBC 4748 II:14.
A-ḫu-ki-nu-um, ú-tul, 3 V:4 / 63:6.
A-ḫu-la-ab-. . ., 44:14.
A-ḫu-um, Aḫ-ḫu-um
1. *dúb-sar*, 126:40.
2. *na-kid*, 15 III:9.
3. YBC 7238:32.

A-ḫu-um-ma. See List of Cities.
A-ḫu-um-dSín, 49:11.
A-ḫu-ni
1. f. of *Im-gur-dSín*, 1 IV:15 / 2 III:26 / 3 III:32 / 4 IX:23 / 9:18, 26 / 15 IV:16.
2. 81:6 / 102:19.

A-ḫu-ši-na, lumt-lăḫ, 118:19.
A-ḫu-šú, s. of *Ka-na-a-a*, 3 II:7.
A-ḫu-šú-nu
1. s. of *Awîl-dNin-šubur, gìr*, 17:21.
2. s. of *Awîl-dNin-šubur, na-kid*, 1 III:25 / 2 V:35 / 6 II:15.
3. s. of *Ka-na-a-a*, 1 IV:32 / 2 V:15.
4. *da-gál*, 106:45.
5. 16 IV:10 / YBC 4853:27.

A-ḫu-ṭa-bu-um, A-ḫu-ṭâbum (*DÚG*)
1. *dumu lugal*, 153:7, 13.
2. *NI-SUR*, 204:5.
3. 171:28.

A-ḫu-wa-qar
1. h. of *fdSín-nu-ri*, 88:15.
2. *du-gab mu*, 141:31.

A-ia-a-ni, 42:19.
Ak-be-la, 159:6.
Ak-be-lum, IŠ, 112:27 / 123:27.
A-ki-ia-ú-a-ú
1. *na-kid*, 233:3, 8.
2. *ú-tul*, 193:11.

A-lam-ma-li-a-at, 127:6.
A-li-i, f. of *dSín-i-qi-šá-am*, 3 II:13 / 4 I:23/ 6 I:26 / 19:17 / 25:13.
A-lí-a-bu-šá, YBC 4744:18.

A-wi-ia-tum, 125 Case:28; Tablet:28 / (?) 139:2.
Awîl-^{d}Amurru
1. *gìr*, 166:12, 27.
2. *mi-lăḫ*, 123:18 / 126:22 / 129:13.

Awîl-^{d}Ašnan, YBC 7260 VI:3.
Awîl-^{d}Dumu-zi-da, *-^{d}Dumu-zi*
1. f. of *Nu-úr-ì-lí-šú*, *^{d}Sín-pi-la-aḫ*, 6 III:2.
2. f. of *Nu-úr-ì-lí-šú*, 3 I:28 / 5 I:9.

Awîl-ga(?)-tum, 147:11.
A-wi-li-ia, 120:2.
A-wi-il-ili, A-wi-il-ì-lí, A-wi-el-ili, A-wi-el-ì-lí
1. s. of *Ka-na-a-a*, b. of *Nu-úr-ì-lí-šú*, 3 II:38 / 5 I:33.
2. s. of *Ka-na-a-a*, *na-kid*, 1 II:21 / 2 V: 4 / 11:5, 14 / 30:20, 29.
3. s. of *Ú-ba-a-a*, 121:10, Seal.
4. *arad*, 71:1.
5. *dam-qar*, 129:2, 4, 10.
6. 4 III:39; IV:6 / 16 IV:9 / (?) 76:8 / 108:8 / 113:4 / 138:2 / YBC 7238: 31.

A-wi-lim, 171:2 / 172:2, 8, 12 / 204:2.
Awîl-^{d}Ma-ma, 80:4 / 102:2.
Awîl-^{d}Ma-.., s. of *Gimil(ŠÚ)-^{d}Lugal*, *arad ^{d}Nannar-gè*, *dúb-sar*, 47:Seal.
Awîl-^{d}Nannar
1. s. of *Nu-úr-ì-lí-šú*, 119:22 / 126:26 / 129:14 / 134:20.
2. b. of *Azag-[^{d}Innina(?)]*, 202:34.
3. 84:8 / 102:6 / 128:8.

Awîl-^{d}NIN-IB, 224:13.
Awîl-^{d}Nin-šubur, f. of *A-ḫu-šú-nu*, 1 III:26 / 2 V:35 / 6 II:15 / 17:21.
Awîl-šá-^{d}Nin-a-zu, f. of *I-ba-áš-ši-ili*, 18:11.
'A-wi-il-ti-ì-lí, w. of *Ì-lí-tu-ra-am*, YBC 4857:11.
A-wi-il-..., *A-wi-el-...*, 194:2 / 217 II:9.
A-wi-lum, 207:32.
Azag-^{d}En-ki, 149:2.
Azag-^{d}Innina
1. f. of *Ur-^{d}En-ki-ka*, 128:12.
2. b. of *Awîl-^{d}Nannar(?)*, 202:27(?), 31, 40(?), 45.
3. 171:19, 21, 22.

Azag-^{d}Nannar
1. s. of *^{d}Nannar-ṭa-bi-..*, *arad ê ^{d}Nannar-gè*, *dúb-sar A-RU-A*, 47:Seal / 51: Seal / 52:Seal.
2. f. of *Gimil(ŠÚ)-...*, 50:Seal.
3. 71:6 / 102:11.

Azag-ni-ia, 49:12.
Azag-^{d}Nin-gal
1. f. of *Še-ṣi-lum*, 141:19.
2. f. of *Ur-^{d}Nannar*, 46:Seal / 47:Seal / 50:Seal / 51:Seal / 52:Seal / 53:Seal / 122:Seal.
3. 126:3.

Azag-^{d}Nin-šubur, YBC 7620 IV:32.
Azag-^{d}..., 171:19.
A-za-ni-tum, f. of *A-na-Ê-a-tak-la-ku*, *^{d}Sín-ášû(A-ZU)*, 5 V:27.
A-zi-ia, YBC 4853:9.
^{d}Babbar-ma-an-sí, 111:14.
^{d}Babbar-zi-ma-an-sí, 253:20.
^{d}Babbar-zi-mu, 114:10.
Bal-mu-nam-ḫe
1. s. of *^{d}Sín-nu-úr-ma-tim*, 122:9.
2. Written *Bal-la-mu-ḫe-ḫi*, 125 Tablet: 10.
3. *gìr*, 150:51 / 227:15.
4. 112:10 / 114:3 / 115:2, 3 / 116:2, 3 / 118:6 / 119:7 / 123:10 / 124:6 / 125 Case:11 / 126:10 / 128:3 / 129:5 / 132:4 / 134:8 / 141:6 / 143 Tablet:7; Case:4 / 145:4 / 146:11, 12 / 147:3 / 193:10 / 253:2, 3 / YBC 4748 I:7.

See also List of Cities.
Ba-la-(?)-.., 246:2.
Ba-a-na-nu-um, 201:1.
Ba-ni-ilu, *na-kid*, 19:13.
^{d}Ba-ú-ga-mi-la-[tum], YBC 4726:13.
Ba-a-zu-um, *na-kid*, 196:7 / 233:5, 10.
Be-gu-um, *dam-qar*, YBC 7260 III:32.
Be-lí-i, *Be-lí*, s. of *Da-da-a*, 142:8 / YBC 6278 Case:3, 7.
Be-lí-ia, 82:3.
Be-lí-ba-áš-ti, YBC 7260 III:30.
Be-lí-i-din-nam, s. of *Azag-^{d}En-ki*, 149:2.
Be-lí-ki-ma-tim, 4 VII:23.
Be-lí-ki-in-i-ma-tim, 18:21.

Be-lí-ta-a-a-ar, *ŠÚ-QA-GAB-A lugal*, 141:24.
Be-lum-ki-im-ma-tim, 39:9.
Be-ta-tum, 171:5 / 172:5 / 178:10 / 205:2.
Bi-na-a. See List of Cities.
Bi-in-Na-ru-um
  1. f. of *A-gu-ú-a*, 1 II:32.
  2. f. of *A-at-ta-a*, 1 II:27.
Bi-tim, 171:3 / 172:3 / 194:3, p.n.(?)
Bi-tu-ú-a, 128:9.
Bîtu(Ê)-ra-bi, 127:22.
Bu-bi-qum, 2 III:9.
Bûr-ia, f. of ^{d}*EN-*. . ., 112:Seal / 129:Seal.
Bûr-^{d}*Nu-nu*, YBC 7260 II:28.
Bur-ra-tum, 129:27.
Bûr-^{d}*Sín*
  1. s. of ^{d}*Nannar-ma-an-sí*, 118:17.
  2. 70:11 / 102:10 / 214:4.
Bu-ur-tim, YBC 4748 I:10.
Bu-ru-um-mu, 224:25, p.n.(?)
Bûr-^{d}. . ., 242:12.
Bu-uz-bu-zu-um
  1. f. of *Iš-me-*^{d}*IM*, 1 III:31.
  2. f. of *Ṣi-lí-*^{d}*Sín*, 126:6, 8.
Bu-zi-ia
  1. *pa*, 80:13.
  2. *šà-tam*, 144:18.
  3. 81:4 / 102:20 / 130:18.
Da-bi-tum, 127:4, 5, 10.
Da-da-a, *Da-da*
  1. s. of *Iš-me-Îr-ra*, 1 VI:22 / 18:14.
  2. f. of *Be-lí-i*, *Be-lí*, 142:8 / YBC 6278 Case:3.
  3. 97:4.
Dam-qi-ì-lí-šú, 223:8.
^{d}*Da-mu-lù-ti*, f. of *Ad-da-kal-la*, 141:29.
^{d}*Da-mu-ma-an-sí*, YBC 7260 III:47.
Da-an-ni-ia, *dìm*, 113:15.
Dân-^{d}*La-ta-ra-ak*
  1. *na-kid*, 1 I:9 / 15 I:26; II:7.
  2. 3 I:7 / 4 I:9, 14; IX:17 / 5 VI:32 / 16 I:18 / 19:19 / 36:6.
Dân-^{d}*Nin-gal*, YBC 4859:5.
Dan-nu-li, 130:6.
Dân-^{d}*Šú-bu-la*
  1. *mu*, 124:23.
  2. *pa mu*, 119:18.
  3. 113:14 / 137:21 / 161:1.
Da-aq-qum, *Da-qum*
  1. s. of *Ar-ši-a-nu-um*, 34:3.
  2. *na-kid*, 6 II:29.
  3. 1 V:43 / 16 I:26 / 26:10 / 39:8.
Da-ar-ri-ku, 132:9.
Di-ba-bu-um, s. of *Za-an-gu-um*, 135:3, 4.
Di-di-i, YBC 7260 I:41.
Di-ma-šum, 4 II:16.
Du-ga-qum, *ká(?)*, 140:17 / 143 Tablet:25; Case:22.
^{d}*Dumu-zi-ba-ni*
  1. f. of *A-ab-ba-a*, 2 V:26 / 4 VII:12 / 5 III:30 / 6 III:16.
  2. f. of *A-ap-pa-a*, 15 II:31.
^{d}*Dumu-zi-i-*. . ., 171:25.
Ê-a-ḫe-gál
  1. b. of *Ê-a-mu-ba-lí-iṭ*, *na-kid*, 1 III:36.
  2. *na-kid*, 30:37.
  3. 3 II:10 / 4 VII:38, 39 / 5 III:36 / 7:3 / 10:23.
Ê-a-mu-ba-lí-iṭ
  1. b. of *Ê-a-ḫe-gál*, *na-kid*, 1 IV:4.
  2. 3 II:19 / 5 IV:6 / 138:15.
Ê-a-na-ṣir
  1. s. of *Ib-ku-Ê-a*, *šà-tam*, 141:14.
  2. *gìr*, 169:20 / 170:16.
  3. YBC 7260 II:15; III:25.
Ê-a-ṣi-lí, 221:4 / YBC 4748 III:19.
Ê-a-še-mi, 14:3 / 120:12.
Ê-a-tu-kúl-ti
  1. *na-kid*, 6 III:12.
  2. 1 IV:28 / 2 IV:39 / 5 IV:18 / 130:15.
Ê-a-. . ., 16 III:2.
E-gál-li-ia, *gìr*, 26:8.
E-la-a, 109:5.
E-la-lí, s. of *A-bil-a-ḫi*, 74:2.
El-la-tum, s. of *Wa-tar-*^{d}*Sín*, 137:16.
E-mu-ú, 129:22.
EN-AN-E-UL, *en* ^{d}*Nannar šàg Uruma*^{ki}, 250:8 / 251:10.
E-en-da-a, f. of *Warad-*^{d}*Nannar*, 119:23.
^{d}*En-ki-ra-*. . ., 106:60.
^{d}*En-lil-be-el-ì-lí*, YBC 7260 III:10.
^{d}*En-lil-ga-mil*, YBC 4864:11.

Ḫi-ba-lum, YBC 4748 II:13; III:11; IV:17; VI:8; VII:29.
Ḫi-ni-ir-šú, 102:13.
Ḫi-ṣi-la-šú, 175:10 / 184:6.
^{f}*Ḫi-iš-šá-tum*
  1. w. of ^{d}*Šamaš-ḫa-zi-ir*, 143 Tablet:6, 16; Case:2, 13.
  2. 195:8 / YBC 4748 I:20; II:10; III:8; IV:13; VI:4, 26; VII:24.
^{f}*Ḫu-na-ba-tum*, 98:3, 14.
Ḫu-na-a-bi, 97:14.
Ḫu-nu-bu-um
  1. s. of ^{d}*Šamaš-iš-ki*, 135:16.
  2. f. of ^{d}*Sín-mu-ba-lí-it*, 126:30.
  3. f. of *Ṣi-lí-Ištar*, 126:25.
Ḫu-nu-ub-tum, w. of ^{d}*Sín-ga-mi-il*, ^{lú}*mà-lal*, 161:4.
Ḫu-pa-tum
  1. s. of ^{d}*Sín-na-ṣir*, 119:20.
  2. *kù-dìm*, 145:8.
  3. *šà-tam*, 144:17.
  4. 189:5 / 190:1 / 195:3 / YBC 7260 II:7.
Ḫu-zi-ra-nu-um, YBC 7260 III:45; IV:22; V:23, 28, 32.
Ḫu-zi-ru-um, 179:7.
Ia-a, YBC 4748 II:18; VII:3.
Ia-a-a-nu-um, f. of *Ì-lí-ṣulûli(AN-KUŠ)* (*-lí*), 134:16.
Ia-ba-nu-m, f. of *Im-gu-ú-a*, 124:22.
Ia-da-a-a-tum, 189:9.
Ia-di-du-um
  1. *na-kid*, 11:20.
  2. 2 II:26 / 3 III:36 / 4 IV:35.
Ia-ia-um, 156:2.
Ia-ta-ru-um, 151:5.
Ia-ú-zi-lum, *arad*, 72:1.
I-ba-lu-. . ., 242:11.
I-ba-áš-ši-ili
  1. s. of *A-bi-ì-lí*, *na-kid*, 15 IV:23.
  2. s. of *A-bi-ì-lí*, 4 V:22, 35 / 50:5.
  3. s. of *Awîl-šá-*^{d}*Nin-a-zu*, 18:11.
  4. s. of *Ku-na-ti*, *Ku-na-tum*, 5 V:19 / 10:13 / 25:5.
  5. *gìr*, 166:39.
  6. ^{lú}*mi-láḫ*, 126:38.
  7. *na-kid*, 1 I:18.
  8. 3 I:16 / 4 II:6, 17; III:21 / 7:1 / 15 I:21 / 16 I:3, 16 / 19:31 / 21:5 / 22:4 / 23:5 / 26:6 / 27:4.
Ib-ga-tum, YBC 7260 II:14.
I-bi-ilu, 22:3.
I-bi-ik-^{d}*Nu-nu*, *-Nu-nu*
  1. f. of ^{d}*Nannar-me-du*, 53:Seal.
  2. f. of ^{d}*Sín-pi-la-aḫ*, 122:Seal.
I-bi-ik-. . ., *dúb-sar*, 155:Seal.
I-bi-^{d}*Nin-šubur*, *I-bí-*^{d}*Nin-šubur*
  1. s. of *A-dan-ni-iš-ì-lí*, 4 V:16.
  2. s. of *I-di-Ištar*, *na-kid*, 16 I:5 / 47:5.
  3. ^{lú}*íl*, 126:35.
  4. *kù-dìm*, 118:18 / 119:24.
  5. 4 II:10 / 145:9 / 253:19 / YBC 7260 II:21.
I-bi-^{d}*Sín*
  1. f. of *Ú-ba-a-a*, 144:23.
  2. 206:3.
I-bi-^{d}*Šà-ḫa-an*, 114:2.
Ib-ku-^{d}*A-ba*, f. of *Zi-ki-ir-ì-lí-šú*, 155:Seal.
Ib-ku-^{d}*Ba-ú*, 131:22.
Ib-ku-^{d}*Da-mu*, 160:4, 8.
Ib-ku-Ê-a, f. of *Ê-a-na-ṣir*, 141:14.
Ib-ku-^{d}*IM*
  1. *gìr*. . .*ú-tul*, 4 X:7 / 9:31 / 10:29 / 11:33 / 13:24 / 15 IV:31 / 16 IV:18 / 30:42 / 55:6 / 57:6.
  2. 14:4 / 22:6 / 39:6 / 107:4, 5 / YBC 4748 III:14; IV:22.
Ib-ku-Ìr-ra, 147:5.
Ib-ku-ir-ṣi-tim, 106:61.
Ib-ku-Ištar
  1. s. of *Ur-Lugal-ban-da*, *na-kid*, 1 III:10.
  2. *gìr*, 170:13.
  3. 98:11 / 127:19.
Ib-ku-^{d}*Na-*. . ., f. of ^{d}*Sín-ra-bi*, 35:5.
Ib-ku-^{d}*Sín*, *dìm*, 145:14.
Ib-ku-šá
  1. s. of *I-ku-un-pî(KA)-*^{d}*Sín*, 118:20.
  2. s. of *Ka-ap-sa-nu-um*, 18:17.
  3. *NI-SUR*, 204:4.
  4. 121:24 / 122:16 / 129:21 / 145:10 / 157:2 / YBC 7260 IV:23.

KÁ-šá-^{d}Amurru
1. s. of *I-din-^{d}*..., 116:Seal.
2. 164:3.

KÁ-šá-^{d}Ištar, -Ištar
1. s. of *^{d}Sín-be-el-ì-lí*, 137:2, 14.
2. s. of *Šú-mi-a-bi-ia*, 131:19.
3. 110:11.

KÁ-^{d}Šamaš, 40:11 / YBC 4859:6.

KÁ-šá-^{d}Nu-muš-da, f. of *^{d}Sín-ma-gir*, h. of *^{f}Ta-ri-ba-tum*, 141:2, 4.

KÁ-šá-^{d}Sín
1. f. of *Im-gur-^{d}Sín, Nu-úr-*..., 3 IV:19.
2. f. of *Im-gur-^{d}Sín*, 1 V:2 / 4 VIII:5, 15 / 15 II:15; III:32.
3. f. of *Nu-úr-^{d}Sín*, 2 III:4.

Ka-...
1. f. of *A-ab-ba-a*, 2 IV:8.
2. f. of *Nu-úr-^{d}Sín*, 19:9.

Ki-eš-i-din-nam, 202:3.

Ki-ma-bi-lí, 2 IV:51.

Ki-ma-tim, na-kid, 6 IV:3.

Kin-na-tum, IŠ, 106:47.

Ki-iš-ti-Ìr-ra
1. f. of...*-i-din-na-am*, 162:Seal / 250: Seal / 251:Seal.
2. YBC 7260 II:8; III:26; V:37.

Ku-bi-na-id, nagar, 141:17.

Ku-du-ur-Ma-bu-uk
1. f. of *Warad-^{d}Sín*, 165:Seal.
2. 114:17 / 119:30 / 122:37 / 127:12 / 128:15 / 137:22 / 167:5 / 202:4, 16, 29, 61, 72 / 207:15, 50 / 216:4.

Ku-uk-^{d}Su-gal-li-it, 191:2.

Ku(or *Aš*)*-lu-ú*, f. of *^{d}Sín-mu-ba-lí-iṭ*, 25:32.

Ku-li-..., *DU-GAB*, 106:54.

Ku-na-bu-um, nu-banda, 126:4, 32.

Ku-na-a-nu-um, 119:4, 5, 12.

Ku-na-ti
1. f. of *I-ba-áš-ši-ili*, 5 V:20 / 25:5.
2. f. of *^{d}Sín-ma-gir*, 16 I:12 / 25:16 / 54:6.

Ku-na-tum
1. f. of *I-ba-áš-ši-ili*, 10:13.
2. f. of *^{d}Sín-ma-gir*, 1 I:27.

Ku-un-nu-rum, YBC 4748 IV:19; VI:15; VII:31.

Ku-ru-um, YBC 4748 IV:23.

Ku-úr-šá-nu-um, 24:2.

Ku-su-ul-lum
1. s. of *Li-it-tum, na-kid*, 10:9.
2. s. of *Li-it-tum*, 6 II:11 / 18:5.
3. 4 III:18 / 13:11.

Ku-ú-zu-um, 140:4.

La-gi-ma, 97:5.

La-ki-bu-um
1. *gìr*, 182:15 / 209:12.
2. 128:10.

^{d}Latarak(LÚ-LÀL)-qar-ra-ad, 117:16.

Li-bi-it-Ištar, 178:1 / YBC 7260 I:22.

Li-bi-it-^{d}Sín, 103:3.

Li-bur-ba-ni, f. in-law of *^{d}Sín-i-din-nam*, 141:28.

Li-ik-tum, 171:4 / 172:4 / 194:5 / YBC 4748 I:21; II:11; III:9; IV:14; VI: 5, 27; VII:26, p.n.(?)

^{d}Li-lum-dân, 131:20.

Lim-maš-^{d}Nannar
1. *pa gême uš-bar*, 123:25.
2. 125 Case:23; Tablet:27.

Li-sa-tum, 238:2 / YBC 4748 II:24; III: 13.

Li-it-tum, f. of *Ku-su-ul-lum*, 6 II:12 / 10:9 / 18:5.

Li-za-qar-ilu, 125:4.

Lù-dingir-ra, s. of *Ur-^{d}Nin-šubur*, *^{f}Šá-at-^{d}Sín*; b. of *Ilu-pî(KA)-^{d}Ba-ú*; *šutug* ..., YBC 5420:2, 10, 16, 20, 28, 30.

Lu-ud-lu-ul-^{d}Sín, 2 VI:33 / 5 VI:37 / 127: 24 / 142:5.

Lù-GA-a-a, f. of *^{d}Sín-mu-ba-lí-iṭ*, 155:Seal.

Lugal-ban-da, 111:3.

Lugal-gi-na, 135:6.

Lugal-^{d}Guškin, f. of *SAG-lugal(?)-*..., 46: Seal / 50:Seal / 53:Seal.

Lugal-lù-ti-na(?), s. of *^{d}Nannar-me-a-*..., *dúb-sar*, 47:Seal / 51:Seal / 52:Seal.

Lugal-nig-gi-na, 149:1.

Lù-ti-la-di-bi, 125 Case:19; Tablet:18.

Ma-di-ia, 110:12.

Ma-di-ka-ar-ku-te-im, YBC 4750 IV:5.

Ma-gur-^{d}Sín, 5 VI:26.

^{f}Ma-ḫa-ni-tum, w. of *Ga-gu-um*, 117:4.

Ma-ku-ur-^{d}Sín
  1. *na-kid*, 30:34, 35, 38.
  2. 2 IV:23 / 3 I:41 / 4 VII:32, 33: VIII:26 / 7:2 / 10:18, 24 / 15 IV:2 / 16 III:11.

Ma-ma-nu-um, 102:25.
^{d}Ma-mi-ia, w. of *^{d}Sín-iš-me-a-ni*, m. of *Ig-mi-il-^{d}Sín*, 123:8.
^{d}Ma-mi-tum-ri-me-ni, m. of *^{f}Um-mi-*. . ., 42:9.
Ma-a-nu-um, f. of *An-na-tum*, 141:30.
Ma-na-a-nu-um. See *Ku-na-a-nu-um*.
Ma-nu-ú-um, 32:3.
Mâr-^{d}Amurru, 41:7, 8.
Mâr-ì-lí, YBC 7260 II:25.
Ma-ri-^{d}Ištar, 108:7.
Mâr-^{d}Sín-be-el-. . ., 102:9.
Mâr-^{d}Sín-tu-kúl-ti, *gìr*, 17:14.
^{f}Ma-ri-tum, 88:14.
Mâr-Uruma^{ki}
  1. f. of *A-bi-ṭa-bu-um*, 4 VIII:13 / 13:20.
  2. 31:5.

Ma-sa-bu-um. See List of Cities.
^{f}Ma-ta-tum, YBC 4726:14.
Ma-ti-ilu, 39:7.
Ma-ti-nu-ru-um
  1. s. of *^{d}Sín-iq-be-i*, b. of *^{d}Sín-êriš(PIN)*, *na-kid*, 1 III:5.
  2. s. of *^{d}Sín-iq-be-e*, 5 II:24.
  3. b. of *^{d}Sín-êriš(PIN)*, 3 III:24.
  4. *na-kid*, 15 I:19 / 19:23, 30.
  5. 16 I:8.

Me-ni-. . ., 44:11.
^{f}Me-éš-li-ba-tum, *géme*, 117:1.
Me-eš-(?)-^{d}Gu-la, 98:5.
^{f}Mu-ba-li-it-tum, m. of *^{f}Šá-at-^{d}Nu-muš-da*, 70:1.
Mu-da-du-um, s. of *Ur-^{d}Nin-gi-na*, 148:48.
Mu-kin-ilu, 49:13.
Mu-na-na-nu-um, 3 III:39.
Mu-na-nu-um, 2 II:30.
Mu-nu-tuk, 27:3 / 31:4.
Mu-na-wi-rum, *-ru-um*, 143 Tablet:4, 14; Case:11 / YBC 7260 V:4.
^{f}Mu-šá-at-^{d}Sín, d. of *A-ma-at-^{d}Za-má-má*, 67:6.
^{d}Muš-dingir-ka-ni, p.n.(?), 42:18.
Mu-ta-bu-um, *šà-tam*, 122:23.
Mu-ti-a-ba-al, YBC 4750 V:9.
Mu-tum-e-el, *Mu-tum-ilu*
  1. s. of *^{d}Sín-êriš(PIN)*, 4 III:6.
  2. s. of . . ., *-mi*, *na-kid*, 19:29.
  3. f. of *I-din-ilu*, 123:Seal / 126:Seal.
  4. 1 V:15 / 2 III:39.

Na-bi-^{d}En-lil
  1. s. of *^{d}Sín-na-ṣi-ir*, *arad ^{d}Amurru*, 125 Case:18; Tablet:17; Seal.
  2. f. of *^{d}Sín-ri-me-ni*, 109:13.
  3. *simug*, 134:21.
  4. 12:6 / 72:6 / 160:4.

Na-bi-ì-lí-šú
  1. s. of *Nu-úr-^{d}Sín*, 1 VI:26.
  2. s. of *^{f}Šá-at-^{d}Sín*, 144:6.
  3. . . ., *^{d}UD*, 132:10.
  4. 133:5, 6 / 151:3.

Na-bi-^{d}Sín, YBC 7260 I:24.
Na-bi-. . ., 122:25.
Na(?)-ab-tum, 98:1.
Na-bu-um-MER(?), 159:2.
Na-din-ilu, 3 III:20 / 7:4 / 15 III:36.
Na-din-iš-ta-al-mu-um, h. of *^{f}Ši-ba-a-a*, f. of *^{d}Sín-êriš(PIN)*, 121:4, 7.
Na-din-tum-^{d}Nin-gal, YBC 4853:21.
Na-aḫ-lum
  1. *na-kid*, 6 IV:27.
  2. 4 VII:42.

Na-ki-mu-um, 20:5.
^{fd}Na-na-a-a-im-gur, *šú-gé*, YBC 4726:10.
^{d}Nannar-a-a
  1. s. of *A-bi-šá-^{d}Sín*, 2 IV:43.
  2. s. of *Nu-úr-maš-ku-ku(?)*, 2 IV:35.
  3. f. of *^{d}Sín-be-el-ì-lí*, (*-ili*), 2 IV:47 / 6 IV:8.
  4. *na-kid*, 1 IV:24 / 5 IV:12 / 6 IV:12 / 33:8.

^{d}Nannar-ašarid(IGI-GUB), 73:9.
^{d}Nannar-e-ra-mu-šú, YBC 7260 I:26.
^{d}Nannar-ma-an-sí
  1. s. of *I-din-Îr-ra*, *lù Zararma^{ki}*, 100:3.
  2. s. of *Î-lí-tu-kúl-ti*, 137:18.
  3. s. of *^{d}Sín-be-el-ì-lí*, 80:2.
  4. f. of *Bûr-^{d}Sín*, 118:17.

5. f. of *Ilu-šú-na-ṣi-ir*, 47:Seal / 50: Seal.
6. *dìm*, 143 Tablet:28; Case:25 / 172: 14.
7. *engar*, 112:25.
8. *gìr*, 168:15.
9. ^{lù}*KID*, 129:23.
10. 102:4 / 113:9 / 122:6 / 144:4, 5, 13 / 148:53 / YBC 4739:43 / YBC 7260 I:23.

^{d}*Nannar-me-a-. . .*, f. of *Lugal-lù-ti-na(?)*, 47: Seal / 51:Seal / 52:Seal.

^{d}*Nannar-me-du*
1. s. of *I-bi-ik-Nu-nu*, 53:Seal.
2. s. of *Warad-Ê-a*, 151:8, 9, Seal.
3. f. of *Ib-ni-Ê-a*, 149:4.
4. f. of *Ib-ni-ia*, 123:Seal.

^{d}*Nannar-ni-maḫ*
1. *DU-GAB*, 141:15.
2. 136:3 / 150:39 / 176:6 / 184:21.

^{d}*Nannar-ni-zu*, 133:16.

^{d}*Nannar-sag-gal*, 133:2.

^{d}*Nannar-sí-ga*, YBC 7260 I:40.

^{d}*Nannar-tab-ba*
1. s. of *Nu-úr-ì-lí-šú*, 125 Case:20; Tablet:19; Seal.
2. 134:22.

^{d}*Nannar-ṭa-bi-. . .*, f. of *Azag-^{d}Nannar*, 47: Seal/ 51:Seal / 52:Seal.

Na(?)-an-na-tum, 143 Tablet:27; Case:24.

Na-an-. . ., 122:26.

Na-ap-li-iṣ-ilu
1. *gìr*, YBC 6505:41.
2. YBC 4748 III:12; IV:18; VII:30.

Na-ra-am-Ê-a, YBC 4748 I:15; II:27, 35; III:3, 30; IV:8; VI:21; VII:21.

Na-ra-am-^{d}Sín
1. f. of *Im-gur-^{d}Sín*, 77:8.
2. YBC 7260 II:19; IV:12; V:18.

Na-ra-am-ta-am, 110:2.

Na-ra-am-tum, 202:46.

Na-ar-bu-um, *dúb-sar*, 126:24.

Na-wi-ru-um-ì-lí, 122:4.

^{d}*Na-. . .*, 2 II:18.

Na-. . .-im, f. of *Warad-^{d}Nannar*, 132:11.

^{d}*Nergal-ki-i*, f. of ^{d}*Sín-ma-gir*, 126:34.

^{d}*Nergal-KU-UB*, 133:18.

Ni-bu-um, 201:3, p.n.(?)

Ni-di-it-tum, 39:2.

Ni-ig-ma-nu-um, 155:4.

Ni-ik-ka-a, 88:8.

Ni-ki-. . ., 118:2, 3.

^{d}*Ninâ(?)-ú-ra-bi*, 8:6 / 102:15.

^{fd}*Nin-gal-la-ma-zi*, *šú-gé*, YBC 4739:13.

^{fd}*Nin-gal-mu-ba-lí-iṭ*, YBC 4739:25.

^{d}*Nin-giš-zi-da-ga-mi-il*, 80:9 / 81:2 / 102:26 / 161:7.

^{d}*Nin-kar-ra-ag-ba-la-ṭu*, *šú-i*, 124:20.

^{d}*Nin-kar-ra-ag-mu-ba-lí-iṭ*, YBC 4739:40.

^{fd}*Nin-kar-ra-ag-um-mi*, YBC 4739:6.

^{d}*Nin-si-an-na-me-du*, f. of *Ilu-šú-i-bi-šú*, 123:Seal / 129:Seal.

^{d}*Nin-subur*, 133:7.

Ni-in-nu-ú-a, 178:3 / YBC 4748 IV:21; VI:17; VII:33.

Ni-ši-i-ni-šú, *nin-dingir*, YBC 7260 III:28.

Nu-na-a
1. f. of ^{d}*Sín-ma-gir*, 2 VI:37 / 5 VII:15.
2. *na-kid*, 6 VI:19.

Nu-na-bu-um, f. of *Zi-zi-bu*, 117:14.

Nu-nu-ú, 148:54.

Nu-úr-a-ḫi
1. s. of *A-qar-ti*, 135:19.
2. s. of *Ilu-rê'û*, 15 I:31.
3. 4 IX:14, 15.

Nu-úr-^{d}Amurru
1. *gìr*, 169:18 / 170:14 / 246:14.
2. 37:3.

Nu-ra-tum, 44:5.

Nu-úr-^{d}Ba-ú, *na-kid*, 33:9.

Nu-úr-^{d}Da-gan, 103:4.

Nu-úr-Ê-a, YBC 7260 V:38.

Nu-úr-ì-lí-šú
1. s. of *A-lí-mu-šá-li*, b. of ^{d}*Sín-ra-bi*, 2 VI:10.
2. s. of *A-lí-mu-šá-li*, *na-kid*, 6 VI:3.
3. s. of *A-lí-mu-šá-al-li*, 4 VIII:8 / 25: 35.
4. s. of *Awîl-^{d}Dumu-zi-da*, b. of ^{d}*Sín-pi-la-aḫ*, 6 III:1.
5. s. of *Awîl-^{d}Dumu-zi-da*, 3 I:28.
6. s. of *Awîl-^{d}Dumu-zi*, *na-kid*, 5 I:8.

dSín-a-da-làl, 107:16.
dSín-a-ḫi-i-din-nam, YBC 4864:2.
dSín-am-ta-ḫa-ar, 98:20.
dSín-âsû(A-ZU), s. of *A-za-ni-tum*, b. of *A-na-Ê-a-tak-la-ku*, 5 V:33.
dSín-a-šá-ri-id, *Sin(EŠ)-a-šá-ri-id*
1. *pa mu*, 141:12.
2. 134:23.
dSín-ba-la-ti
1. *na-kid*, 1 IV:19 / 6 II:4 / 11:11 / 30:24.
2. 4 IV:5 / 5 III:24 / 16 IV:11.
dSín-ba-lí-iṭ, 106:56 / 120:11.
dSín-ba-ni
1. *na-kid*, 6 III:33.
2. 4 IV:16 / 16 IV:6.
dSín-ba-..., 1 V:31.
dSín-be-el-ap-lim, 241:2.
dSín-be-el-ì-lí, *-ili*
1. s. of *dNannar-a-a*, *na-kid*, 2 IV:47 / 6 IV:7.
2. f. of *KÁ-šá-Ištar*, 137:14.
3. f. of *dNannar-ma-an-sí*, 80:3.
4. 119:25.
dSín-bi-...-ki, 139:17.
dSín-êriš(PIN)
1. s. of *dIM-na-ṣi-ir*, b. of *A-bil-ku-bi*, 5 I:21.
2. s. of *dIM-na-ṣi-ir*, b. of *dSín-a-ba*, 4 VII:2, 7.
3. s. of *dIM-na-ṣi-ir*, *na-kid*, 6 II:19 / 15 II:24.
4. s. of *dIM-na-ṣi-ir*, 25:41 / 56:8.
5. s. of *Na-din-iš-ta-al-mu-um*, *fŠi-ba-a-a*, 121:6, 9.
6. s. of *dSín-iq-be-i*, *na-kid*, 1 II:36 / 2 II:1 / 54:10.
7. s. of *dSín-na-be-i*, 4 II:34.
8. f. of *Mu-tum-ilu*, 4 III:7.
9. b. of *Ma-ti-nu-ru-um*, 3 III:28.
10. *na-kid*, 15 I:19 / 19:23, 30.
11. *lù Umma^{ki}*, 166:7.
12. 16 I:8 / 175:9 / 184:5 / 209:2.
dSín-ga-mi-il, *-ga-mi-el*, *-ga-mil*
1. s. of *A-bi-um-mu*, *dìm*, 131:26.
2. s. of *Ti-...*, 122:20.
3. h. of *fḪu-nu-ub-tum*, *mà-lal ê-dúb(?)*, 161:5.
4. f. of *fE-ri-iš-tum*, 125 Case:7, 10; Tablet:9.
5. f. of *Zi-ia-tum*, 123:Seal.
6. 48:5 / 134:3, 9, 11, 15.
dSín-ga-ti-ṣa-ba-at, *gìr*, 169:17 / 170:12 / 182:14 / 185:15.
dSín-ḫa-zi-ir, YBC 4750 V:8.
dSín-ia, s. of *Ḫa-ba-tum*, f. of *dEn-lil-na-id*, 131:3, 4, 5, 13, 17.
dSín-ia-tum, *^{lù}ŠE*, 123:20. Cf. *Zi-ia-tum*, 123:Seal.
dSín-i-din-na, s. of *A-ab-ba*, 4 VI:7, 9.
dSín-i-din-nam
1. s. of *A-ab-ba*, *na-kid*, 1 III:19.
2. s. of *A-ab-ba*, 52:5.
3. f. in law of *Li-bur-ba-ni*, 141:28.
4. *lugal Zararma^{ki}*, 140:24 / 168:22 / 173:9 / 174:29 / 212:4.
5. *lugal*, 111:19 / 169:24 / 170:21 / 213:8.
6. *dumu lugal*, 153:10.
7. 171:7 / 194:10 / YBC 4748 VII:15.
dSín-i-din-na-áš, *gìr arad*, 152 Tablet:4, 6; Case:4.
dSín-i-din-na-šú, 151:1.
dSín-i-din-..., 16 II:10.
dSín-ilu, 191:4 / 235:3.
dSín-im-gur-ra-an-ni, *-im-gur-an-ni*, YBC 4750 V:5 / YBC 7249 III:26 / YBC 7260 IV:20.
dSín-i-mi-ti, s. of *...-i-din(?)*, *arad dSín-i-ri-ba-am*, 155:Seal.
dSín-ip-pa-al-za-am, 144:19.
dSín-iq-be-i, *-iq-be-e*
1. f. of *Ma-ti-nu-ru-um*, 1 III:6 / 5 II:25.
2. f. of *dSín-êriš(PIN)*, 1 II:37 / 2 II:2 / 54:11.
dSín-i-qi-šá-am
1 s. of *A-li-i*, *na-kid*, 6 I:25 / 19:17.
2. s. of *A-li-i*, 3 II:13 / 4 I:22 / 25:13.
3. s. of *Ḫa-na-bi*, 152 Case:6.
4. s. of *Ur-mêš-šun(?)-na*, 2 I:32.
5. *lugal*, 62:14 / 160:14.

6. master of *Ib-ni-ia*, 123:Seal. (=*lugal?*)
7. *a-bal(?)*, 140:6.
8. 1 VI:9 / 64:10 / 81:3 / 102:18 / YBC 7260 II:18; IV:7.

ᵈSín-i-qi-šam (written *Ú*) (*?*), *lugal*, 159:7.

ᵈSín-i-ri-ba-am, *-e-ri-ba-am*
1 s. of *Za-a-a*, 134:18.
2 f. of *Ḫa-zi-ru-um*, 106:Seal.
3. *lugal*, 133:14, 24 / 155:8 / 156:7 / 157:7 / 158:6 / master of *ᵈSín-i-mi-ti*, 155:Seal.
4. *lugal Unug*[ki], 124:15.
5. *na-kid*, 196:5 / 233:4, 9.
6. *nu-giš-sar*, 146:4, 14.
7. 22:5 / 69:5 / 80:12 / 118:16 / 131:7 / 138:16 / 189:4 / YBC 7260 III:33, 50.

ᵈSín-iš-me-ni, *-iš-me-a-ni*
1. s. of *Gimil(ŠÚ)-ᵈNa-na-a-a*, (*-ᵈNa-na-a*), 4 VII:15 / 16 III:19 / 18:39 / 42:21 / 43:5.
2. s. of *ᵈSín-ri-me-ni*, 126:36.
3. s. of *ᵈŠamaš-na-ṣi-ir*, 126:27.
4. h. of *ᶠᵈMa-mi-ia*, f. of *Ig-mi-il-ᵈSín*, 123:6, 7.
5. b. of *A-ta-na-aḫ-ì-lí*, 1 V:35.
6. *ˡᵘsimug*, 119:2, 21.
7. 3 III:48 / 20:6 / 49:4 / 102:8 / 139:4 / 208 II:36 / YBC 7260 II:26.

ᵈSín-it-ti, 76:7.

ᵈSín-i-. . ., 148:6.

ᵈSín-ki-ma-ì-lí-a, 133:17.

ᵈSín-li-ta-la-al, 84:6.

ᵈSín-li-ta-am, 109:4.

ᵈSín-ma-gir
1. s. of *Gub-ba-ni-dúg*, 135:21.
2. s. of *I-la-ni* (or *lí*), *nagar*, 141:21.
3. s. of *Ì-lí-e-mu-qi*, 34:7.
4. s. of *KÁ-šá-ᵈNu-muš-da*, *ᶠTa-ri-ba-tum*, 141:1.
5. s. of *Ku-na-ti*, *na-kid*, 54:6.
6. s. of *Ku-na-ti*, 16 I:12 / 25:16.
7. s. of *Ku-na-tum*, *na-kid*, 1 I:26.
8. s. of *ᵈNergal-ki-i*, 126:34.
9. s. of *Nu-na-a*, 2 VI:37 / 5 VII:14.
10. s. of *[Um]-mi-a-ḫi-ia*, 162:Seal.
11. s. of *Ur-ᵈNin-a-zu*, *na-kid*, 6 III:40.
12. s. of *Wi(Pi)-ra-a-a*, *arad ᵈEn-ki*, 106:Seal.
13. *dam-qar*, YBC 7260 III:21.
14. *na-kid*, 15 I:16.
15. *simug*, 114:14.
16. 3 II:4 / 4 II:24, 30 / 6 IV:24 / 45:3 / 82:2 / 97:10 / 175:35 / 176:7 / 184:20, 22 / 253:17 / YBC 7260 II:12, 24.

ᵈSín-ma-ha-aṣ (perhaps *ᵈSín-ma-gir*)
1. *šabra*, YBC 7260 III:27.
2. 128:11.

ᵈSín-ma-ilu, 242:3.

ᵈSín-ma-an-sí, 136:11.

ᵈSín-ma-(?), 73:8.

ᵈSín-mu-ba-lí-iṭ
1. s. of *Ap-pa-tum*, YBC 6278 Case:18.
2. s. of *Ḫu-nu-bu-um*, 126:30.
3. s. of *Im-gur-ᵈSín*, 135:17.
4. s. of *Ku* (or *Aš*)*-lu-ú*, 25:32.
5. s. of *Lù-GA-a-a*, *arad ᵈSín-*. . ., 155: Seal.
6. *na-kid*, 6 VI:12 / 15 II:5.
7 2 VI:29 / 4 IX:7, 8 / 5 VII:8 / 67:3/ 224:16.

ᵈSín-mu-pa-ḫi-ir
1. *na-kid*, 104 Tablet:6; Case:5.
2. 4 V:12 / 132:8.

ᵈSín-mu-uš-ta-al, *šá-pi-ir Zararma*[ki], 227: 12.

ᵈSín-na-be-i, f. of *ᵈSín-êriš(PIN)*, 4 II:35.

ᵈSín-na-id, s. of *Ab-di-ra-aḫ*, 137:20.

ᵈSín-na-kid, 146:22.

ᵈSín-na-ṣi-ir, *-na-ṣir*
1. f. of *Ḫu-pa-tum*, 119:20.
2. f. of *Na-bi-ᵈEn-lil*, 125:Seal.
3. f. of *Warad-ᵈNannar*, 144:21.
4. 16 III:13 / (*?*) 246:1.

ᵈSín-na-ši, 2 III:30 / 139:3 / YBC 7260 II:20.

ᵈSín-na-tum
1. s. of *ᵈSín-pi-la-aḫ*, b. of *Gi-mi-lum*, 56:5.
2. 4 VI:25, 32 / 43:4.

ᵈSín-na-wi-ir, 113:3, 6 / 174:8.

3. *nu-banda*, 65:8.
4. 167:9 / 234:3 / YBC 5784:2.

Ṣi-lí-^{d}*Sín*
1. s. of *Bu-uz-bu-zu-um*, 126:7, 9.
2. 115:12 / 116:12 / YBC 4739:36.

Ṣi-lí-^{d}*Šamaš*
1. s. of *Si-'-mu-ug-ra*, 172:7 / 174:9.
2. *gìr*, 166:12, 27.
3. 171:12 / 176:6 / 181:30 / 182:4 / 186:2 / 191:5 / YBC 4864:8.

Ṣi-lí-Uruk^{ki}, f. of *I-din-*^{d}*En-lil*, 126:37.
Ṣi-lí-Uruma^{ki}, *DIN*, 148:49.
Šá-^{d}*Amurru*, b. of ^{d}*Sín-še-mi*, 2 VI:20.
Šá-ma-a-a, 24:3 / 107:14.
Šá-ma-al-lu-um, 144:2, 20.

^{d}*Šamaš-ga-mil*, *-ga-mi-il*, *-ga-mi-el*
1. b. of *Ri-'-(?)*, 134:19.
2. 75:3 / 121:23 / YBC 4748 III:17; IV:25.

^{d}*Šamaš-ḫa-zi-ir*
1. h. of ^{f}*Ḫi-iš-šá-tum*, 143 Tablet:5, 15; Case:1, 12.
2. *gìr*, 246:13.
3. YBC 4748 VII:36 / YBC 7260 III:19.

^{d}*Šamaš-ḫe-gál*, f. of ^{d}*Sín-a-ba*, 141:18.
^{d}*Šamaš-idinnam(MA-AN-SÍ)*. See ^{d}*Babbar-ma-an-sí*.
^{d}*Šamaš-ilu*, 242:4.
^{d}*Šamaš-i-pu-uš*, *IŠ*, 106:50.
^{d}*Šamaš-iš-ki*, f. of *Ḫu-nu-bu-um*, 135:16.
^{d}*Šamaš-iškun*. See List of Cities.
^{d}*Šamaš-ki-ma-ili-šú*, 103:7 / YBC 7260 IV:33.
^{d}*Šamaš-mu-še-zi-ib*, YBC 4864:7, 10.
^{d}*Šamaš-napišti-idinnam*. See ^{d}*Babbar-zi-mu*, ^{d}*Babbar-zi-ma-an-sí*.

^{d}*Šamaš-na-ṣi-ir*, *-na-ṣir*
1. f. of ^{d}*Sín-iš-me-ni*, 126:27.
2. 138:19.

^{d}*Šamaš-nu-ri*, YBC 4744:7.
^{d}*Šamaš-ra-bi*, 139:5.
^{d}*Šamaš-še-mi*, 125 Case:25; Tablet:23.

^{d}*Šamaš-tu-kúl-ti*
1. *nu-banda*, 65:12.
2. YBC 4748 II:17; VII:2.

Šá-ma-a-a-tum, *Šá-a-ma-a-a-tum*
1. *na-kid*, 212:68, 74.
2. 192:10, 14 / 208 I:12; III:8; IV:14.

Šar-ḫi-ilu, *na-kid*, 1 VI:19 / 6 II:25.
Šar-ḫu-um, 1 VI:15 / 3 II:46 / 4 VI:31 / 5 II:18 / 56:7.
Šarru-aplu(TUR-UŠ), 112:2.
Šarru-daiân, 109:10 / 111:13.
Šarru-ra-..., 122:31.
Šar-ru-ut-^{d}*Sín*, *mà-laḫ(DU)*, 143 Tablet:23; Case:21.
Šarru-ut-^{d}*(?)*, 102:1.
^{f}*Šá-at-Ê-an-na*, 88:13.
Šá-at-^{d}*En-lil*, YBC 4748 IV:15; VI:6, 28; VII:27.
Šá-at-ib-bi, 171:6 / 172:6 / 194:4 / 195:7.
^{f}*Šá-at-Ištar*, w. of *Û-ma-a-a-tum*, 137:5.
Šá-at-^{d}*Mà-an-na*, *-*^{d}*Mà-na*, 127:4, 5, 10.
Šá-at-^{d}*Nin-šubur*, 194:7. (*dumu-sal.*)
^{f}*Šá-at-*^{d}*Nu-muš-da*, d. of ^{f}*Mu-ba-li-it-tum*, 70:2.

^{f}*Šá-at-*^{d}*Sín*
1. w. of *Ur-*^{d}*Nin-šubur*, m. of *Ilu-pî (KA)-*^{d}*Ba-ú*, *Lù-dingir-ra*, YBC 5420: 4, 17, 21.
2. m. of *Na-bi-ì-lí-šú*, 144:7.
3. YBC 4744:14.

Še-in-gál-lum, YBC 7260 II:29.

Še-ru-um-ì-lí
1. *gìr*, 169:19.
2. 148:34.

Še-ṣi-lum, s. of *Azag-*^{d}*Nin-gal*, *nagar*, 141:19.
Šeš-pa-tuk, 8:3 / 102:14 / 111:4 / YBC 7260 I:12.
ŠEŠ-...-PÁD, 111:15.
^{d}*ŠE-(?)-GAL-GA*, s. of *Warad-*^{d}*Nannar*, 250:Seal.
^{f}*Ši-ba-a-a*, w. of *Na-din-iš-ta-al-mu-um*, m. of ^{d}*Sín-êriš(PIN)*, 121:5, 8.
Ši-bar(maš)-. See *Lim-maš-*.

Ši-ip-^{d}*Sín*
1. *gu-za-lal*, 119:15 / 122:17 / 124:17.
2. *íl(?)*, 131:23.
3. 206:4.

Ši-ri-im-tum. See List of Cities.
Šú-ub-na-AN, h. of ^{f}*A-ḫa-a-tum*, 110:4, Seal.

9. 109:11 / 125 Case:27; Tablet:25 / 126:31 / 136:10 / 140:15 / 142:7 / 143 Tablet:21; Case:18 / 145:18 / 147: 10 / 175:20 / 180:2 / 186:12 / 199:4 / 253:15 / YBC 4748 II:15.

Warad-NE-NE, lugal Unug^{ki}, *Unug*^{ki}*(-ga)*, 141:36 / 147:21.

Wa-ra-ad-^{d}*Nin-gal*, 86:3.

Warad-^{d}*Nin-šubur*, 140:2.

Warad-^{d}*Sín*
1. s. of *Im-gur*^{d}*Sín, na-kid*, 1 V:19 / 2 III:46 / 4 IX:28 / 9:23.
2. s. of *Ku-du-ur-Ma-bu-uk, lugal Zararma*^{ki}*(-ma)*, 165:Seal.
3. *lugal Zararma*^{ki}, 124:14.
4. *lugal*, 12:11 / 15 IV:34 / 121:17 / 125 Case:17 / 126:19 / 130:13 / 161:10 / 199:10.
5. [*lugal*], 122:Seal / 127:12.
6. master of *Ur-*^{d}*Nannar*, 46:Seal / 47: Seal / 50:Seal / 51:Seal / 52:Seal / 53:Seal, (*lugal?*).
7. f. of *A-bi-ṭa-bu-um*, 53:5.
8. f. of *U-bar-*^{d}*Sín*, 5 V:39 / 30:5.
9. *arad*, 69:1.
10. 48:11 / YBC 4726:19 / 4750 VI:10.

Warad-^{d}*Šamaš*, YBC 7260 II:30.

Warad-šarri, 41:6.

Warad-ti-tu-ri-im, 89:5 / 91:8 / 94:19.

Warad-^{d}..., 242:14.

Wa-ar-da-a-ni, Wa-ar-da-ni, Warda(-da)-ni
1. *pa géme uš-bar*, 134:17.
2. 119:3 / 125 Case:24; Tablet:22.

Wa-ar-da-nu-um, 151:4.

Wa-tar-^{d}*Sín*, f. of *El-la-tum*, 137:16.

Wa-tar-^{d}*Šamaš, nagar*, 141:16.

Wi(PI)-ra-a-a, f. of ^{d}*Sín-ma-gir*, 106:Seal.

Wu-ú-ur-ru-ki-im, 212:35.

Za-a-a, f. of ^{d}*Sín-i-ri-ba-am*, 134:18.

Za-li-lum
1. *na-kid*, 1 I:22 / 6 I:11.
2. 2 I:36 / 5 VI:6 / 64:9.

^{d}*Za-má-má-mu-šá-lim*, 189:7 / 190:3 / 195:5.

Za-am-ma-a-nu-um, šú-i, 122:3, 28.

Za-am-bi-ia, lugal I-si-in^{ki}, 3 V:9.

Za-an-qu-um, f. of *Di-ba-bu-um*, 135:5.

Za-ni-ik-pî(KA)-^{d}*Šamaš, IŠ*, 106:48, Seal.

Za-pi-i-pi, Za-pi-i-pi-i
1. *na-kid*, 6 I:19.
2. 5 VI:20.

Za-ar-ri-qum, s. of *E-nu-um-li-bur*, b. of *Ti-iz-qa-ru-um*, 112:5, 8, 18.

Za-ar-ri-..., 139:15.

Za-a-ṣu-uš(?), s. of ^{d}*Sín-pa-la-šú*, 147:15.

Zer-ia-kul-ti, lù Unug^{ki}, 124:21.

Zi-ba-tum, YBC 4750 IV:10.

Zi-ib-na-tum. See List of Cities.

Zi-ia-tum
1. s. of ^{d}*Sín-ga-mi-il*, 123:Seal. (=^{d}*Sín-ia-tum*, 123:20.)
2. ^{lú}*ŠE*, 132:12 / 143 Tablet:20; Case: 17 / 146:20.
3. 197:2 / 253:18.

Zi-ki-ir-ì-lí-šú
1. s. of *Ib-ku-*^{d}*A-ba, arad Nu-úr-*^{d}*IM*, 155:Seal.
2. 101:2 / YBC 7260 III:24.

Zi-li-..., 140:1.

Zi-na-tum
1. s. of ^{d}*Sín-pi-la-aḫ*, 1 IV:37 / 3 II:22 / 45:4.
2. *(?)-na lugal*, 113:10.

Zi-zi-bu, s. of *Nu-na-bu-um*, 117:14.

Zu(?)-ḫa-a-a, 140:7.

Zu-ki-im, 121:3.

Zu-ni-ba-la-..., 122:21.

Zu-ru-um, YBC 4748 III:15.

...*-a-a*, f. of *Nu-úr-ì-lí-šú*, 13:15.

..., *-bi*
1. s. of ^{d}*IM-na-ṣi-ir*, 18:33.
2. s. of ^{d}*KAL-šá-*^{d}*Šamaš*, 79:4.

...*-êriš(PIN)*, 6 VI:22.

...*-ga-*^{d}*Nannar*, 136:9.

...*-i-din-na-am*, s. of *Ki-iš-ti-Îr-ra, arad* ^{d}*Nergal(Nér-Urú-Gal)*, 162:Seal / 250: Seal / 251:Seal.

...*-la-ti*, 3 III:16.

...*-ma-lum*, 107:6.

...*-na-id, pa géme uš-bar*, 129:16.

...*-nu-um*, 81:8.

...*-ra-bi*, s. of *Ur-méš-ban-da*, b. of *U-bar-*^{d}*Šamaš*, 3 III:8.

. . . *-ru-um*, 4 IX:35.

. . . *-dSín*

1. *dam-qar*, 51:Seal.
2. 4 I:38 / 16 IV:2 / 19:18 / 202:59 / 212:33.

. . . *-dŠamaš*, f. of *Im-gur-d*. . ., 174:16.

. . . *-ta-a-a-ar*, s. of *Ur-ê-gal*, b. of *Im-gur-dSín*, 3 II:35.

. . . *-ti-ilu*, 142:2.

. . . *-tum*, 98:9.

. . . *-ṭa-bu-um*, 2 III:13.

. . . *-ut-tum*, 98:10

Gods and Substitutes or Epithets.

dA-ba, in names under *Ib-ku*—.

A-bi, *A-bu*, in names under *A-bi*—, *A-bu*—.

Ad-da, in names under *Ad-da*—.

A-ḫi, in names under *A-bil*—, *A-ḫi*—, *Nu-úr*—.

A-lí, in names under *A-lí*—.

dAl-la-zun, in names under *dAl-la-zun*—.

dAmurru, 106:Seal / 125:Seal / 126:Seal / 129:Seal; and in names under *A-bil*—, *Awîl*—, *KÁ-šá*—, *Mâr*—, *Nu-úr*—, *Ṣi-lí*—, *Šá*—, *Ur*—, *Warad*—.

Ana, 106:64 / 139:21 / 149:8 / 150:9, 53 / 218:40 / 219:24 / 221:12 / 222:32 / 223:2, 7 / 224:34 / 225:2 / 229:2 / 230:2 / 242:16 / 246:17 / 247:2 / 248:2.

A-nu-um, in names under *Ar-ši*—, *Ku-na*—, *Ma*—, *Ma-na*—, *Ra-bi*—, *Sa-bi*—.

dAšnan(ŠE-TIR), 221:14 / 222:34; and in names under *Awîl*—.

dA-tuk-tuk, in names under *Ur*—.

dBabbar, 69:3 / 106:42 / 107:12 / 126:18 / 133:13 / 137:12 / 138:13 / 167:13; in List of Temples; in List of Officials and Occupations; and in names under *dBabbar*—, *Gar-ra*—.

dBara, in List of Temples; and in names under *Ur*—.

dBàr-ul-e-gar-ra, in List of Temples.

dBa-ú, in *šutug dBa-ú* in List of Officials and Occupations; and in names under *dBa-ú*—, *Ib-ku*—, *Ilu-pî*—, *Nu-úr*—, *Ṣi-lí*—, *U-bar*—, *Warad*—.

Be-lí, *Bi-lí*, *Be-lum*, in names under *Be-lí*—, *Be-ium*—, *Ki-ma*—.

dDa-gan, in names under *Nu-úr*—.

dDa-mu, in names under *dDa-mu*—, *Gimil*—, *Ib-ku*—, *I-din*—.

dingir-ra, in names under *Lù*—.

dDumu-zi-da, *dDumu-zi*, in names under *Awîl*—, *dDumu-zi*—, *Gimil*—, *U-bar*—.

Ê-a, in names under *A-na*—, *Ê-a*—, *Ib-ku*—, *Ib-ni*—, *I-din*—, *Î-lí*—, *Im-lik*—, *Iš-ku-un*—, *It-ti*—, *Na-ra-am*—, *Nu-úr*—, *Warad*—.

dÊ-nim-ma, in names under *Ṣi-lí*—.

dEn-ki, 46:Seal / 47:Seal / 50:Seal / 51:Seal / 52:Seal / 53:Seal / 106:64, Seal / 122:Seal / 139:21 / 149:8 / 150:3, 9, 53 / 217 I:8, 23; IV:27 / 218:2 / 219:24 / 220:1 / 221:12 / 222:32 / 223:2, 7 / 224:34 / 225:2 / 229:2 / 230:2 / 242:16 / 246:17 / 247:2 / 248:2; in List of Temples; in List of Officials and Occupations; and in names under *Azag*—, *dEn-ki*—, *KÁ*—, *Ur*—.

dEn-lil, *dEn-lil-lá*, 79:28 / 106:64 / 139:21 / 149:8 / 150:3, 9, 53 / (?) 167:13 / 203:6 / 204:11 / 217 I:3, 8, 23; IV:27 / 218:2, 40 / 219:24 / 220:1 / 221:12 / 222:32 / 223:2, 7 / 224:34 / 225:2 / 229:2 / 230:2 / 242:16 / 246:17 / 247:2 / 248:2; and in names under *dEn-lil*—, *Gimil*—, *I-din*—, *Na-bi*—, *dSín-a-bil*—, *Šá-at*—.

E-nu-um, in names under *E-nu-um*—.

dGirru (BIL-GI), in names under *Im-gur*—.

dGÚ-AN-NA, 129:Seal.

dGu-la, in names under *Me-eš-(?)*—, *U-bar*—.

Temples.

ê ^{d}*Innina*, 171:16 / 172:8.
ê ^{d}*Innina* ^{d}*Nannar ù* ^{d}*En-ki*, 202:18 / 207: 19, 63.
Ê-kalam-ta-ní-gúr ê ^{d}*Innina Zabalam*^{ki}, 253: 25–6.
ê Keš^{ki}, 226:3.
Ê-kúr, 149:10 / 150:10, 55.
ê ^{d}*Nannar*, 2:L.E.; VI:1 / 4 VIII:28; X:5, 9 / 5 VI:33; VII:20 / 6 V:2 / 15 I:3 / 16 IV:17 / 18:41 / 47:Seal / 51:Seal / 52:Seal / 54:17 / 56:14 / 57:7 / 59:9 / 60:5 / 61:8 / 122:11 / 162:8 / 173:2 / 202:2, 17, 61, 72 / 207:15, 50.
ê ^{d}*Nannar* ^{d}*Nin-*... ^{d}*Babbar-ra*, 124:27–8.
ê ^{d}*Nin-ê-gal*, 237:4.
ê ^{d}*Nin-gal*, 4 IX:39; X:6 / 5 VII:16, 21.
ê ^{d}*Nin-gal* ^{d}*Babbar*, 125 Case:34–5.
ê ^{d}*Nin-lil* 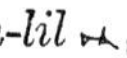, 127:29 / 202:13, 49 / 207: 6.
ê ^{d}*Nin-lil nim-ma*, 201:9.
ê ^{d}*Nin-mar-ki*, 201:10 / 202:73.
Ê-nun-maḫ, *Ê-nun-maḫ ê* ^{d}*Nannar(-šù)*, 15 I:4 / 122:14 / 253:24.
ê ^{d}*Sín*, 169:9.
kisal-maḫ ^{d}*Babbar*, 7:12 / 22:8 / 24:8 / 26:12 / 27:6 / 33:12 / 39:11 / 42:24 / 43:8 / 47:9 / 48:19 / 67:11 / 70:13 / 73:12 / 77:10 / 85:7 / 104:14.
kisal-maḫ ^{d}*Nannar*, 118:24 / 120:16.

Officials and Occupations.

^{lù}*a-bal*, 42:4 / 140:9.
^{lù}*a-bal*^{meš}, 40:8.
arad, 40:1, 2, 3 / 42:1 / 46:Seal / 47:Seal / 50:Seal / 51:Seal / 52:Seal / 53: Seal / 71:1 / 72:1 / 77:4 / 106:Seal / 115:2 / 116:2 / 122:Seal / 123:Seal / 125:Seal / 126:Seal / 129:Seal / 155: Seal / 222:1 / 250:Seal / 251:Seal / 253:2 / YBC 5420:Seal.
See also *sag arad*.
arad ê-gal, 117:3.
^{lù}*BIL(?)*, 219:16.
BIR-ŠÚ-BU-BU(=barû), 171:26.
DA-GÀL, 106:45.
dam-qar, 51:Seal / 129:4, 22 / 139:18 / 141:25, 26 / 154:2, 6, 8, 11 / 203:3.
dam-qar^{meš}, 186:7.
dìm, 113:15 / 123:26 / 127:16 / 131:27 / 134:24 / (?) 137:17 / 143 Case:20, 25 / 145:14 / 172:14 / YBC 6278 Case:14–16.
DIN (muttaggišu), 148:49.
dúb-sar, 46:Seal / 47:Seal / 50:Seal /51: Seal / 52:Seal / 53:Seal / 121:26 / 126:24, 40 / 133:21 / 134:25 / 155: Seal.
dúb-sar A-RU-A(?), 47:Seal / 51:Seal / 52: Seal.
DU-GAB, 106:54 / 141:15.
DU-GAB mu, 141:31.
en ^{d}*Babbar*, 152 Tablet:8; Case:12 / 153: 16 / 154:16.
en dúb ^{d}*IM*, 177:4, 12 / 183:8.
en ^{d}*En-ki*, 194:11.
en ^{d}*Nannar*, 28:10 / 29:6 / 46:Seal / 50: Seal / 51:Seal / 250:9 / 251:11.
engar, 112:24, 25.
erim dumu lugal, 151:7.
erim šàg-ga. See ^{lù}*šàg-ga*.
géme, 73:1 / 117:2, 10 / 194:6 / 207:39 / 222:2, 8–11, 15, 18.
géme^{zun}, 178:9 / 207:27 / 222:19, 23, 26.
géme-arad^{zun}, 175:25 / 178:2 / 184:10 / 222: 3, 5.
géme uš-bar, 77:2. See also *pa géme uš-bar*.
gìr, 17:6, 12, 21 / 26:8 / 100:6 / 121:19 / 126:39 / 150:50 / 153:8 / 166:12, 27, 38 / 168:13 / 169:16 / 170:11 / 171:17 / 182:13 / 185:14 / 205:5 / 209:12 / 221:3 / 227:15 / 246:13.
gìr arad (=šakkannakku), 152:4.
gìr dam-qum, 166:8.

^{lú}*SA-GAZ*, 33:7 / 46:2 / 47:4 / 50:4 / 51:4 / 52:4 / 53:3.
sangu ^{d}*Innina*, YBC 4857:13
síb, 106:67 / 149:11 / 150:5, 11, 56 / 217 I: 10, 25; IV:29 / 218:4, 43 / 220:3 / 221:15 / 222:35 / 224:37 / 225:5 / 246:20 / 247:5 / 248:5.
síb-e-ne, 3 V:4 / 4 X:4 / 13:1, 23 / 15 IV: 30 / 16 IV:16 / 55:5 / 57:5 / 61:7 / 63:5 / 181:20.
síb áb-udu-e-ne. 175:11 / 184:7.
simug, 114:14 / 119:21, 26, 27 / 134:21 / 145:19.
simug gìr arad, 119:17 / 123:19 / 126:21.
^{lú}*simug šá ê A-ab-ba-a*, 195:9.
šabra, YBC 7260 III:27.
^{lú}*šàg-ga*, ^{erim}*šàg-ga*, 175:6 / 181:4, 10, 16 / 184:3.
šá-pi-ir Ararma^{ki}, 227:13.
šar-ra-ni(?), 149:6.
šar-ri-im, 208 I:31 / 212:32, 61 / 217 II: 36; IV:15.
šà-tam, 119:16 / 122:22, 23 / 141:13, 14 / 144:17, 18, 20 / 163:14.
šà-tam-e-ne, 1 VI:30 / 3 V:6 / 5 VII:22 / 9:32 / 10:28 / 11:34 / 13:24 / 15 IV:32 / 16 IV:19 / 19:34 / 25:43 / 30:43 / 33:10 / 46:6 / 47:7 / 50:8 / 51:7 / 52:7 / 53:6 / 55:7 / 59:6 / 95:11 / 102:32 / 104:12 / 155:6 / 162:6 / 214:6 / 250:6 / 251:8.
^{lú}*ŠE*, 123:20 / 132:12 / 143 Case:17 / 146: 20.
^{lú}*ŠE-íl*, 166:18, 23, 34 / 170:8 / 185:10 / 209:8.
^{lú}*ŠE-KIN-KUD*, 181:5, 11, 17.
^{lú}*ŠE*^{meš} *šá Ni-in-nu-ú-a*, 178:3.
šú-gé, YBC 4726:10 / YBC 4739:13.
šú-ḫa, ^{lú}*šú-ḫa*, 97:7 / 174:13.
šú-ḫa-e-ne, 97:9.
šú-i, 122:3 / 124:20 / 163:24.
ŠÚ-QA-GAB-A lugal, 141:24, 27.
šutug, 135:11 / 137:19.
šutug..., YBC 5420:2, 10, 16.
šutug ^{d}*Ba-ú*, YBC 5420:Seal.
šutug ^{d}*En-ki*, 143 Case:19.
šutug ^{d}*Nin-azag-nun-na*, 135:1.
šutug ^{d}*Nin-giš-zi-da*, 132:14.
šutug simug(?) ^{d}*Nannar*, 46:Seal / 47:Seal / 50:Seal / 51:Seal / 52:Seal / 53:Seal.
šutug simug(?) pisan dúb-ba ^{d}*Nannar*, 122: Seal.
ukuš lugal, 144:22.
UM(?) nagar, 143 Case:23 / 147:13.
uš-bar, ^{lú}*uš-bar*, 147:12 / 177:6.
ú-tul, 193:11. See also *gìr*...*ú-tul*.

Countries and Cities.

uru^{ki} *A-bi-sa-ri-e*, 175:32 / 184:16.
Adab^{ki}, 140:23 / 143 Tablet:32 / 144:27 / 168:21 / 169:23 / 170:20 / 171:36 / 172:19 / 173:8 / 174:28 / 175:39 / 212:3.
uru^{ki} *A-ḫu-um-ma*, 106:8, 10.
uru Al-gu-um, 17:25.
uru^{ki} *AN-BAR*, 153:2.
AN-ZA-QAR Bal-mu-nam-ḫe, 181:13.
Ararma^{ki}, *Ararma*^{ki} (*-ma*), 16 IV:22 / 17:5 / 48:20 / 80:15 / 85:8 / 100:5 / 106:3 / 109:16 / 124:14 / 140:25 / 164:6 / 165:Seal / 168:23 / 172:21 / 173:10 / 174:30 / 186:3 / 199:7 / 202:15, 57 / 203:5 / 207:12, 19, 44, 63 / 208 I:34 / 212:4, 34 / 227:11; and in *šá-pi-ir Ararma*^{ki} in List of Officials and Occupations.
Bâbilu (DIN-TIR-KI), *uru*^{ki} *Bâbilu (KÁ-DINGIR)*, 38:5, 13 / 141:35 / 147: 20 / 181:13.
BÁD[1]*(?)*^{ki}, *lù BÁD*^{ki}, 124:4 / 204:12.
Bal-mu-nam-ḫe. See *AN-ZA-QAR Bal-mu-nam-ḫe*.

[1] To be read BÀD(?). Cf. Strassmaier *Warka*, No. 18; Meissner *Alt-Bab. Privatrecht*, No. 108; Langdon in *Babyloniaca*, VII, p. 43.

uru^{ki} *Bi-na-a,* 196:13.
Du-un-nu-um^{ki}, 218:41 / 219:25.
Ê-ŠÚ-^{d}*Sín-na*^{ki}, *Ê-ŠÚ-*^{d}*Sín-na,* 243:6 / 252:2.
uru^{ki} *Gar-ra-*^{d}*Babbar,* 132:17 / 145:23 / 146:25 / 192:16 / 193:13 / 194:16 / 195:14 / 196:15 / 197:6 / 198:6 / 208 I:5, 32; II:34; IV:16 / 231:13.
uru^{ki} *Gar-ra-*^{d}*Nergal (Nér-Urú-Gal),* 235:5.
uru^{ki} *Gimil (ŠÚ)-*^{d}*En-lil-lá,* 202:7.
uru^{ki} *ḪAL,* 150:7 / 217 I:12, 27; IV:31 / 220:5.
uru^{ki} *I-di-*^{d}*IB,* 166:40.
IM^{ki}, 232:7 / 233:14.
uru^{ki} *Im-gur-*^{d}*Girru (BIL-GI),* 107:21.
Ì-si-in^{ki}, *I-si-in*^{ki}, *Ì-si-in-na, Ì-si-in-na*^{ki}, *Ì-si-in*^{ki}*-na,* 3 V:10 / 83:7 / 95:16 / 106:65 / 139:22 / 141:34 / 147:19 / 205:8 / 206:6 / 218:42 / 219:26 / 223:9 / 249:5.
uru^{ki} *Iš-ku-un-Ê-a,* 175:27 / 184:12 / 188:4 / 193:9 / 201:6 / 244:2.
uru^{ki} *Iš-ku-un-*^{d}*Nergal (GÌR-UNU-GAL),* 234:14.
Iškun-^{d}*Šamaš.* See *Gar-ra-*^{d}*Babbar.*
uru^{ki} *KÁ,* 148:35.
uru^{ki}, *KÁ-*^{d}..., 168:2.
uru^{ki} *KAB-EN(?)...,* 38:9.
Ka-ṣal-lu^{ki}, 4 X:11 / 14:6 / 16 IV:21 / 30:45 / 31:7 / 32:6 / 46:8 / 49:15 / 50:10 / 51:9 / 52:10 / 53:8 / 65:21 / 68:5 / 72:9 / 78:5 / 81:12 / 88:18.
Ki-sur-ra^{ki}, 203:5 / 204:9.
uru^{ki} *Ma-sa-bu-um,* 170:17 / 185:2.
Maš-gan-šabra^{ki}, *Maš-gan-šabra,* 99:2 / 112:33 / 113:20 / 127:30 / 165:5 / 176:11 / 177:14 / 178:14 / 179:10 / 180:8 / 181:32 / 182:18 / 183:10 / 184:25 / 185:20 / 186:14 / 202:13, 49 / 207:6 / 209:16 / 210:7 / 211:5 / 212:6, 76 / 213:9 / 214:8 / 215:3 / 216:10.
uru^{ki} *Na-za-rum,* ^{uru}*Na-za-rum,* 236:4 / 237:9 / 238:8.
^{d}*Nergal-iškun.* See *Gar-ra-*^{d}*Nergal, Iš-ku-un-*^{d}*Nergal.*
Nibru^{ki}, 5 VII:25 / 25:45 / 61:10 / 63:9 / 71:9 / 135:24 / 167:11.
^{kúr}*Nim*^{ki}, *Nim*^{ki}*-ma,* ^{kúr}*Nim*^{ki}*-ma,* 2 L.E. / 3 V:8 / 18:43 / 36:9 / 60:7 / 76:12.
uru^{ki} *Nu-úr-*^{d}*IM,* 212:32, 61.
Ra-bi-qum^{ki}, 141:35 / 147:20.
uru^{ki} *Ra-ḫa-bu-um,* ^{uru}*Ra-ḫa-bu,* 106:5 / 172:12 / 217 IV:18.
Rù-um-ma, uru^{ki} *Rù-um*^{ki}, 152:5 / 202:73.
uru^{ki} *sag maḫ.* See *Du-un-nu-um*^{ki}.
uru^{ki} *SAG-PA-KAB-DU-GA,* ^{uru}*SAG-PA-KAB-DU,* ^{uru}*SAG-PA-KAB-DU*^{ki}, *uru*^{ki} *SAG-PA-KAB-GA,* 58:12 / 115:15 / 116:15 / 126:43 / 129:31 / 164:9 / 202:11, 43.
uru^{ki} ^{d}*Sín-nu-úr-ma-tim,* 181:7 / 182:2 / 212:72 / 217 II:2, 35; III:23.
Su-ti-um^{ki}, 141:35 / 147:20.
^{d}*Šamaš-iškun.* See *Gar-ra-*^{d}*Babbar.*
Šir-bur-la^{ki}. See List of Canals.
uru^{ki} *Ši-ri-im-tum*^{ki}, *uru*^{ki} *Ši-ri-im-tum,* 114:7 / 181:19.
Umma^{ki}, *lù Umma*^{ki}, 166:7 / 233:11.
UNU^{ki} *(-ma)* = *Zararma*^{ki} *(-ma)(?),* 22:9 / 39:12.
Unug^{ki}, *Unug*^{ki} *(-ga), Unug(?), lù Unug*^{ki}, 79:29 / 124:15, 21 / 141:34, 36 / 147:19, 21 / 149:12 / 150:11, 57 / 172:9 / 217 I:4.
Uruk^{ki}, in personal names under *I-ta-na-aḫ—, Ṣi-lí—.*
Uruma^{ki}*(-ma), Uruma*^{ki}, 103:2 / 121:29 / 123:31 / 149:15 / 150:12, 59 / 163:28 / 174:12, 17, 19 / 201:8 / 202:8, 38 / 214:3 / 250:9 / 251:11; and in personal names under *Mâr—,* ^{d}*Sín-ri-im—,* ^{d}*Sín-šar—, Ṣi-lí—.*
Ú-zar-pa-ra^{ki}, *Ú-za-ar-bar-ra,* 243:7 / 252:3.
uru^{ki} *Wa-qar-tum,* 106:7, 12.
Zabalam^{ki},[1] 172:11 / 207:57 / 253:26.
Zar-bí-lum^{ki}, 26:7 / 199:9 / 207:33 / 218:3 / 224:35 / 225:3; and in *pa dam-qar Zar-bí-lum*^{ki} in List of Officials and Occupations.
uru^{ki} *Zi-ib-na-tum,* 107:22.

[1] So read Delitzsch *Sumerisches Glossar,* p. 218.

Canals.

CATALOGUE.

The following system of notations and abbreviations for the list of dates has been adopted: Figures indicate known years of definite reigns; as, *W-S* 1 is the first year of *Warad-Sin.* Dates with Roman letters, like *W-S* a, belong to *Warad-Sin;* but the order in the reign is undetermined. Dates with a Greek letter, like *W-S* α are only conjecturally assigned to the reign. U a, U b, etc., indicate unindentified formulæ which probably belong to the Larsa Dynasty.

Text.	Reign.	Year.	Month.	Day.	YBC.	Description.
1	*Sin-idinnam(?)*	α	7	. .	4752	Record of sheep and their shepherds.
2	*Sin-idinnam(?)*	α	12	. .	4746	Record of sheep belonging to the temple of *Nannar.*
3	*Sin-idinnam(?)*	α	11	30	4728	Record of sheep brought in by shepherds.
4	*Warad-Sin*	α	12	. .	4747	Account of sheep belonging to the temples of *Nannar* and *Ningal.*
5	*Warad-Sin*	b(?)	1	. .	4837	Account of sheep belonging to the temples of *Nannar* and *Ningal.*
6	Date broken off	. .	. .	. .	4749	Record of sheep and their shepherds.
7	*Warad-Sin*	c	13	22	4737	Summary of sheep.
8	*Ṣili-IM(?)*	a	. .	. .	4846	Round tag for dates.
9	*Ṣili-IM*	a	12	. .	4735	Record of flocks and their shepherds.
10	*Ṣili-IM*	a	12	. .	4731.	Record of flocks and their shepherds.
11	*Ṣili-IM*	a	12	. .	4724	Record of flocks and their shepherds.
12	*Warad-Sin*	1	7–9	. .	4813	Receipt for dates.
13	U	f	4	14	4733	Balance of sheep brought in by shepherds.
14	*Warad-Sin*	α	5	16	4796	Note concerning a calf.
15	*Warad-Sin*	1	8	. .	4743	Shepherds' account for one year.
16	*Warad-Sin(?)*	α	2	. .	4838	Summary of sheep brought in by shepherds.
17	U	e	5	17	4734	Account of payments in sheep.
18	*Sin-idinnam(?)*	α	12	. .	4742	Temple record of sheep.
19	Date broken off	. .	. .	. .	4738	Account of sheep and their shepherds.
20	*Warad-Sin*	c	8	. .	4810	Record of sheep and cattle for sacrifice.
21	U	f	9	. .	4816	Note concerning cattle.
22	U(*W-S?*)	i	6	. .	4827	Note concerning cattle.
23	U	f	4	. .	4822	Note concerning cattle.
24	*Warad-Sin*	c	8	16	4807	Record of cattle for sacrifice.
25	*Warad-Sin(?)*	b(?)	1	. .	4732	Record of sheep brought by shepherds.
26	*Warad-Sin*	c	4	. .	4860	Account of payments in cattle.
27	*Warad-Sin*	c	4	21	4814	Note regarding cattle.
28	*Warad-Sin*	d	8	18	4798	Note regarding two female slaves.
29	*Warad-Sin*	d	3	18	4791	Note concerning a goat.
30	*Warad-Sin*	α	12	13	4741	Record of flocks.

Text.	Reign.	Year.	Month.	Day.	YBC.	Description.
31	*Warad-Sin*	*a*	12	..	4801	Note regarding sheep.
32	*Warad-Sin*	*a*	4	..	4802	Note concerning two cows.
33	*Warad-Sin*	c	11	21	4865	Note in regard to sheep for *SA-GAZ*.
34	*Warad-Sin*	b	1	6	4722	Record of sheep.
35	U	f	12	..	4842	Note regarding a sheep.
36	*Sin-idinnam(?)*	*a*	12	20	4855	Account of payment in goats.
37	U	f	6	..	4849	Note regarding sheep.
38	U(*Sin-idinnam?*)	d	12	..	4832	Certificate of inspection of sheep for sacrifice.
39	U(*W-S?*)	i	6	..	4836	Note concerning cattle and sheep.
40	U	f	7	..	4784	Record concerning three slaves.
41	U	f	12	..	4790	Account of slaves.
42	*Warad-Sin*	c	8	..	4782	Account of slaves, cattle, and sheep.
43	*Warad-Sin*	c	9	..	4817	Note concerning sheep.
44	*Warad-Sin*	c	2	1(?)	4783	Record of sheep and cattle.
45	U	g	1	23	4763	Note regarding sheep.
46	*Warad-Sin*	*a*	9	..	4854	Square tag for sheep for *SA-GAZ*.
47	*Warad-Sin*	c	10	13	4772	Square tag for sheep for *SA-GAZ*.
48	*Warad-Sin*	c	3	29	4804	Account of sheep.
49	*Warad-Sin*	*a*	7	..	4823	Account of sheep.
50	*Warad-Sin*	*a*	9	..	4771	Square tag for sheep for *SA-GAZ*.
51	*Warad-Sin*	*a*	7	..	4862	Square tag for sheep for *SA-GAZ*.
52	*Warad-Sin*	*a*	7	..	4769	Square tag for sheep for *SA-GAZ*.
53	*Warad-Sin*	*a*	7	..	4762	Square tag for sheep for *SA-GAZ*.
54	*Ṣili-IM*	a	12	..	4776	Account of wool.
55	*Ṣili-IM*	a	12	..	4847	Round tag for records of shepherds.
56	*Ṣili-IM*	a	12	5	4765	Account of wool.
57	*Ṣili-IM*	a	12	..	4833	Round tag for records of shepherds.
58	*Warad-Sin*	11	12	..	4839	Round tag for reeds.
59	*Gungunu(?)*	14	12	..	4834	Round tag for records of sheep.
60	*Sin-idinnam(?)*	*a*	..	..	4848	Round tag for records of sheep.
61	*Sin-iqîsham*	c	12	14	4835	Round tag for records of sheep.
62	*Sin-iqîsham*	1	13	..	4851	Round tag for the receipt of sacrificial sheep.
63	*Warad-Sin*	a(?)	1–12	..	4794	Round tag for records of sheep.
64	U	f	12	..	4826	Account of sheep.
65	*Warad-Sin*	*a*	8	..	4781	Account of laborers.
66	*Warad-Sin*	b	1	..	4845	Note regarding a cow.
67	*Warad-Sin*	c	11	..	4841	Note concerning female slaves.
68	*Warad-Sin*	*a*	7	..	4844	Note in regard to a female slave.
69	U	f	9	..	4856	Note regarding a slave.
70	*Warad-Sin*	c	4	..	4773	Record of female slaves and silver brought for *Ningal*.
71	*Warad-Sin(?)*	b(?)	1	..	4811	Note concerning a slave.
72	*Warad-Sin*	*a*	7	..	4815	Note concerning a slave.

Text.	Reign.	Year.	Month.	Day.	YBC.	Description.
73	*Warad-Sin*	c	10	..	4840	Account of female slaves.
74	U	f	11	..	4812	Rece'pt for a slave.
75	U(*Sin-idinnam?*)	c	4	..	4805	Temple record.
76	*Sin-idinnam(?)*	*a*	11	21	4785	Receipt for slaves.
77	*Warad-Sin*	c	10	..	4858	Receipt for slaves.
78	*Warad-Sin*	*a*	7	..	4829	Note concerning a female slave.
79	*Rîm-Sin*	22	12	..	4730	Account of silver and gold for gods.
80	U	f	8	3	4767	List of payments.
81	*Warad-Sin*	*a*	11	1	4825	List of payments in grain.
82	*Warad-Sin*	a	13	Broken	4787	Temple record.
83	*Rîm-Sin*	32	8	..	4818	Receipt for silver.
84	*Warad-Sin*	c(?)	5	Broken	4852	Receipt for grain.
85	*Warad-Sin*	c	9	7(?)	4806	Temple record.
86	U	f	11	..	4830	Note with regard to a cow.
87	....	..	12	30	4828	Receipt for grain paid for reeds.
88	*Warad-Sin*	*a*	9	..	4779	Account of dates paid to women.
89	....	..	2	..	4780	Temple record.
90	Broken				4824	Record of bitumen.
91	Undated				4766	Temple record.
92	U	f	2	..	4789	Note concerning a slave.
93	*Warad-Sin*	c	9	14	4799	Account of sesame.
94	Undated				4736	List of garments.
95	*Rîm-Sin*	33(?)	12	30	4797	Account of sesame, oil, etc.
96	Undated				4820	List of garments.
97	Undated				4778	List of laborers.
98	Undated				4729	Obverse, list of payments to women; Reverse, beginning of a letter.
99	*Rîm-Sin*	8	6	11	4821	Date formula.
100	U	f	10	..	4850	Note concerning a boat.
101	Date broken				4800	Record concerning reeds.
102	Date broken				4740	Account of grain paid to overseers of women weavers.
103	*Rîm-Sin*	1	1	7	4721	Account of grain for various cities.
104	*Warad-Sin*	c	12	4	4777	Account of wool delivered.
105	Undated				4745	Exercise tablet.
106	*Rîm-Sin*	38	1	..	4751	Partition contract.
107	*Rîm-Sin*	18	3	..	4774	Deed for storehouse.
108	....	..	6	..	4819	Promissory note for grain and oil.
109	U	f	5	20	4809	Promissory note for loan, without interest, of silver and sesame.
110	Undated				4803	Contract respecting penalty for non-delivery of slaves.
111	*Sin-idinnam*	1	4	..	5315	Contract for the return of a boat.
112	*Rîm-Sin*	8	4	8	5567	Deed for improved property.
113	*Rîm-Sin*	8	11	..	4458	Partition contract.

Text.	Reign.	Year.	Month.	Day.	YBC.	Description.
114	*Warad-Sin*	9	8	. .	6170	Contract for the payment of a debt in sesame.
115	*Warad-Sin*	11	5	. .	6225	Contract for the hire of a slave.
116	*Warad-Sin*	11	5	. .	6226	Contract for the hire of a slave.
117	*Ṣili-IM*	1	9	. .	4760	Contract for the transfer of a female slave.
118	*Warad-Sin*	8	5	. .	6166	Deed for real estate.
119	*Warad-Sin*	9	13	. .	5686	Deed for improved property.
120	*Warad-Sin*	8	1	. .	8762	Deed for an orchard.
121	*Warad-Sin*	10	4	. .	6152	Deed for improved property.
122	*Warad-Sin*	9	3	. .	5709	Deed for a storehouse.
123	*Warad-Sin*	10	12	. .	6153	Deed for real estate.
124	*Warad-Sin*	a	4	25	5579	Slave sale contract.
125	*Warad-Sin*	a	13	. .	7475	Deed for real estate.
126	*Warad-Sin*	11	4	. .	6147	Deed for real estate.
127	*Warad-Sin*	12	9	25	5726	Deed for improved property.
128	*Warad-Sin*	9	8	. .	5698	Contract for loan of grain without interest.
129	*Warad-Sin*	11	7	. .	7227	Deed for improved property.
130	*Warad-Sin*	12(?)	Broken		8763	Deed for real estate.
131	*Warad-Sin*	c	6	. .	4275	Deed for an orchard.
132	*Rîm-Sin*	11	10	25	6208	Receipt for a female slave paid for taxes.
133	*Sin-iribam*	1	13	. .	8755	Contract for purchase of orchards.
134	*Warad-Sin*	a	13	. .	5721	Contract for exchange of real estate.
135	*Warad-Sin(?)*	a(?)	11	. .	5369	Contract for purchase of right to serve as priest for five days.
136	*Rîm-Sin*	10	11	. .	5427	Contract for loan of silver without interest.
137	*Rîm-Sin*	6	. .	. .	8746	Deed for granary.
138	*Rîm-Sin*	27	7	1	5175	Deed for unimproved property.
139	*Rîm-Sin*	31	12	. .	8760	Deed for a field.
140	*Rîm-Sin*	7	12	14	8757	Contract for the transfer of slaves.
141	*Rîm-Sin*	15	5	6	7226	Contract for the purchase of a slave from his parents.
142	*Rîm-Sin*	10	12	. .	5448	Deed for improved real estate.
143	*Rîm-Sin*	7	12	18	6146	Deed for granary.
144	*Rîm-Sin*	7	11	. .	8759	Deed for real estate.
145	*Rîm-Sin*	11	11	. .	5584	Contract for the transfer of a female slave.
146	*Rîm-Sin*	11	6	. .	6111	Contract for delivery of produce of orchards.
147	*Rîm-Sin*	15	11	. .	6205	Promissory note for silver.
148	U	f	6	. .	7076	Partition contract.
149	*Rîm-Sin*	24	9	. .	5363	Witnesses, etc., from contract for hire of a slave.
150	*Rîm-Sin*	24	8	x+3	7098	Record of cattle for two years.
151	*Nûr-IM*	b	1	10	5326	Receipt for slaves.
152	*Nûr-IM*	c	8	7	4282	Receipt for silver.
153	*Nûr-IM*	c	12	. .	4300	Receipt for sesame.
154	*Nûr-IM*	c	10	4	4761	Record of payments in silver.

Text.	Reign.	Year.	Month.	Day.	YBC.	Description.
155	*Sin-iribam*	1	5	4	3320	Receipt for lambs.
156	*Sin-iribam*	1	4	..	5092	Receipt for silver (?) in payment of a debt.
157	*Sin-iribam*	1	13	5	5093	Receipt for grain in payment of a debt.
158	*Sin-iribam*	1	8	..	5215	Receipt for silver in payment of a debt.
159	*Sin-iqîsham(?)*	1	5	1–29	5091	Record of payment in grain.
160	*Sin-iqîsham*	b	4	..	5650	Record of payments in silver.
161	*Warad-Sin*	2(?)	1	..	4985	Record of the transfer of a slave.
162	*Warad-Sin*	8	7	16	6197	Note concerning garments.
163	*Warad-Sin*	10	10	..	5418	Account of food and drink for workmen.
164	*Warad-Sin*	11	5	21	7188	Record of grain paid out.
165	*Warad-Sin*	c	12	16	6978	Receipt for garments.
166	*Warad-Sin*	c	4	10	5586	Balanced account of grain.
167	*Warad-Sin(?)*	a(?)	2	29	4405	Record of payments of drink.
168	*Rîm-Sin*	7	3	29	5494	Balanced account of grain.
169	*Rîm-Sin*	7	4	4	7187	Balanced account of grain.
170	*Rîm-Sin*	7	3	27	7310	Balanced account of grain.
171	*Rîm-Sin*	7	4	30	6143	List of payments in oil.
172	*Rîm-Sin*	7	12	x+6	7185	List of payments in oil.
173	*Rîm-Sin*	7	10	24	5529	Record of receipt and delivery of grain.
174	*Rîm-Sin*	7	5	Broken	5829	Record of payments in grain.
175	*Rîm-Sin*	7	12	..	7195	Account of payments in grain.
176	*Rîm-Sin*	8	13	6	8761	Record of grain paid out.
177	*Rîm-Sin*	8	10	19	4415	Receipt for wool.
178	*Rîm-Sin*	8	10	1	8758	Record of silver paid to laborers.
179	*Rîm-Sin*	8	7	23	5518	Receipt.
180	*Rîm-Sin*	8	10	14	4446	Receipt for wool.
181	*Rîm-Sin*	8	12	..	7211	Account of grain paid out in one year.
182	*Rîm-Sin*	8	11	..	5580	Balanced account of grain.
183	*Rîm-Sin*	8	4	8	4414	Receipt for grain.
184	*Rîm-Sin*	8	12	..	7202	Account of grain for one year.
185	*Rîm-Sin*	8	4	6	6985	Balanced account of grain.
186	*Rîm-Sin*	8	9	8	5568	Receipt for sesame, wool, and sheep.
187	*Rîm-Sin*	10	1	17	7308	Record of grain paid out.
188	*Rîm-Sin*	10	7	10	5768	Record of grain paid out.
189	*Rîm-Sin*	10	10	5	6216	Record of grain paid out.
190	*Rîm-Sin*	10	6	9	7032	Record of grain paid out.
191	*Rîm-Sin*	10	9	17	7190	Record of grain paid out.
192	*Rîm-Sin*	11	12	30	5583	Record of balances of sheep and wool.
193	*Rîm-Sin*	11	12	18	7182	Record of payments in sheep and wool.
194	*Rîm-Sin*	11	2	30	6219	Record of payments in oil.
195	*Rîm-Sin*	11	3	9	7313	Record of grain paid out.
196	*Rîm-Sin*	11	12	25	6209	Account of sheep and their wool.
197	*Rîm-Sin*	11	9	..	5535	Note recording the receipt and delivery of silver.

Text.	Reign.	Year.	Month.	Day.	YBC.	Description.
198	*Rîm-Sin*	11	10	10	8775	Note recording the receipt and delivery of silver.
199	*Rîm-Sin*	2	2	5	7030	Receipt for wool for garments.
200	*Rîm-Sin*	12	11	14	7184	Receipt for cattle.
201	*Rîm-Sin*	9	3	5	8756	List of payments in grain.
202	*Rîm-Sin*	3	12	. .	7477	Account of grain delivered during nine years.
203	*Rîm-Sin*	21	11	28	5793	Receipt given by a merchant.
204	*Rîm-Sin*	21	2	5	8744	Record of sesame paid out.
205	*Rîm-Sin*	35	7	19	8731	Receipt for silver (?).
206	*Rîm-Sin*	61	3	15	4465	Receipt for silver.
207	*Rîm-Sin*	4	1	29	7473	Account of sesame, slaves, garments, etc., delivered during five years.
208	*Rîm-Sin*	11	12	. .	7478	Annual account of sheep and their wool.
209	*Rîm-Sin*	8	5	6	8774	Balanced account of grain.
210	*Rîm-Sin*	8	13	. .	4413	Receipt for wool.
211	*Rîm-Sin*	8	2	8	4445	Receipt for wool for garments.
212	*Rîm-Sin*	8	13	4	7476	Annual account of sheep and their wool.
213	*Sin-idinnam*	a	1(?)	. .	5170	Receipt.
214	*Sin-idinnam*	a	1(?)	6	4969	Note concerning payment of sheep.
215	*Sin-idinnam*	a	7	30	5276	Date formula.
216	*Sin-idinnam*	a	9	21	5265	Record of payments.
217	*Rîm-Sin*	23	12	14	7261	Annual account of sheep and their wool.
218	*Rîm-Sin*	30	12	Broken	7099	Annual account of sheep and their wool.
219	*Rîm-Sin*	30	8	Broken	7183	Account of food for cattle and sheep for one day.
220	*Rîm-Sin*	23	. .	. .	7260	Date formula.
221	*Rîm-Sin*	25	4	4	5814	Receipt for gold.
222	*Rîm-Sin*	25	5	11	7214	Annual account concerning slaves.
223	*Rîm-Sin*	25, 26	. .	. .	7249	Date formulæ from an annual account.
224	*Rîm-Sin*	29	6	8	5836	Account of garments.
225	*Rîm-Sin*	30	1	25	6505	Date formula.
226	*Rîm-Sin* II.	c	2	10	7238	Date formula.
227	*Rîm-Sin* II.	c	10	23	5701	Temple record.
228	*Rîm-Sin*	1	5	29	6588	Note from temple records.
229	*Rîm-Sin*	27	12	. .	5420	Date formula.
230	*Rîm-Sin*	27	8	. .	5576	Date formula.
231	*Rîm-Sin*	12	1	8	5534	Record of bitumen.
232	*Rîm-Sin*	13	7	. .	6571	Record of payment.
233	*Rîm-Sin*	14	1	10	7179	Account of receipts from shepherds.
234	*Rîm-Sin*	14	1	20	5360	Record of bitumen.
235	*Rîm-Sin*	14	9	19	4422	Receipt for bronze.
236	*Rîm-Sin*	16	2	. .	3339	Note recording the delivery of silver.
237	*Rîm-Sin*	16	11	. .	8748	Note recording the delivery of silver.
238	*Rîm-Sin*	16	12	6	8747	Record of payments in silver.

Text.	Reign.	Year.	Month.	Day.	YBC.	Description.
239	*Rîm-Sin*	17	1	15	6188	Note concerning bitumen.
240	*Rîm-Sin*	17	3	20	6195	Receipt for sheep.
241	*Rîm-Sin*	17	6	24	7036	Receipt for one talent of wool.
242	*Rîm-Sin*	27	6	16(?)	8730	Promissory note for silver.
243	*Rîm-Sin*	19	6	10	6593	Temple record.
244	*Rîm-Sin*	20	4	13	8754	Record of the delivery of sheep.
245	*Rîm-Sin*	20	1	25	6292	Record of payments.
246	*Rîm-Sin*	28	8	27	7305	Balanced account of dates.
247	*Rîm-Sin*	28	8	. .	5573	Date formula.
248	*Rîm-Sin*	28	4	4(?)	5784	Date formula.
249	*Rîm-Sin*	34	11	20	7835	Receipt for dates.
250	*Warad-Sin*	d	6	. .	7037	Record of a payment.
251	*Warad-Sin*	d	10	23	6178	Record of payments.
252	*Rîm-Sin*	19	13	. .	6278	Date formula.
253	*Warad-Sin*	e	3	16	5728	Contract for hire of a slave.

AUTOGRAPHED TEXTS

1 OBVERSE

Col. I. Col. II. Col. III.

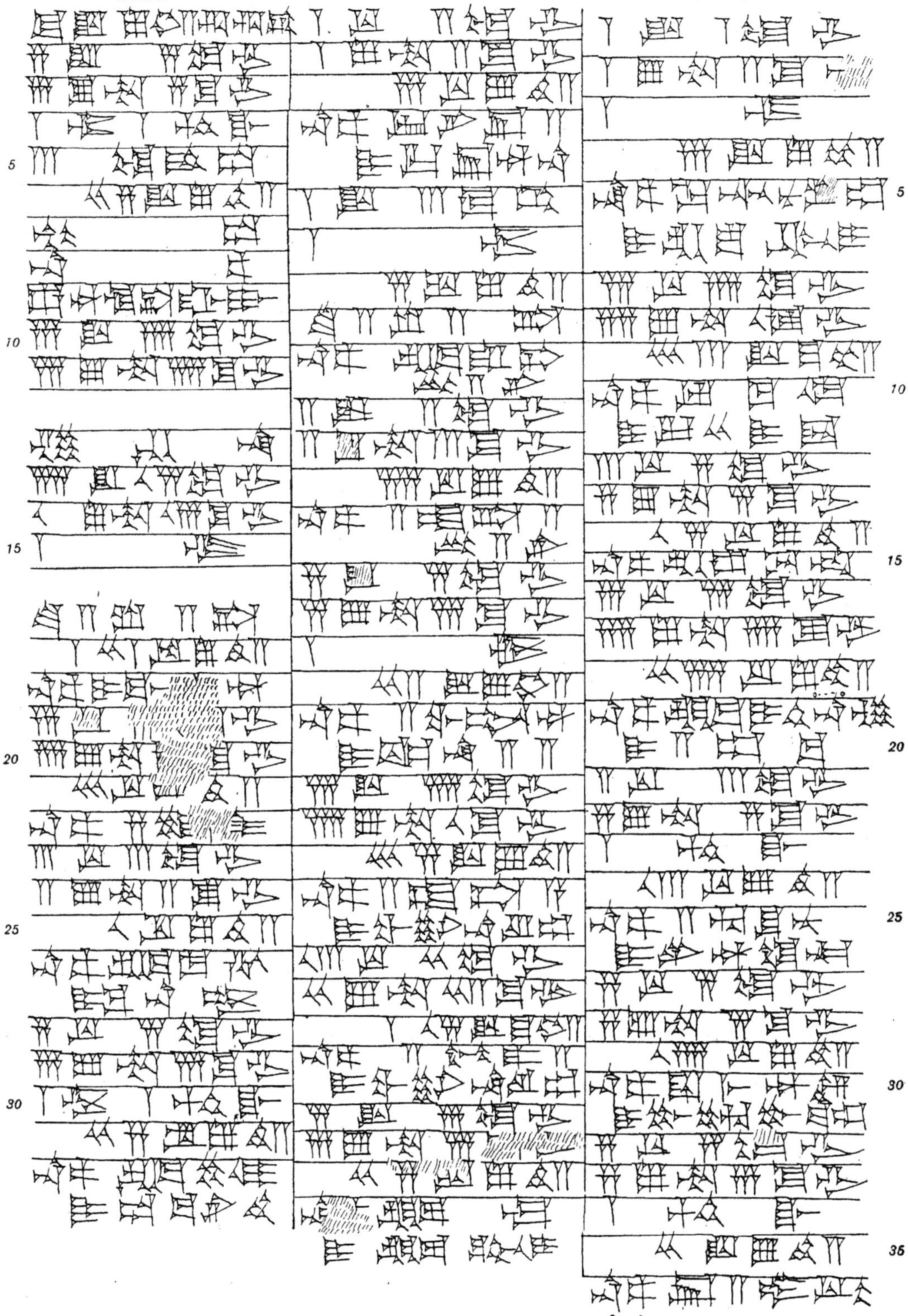

Omit, mistake of scribe.

1 REVERSE

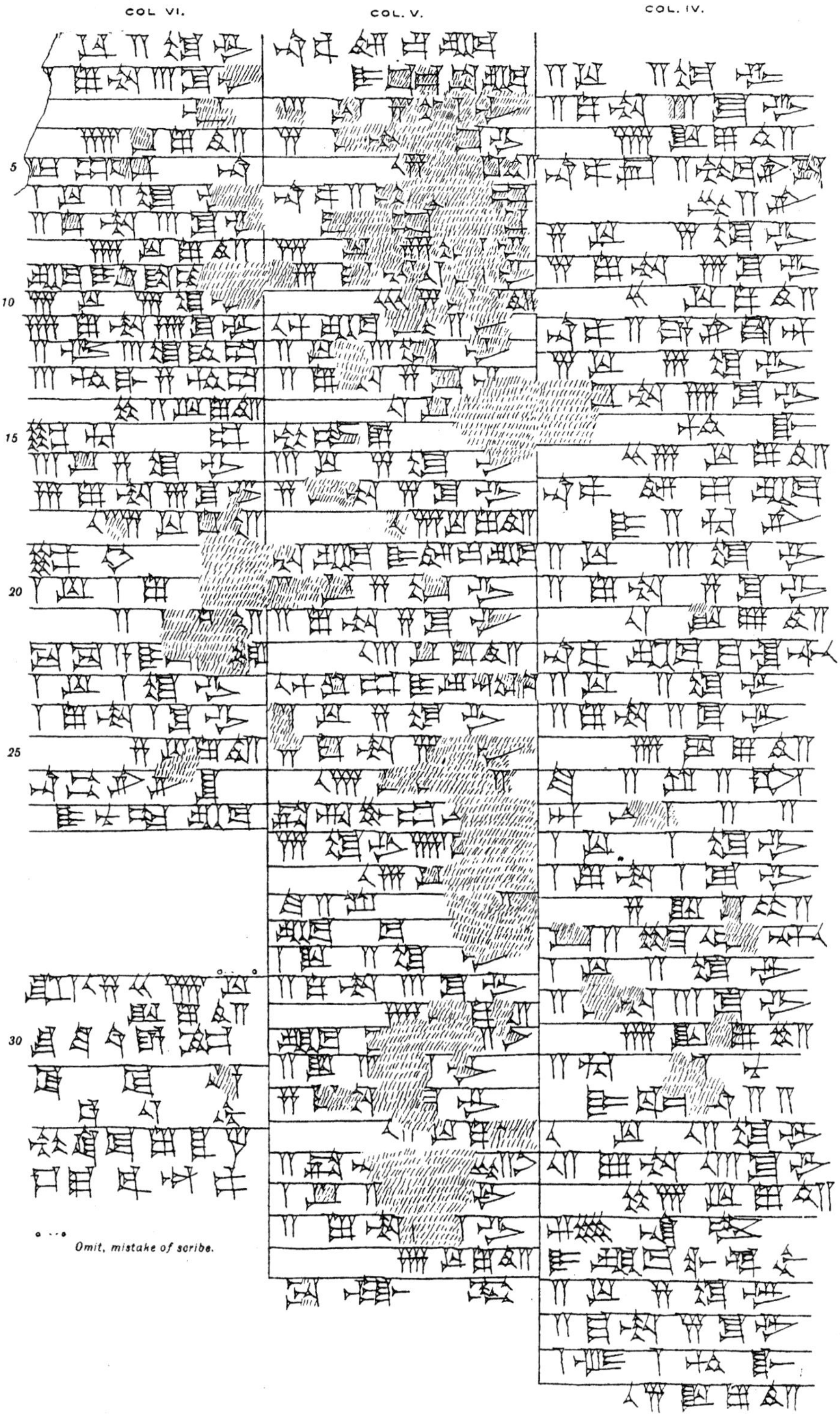

2 OBVERSE

COL. I. COL. II COL. III.

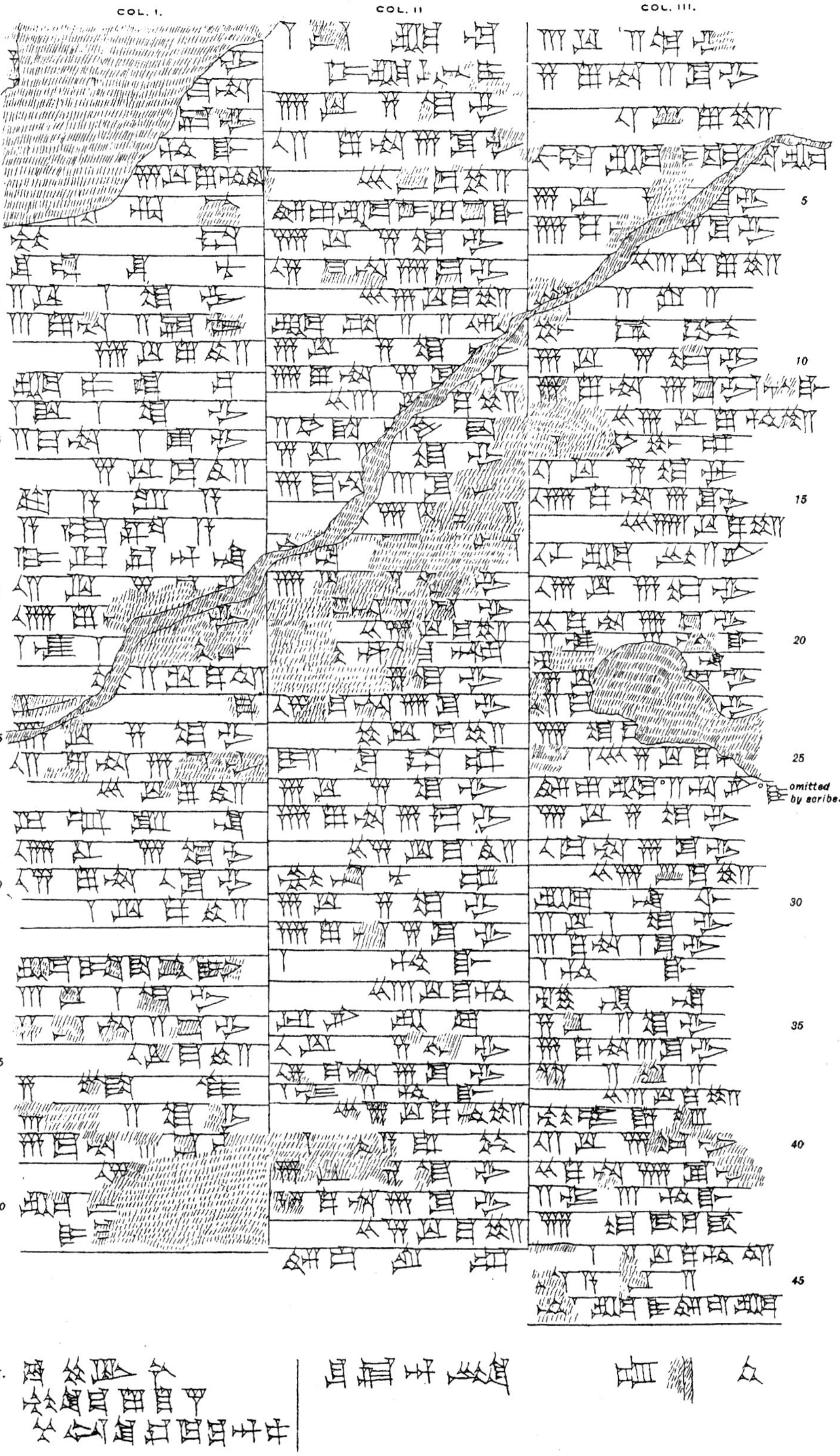

omitted by scribe.

L. E.

PLATE IV

2 REVERSE

Col. VI. Col. V. Col. IV.

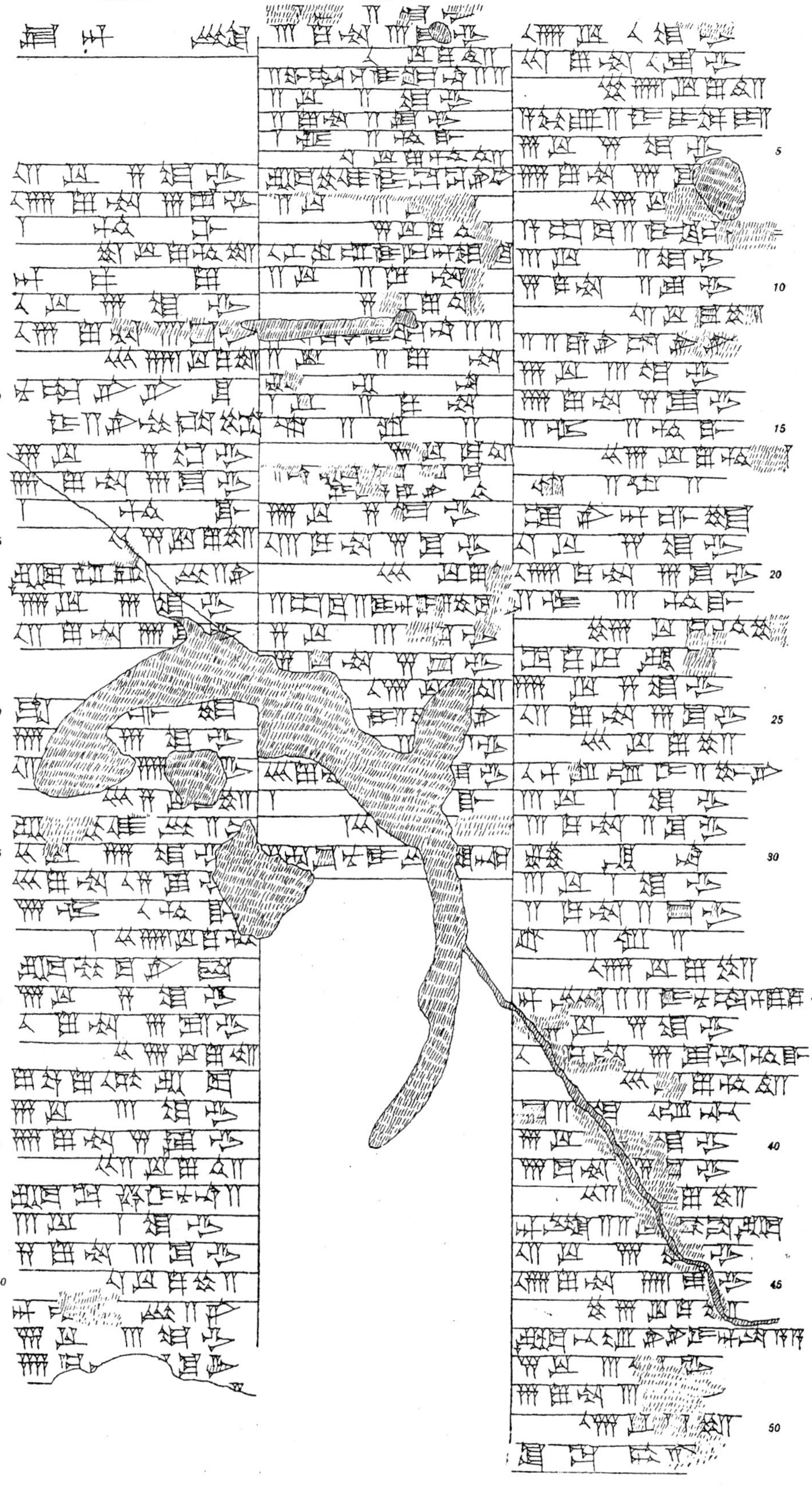

COL. I. 3 OBVERSE COL. II.

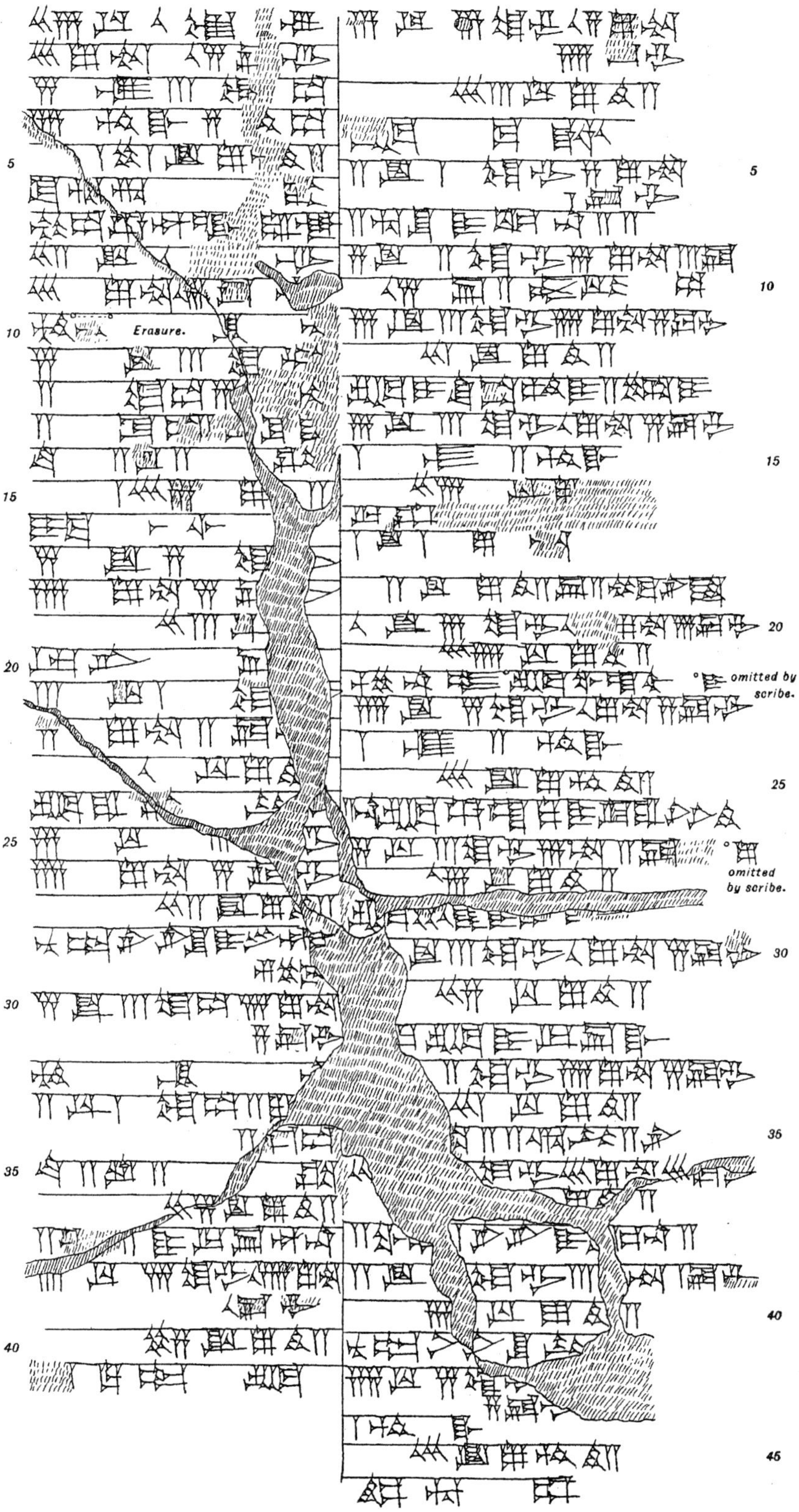

3 REVERSE

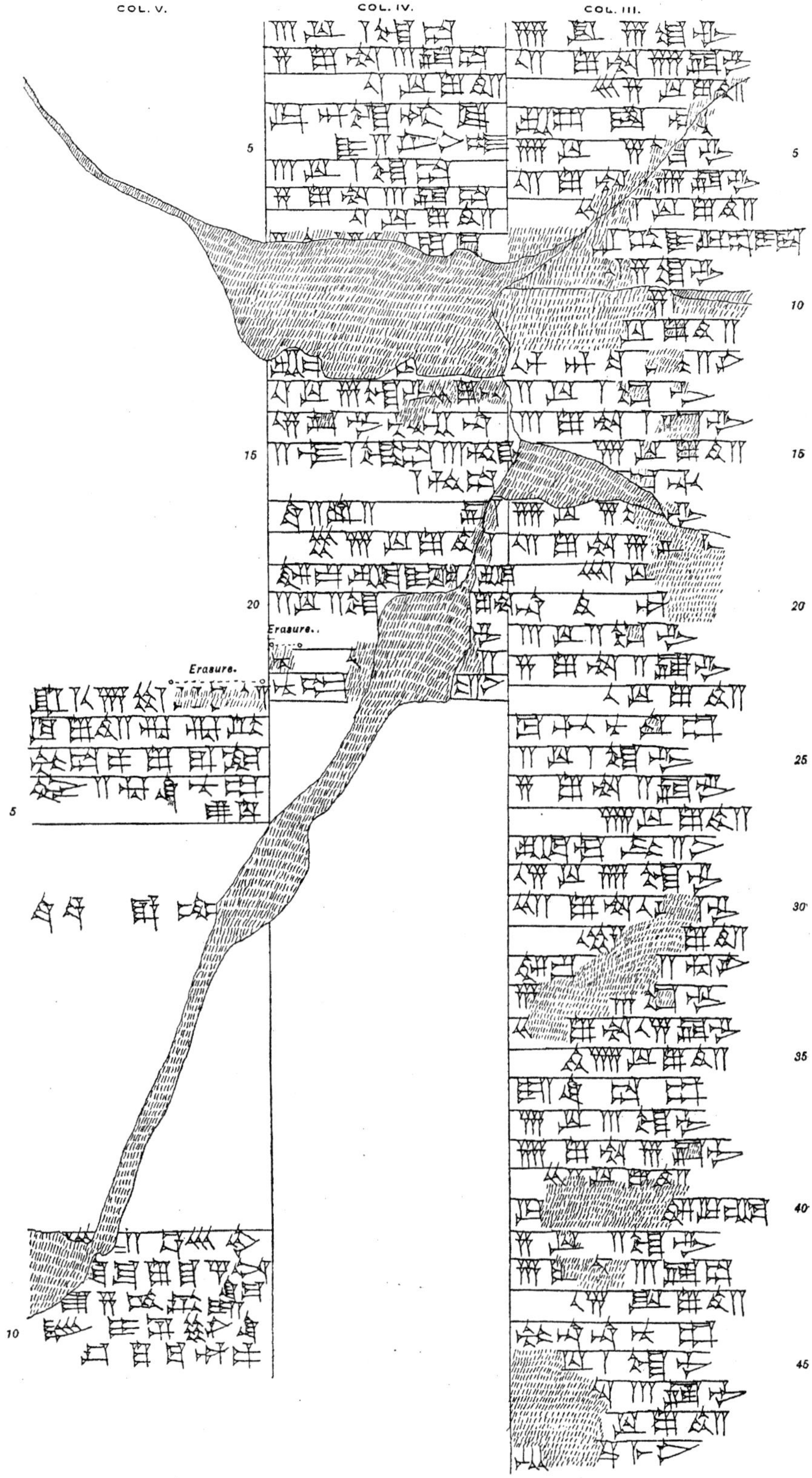

4 OBVERSE

Col. I. Col. II. Col. III. Col. IV. Col. V.

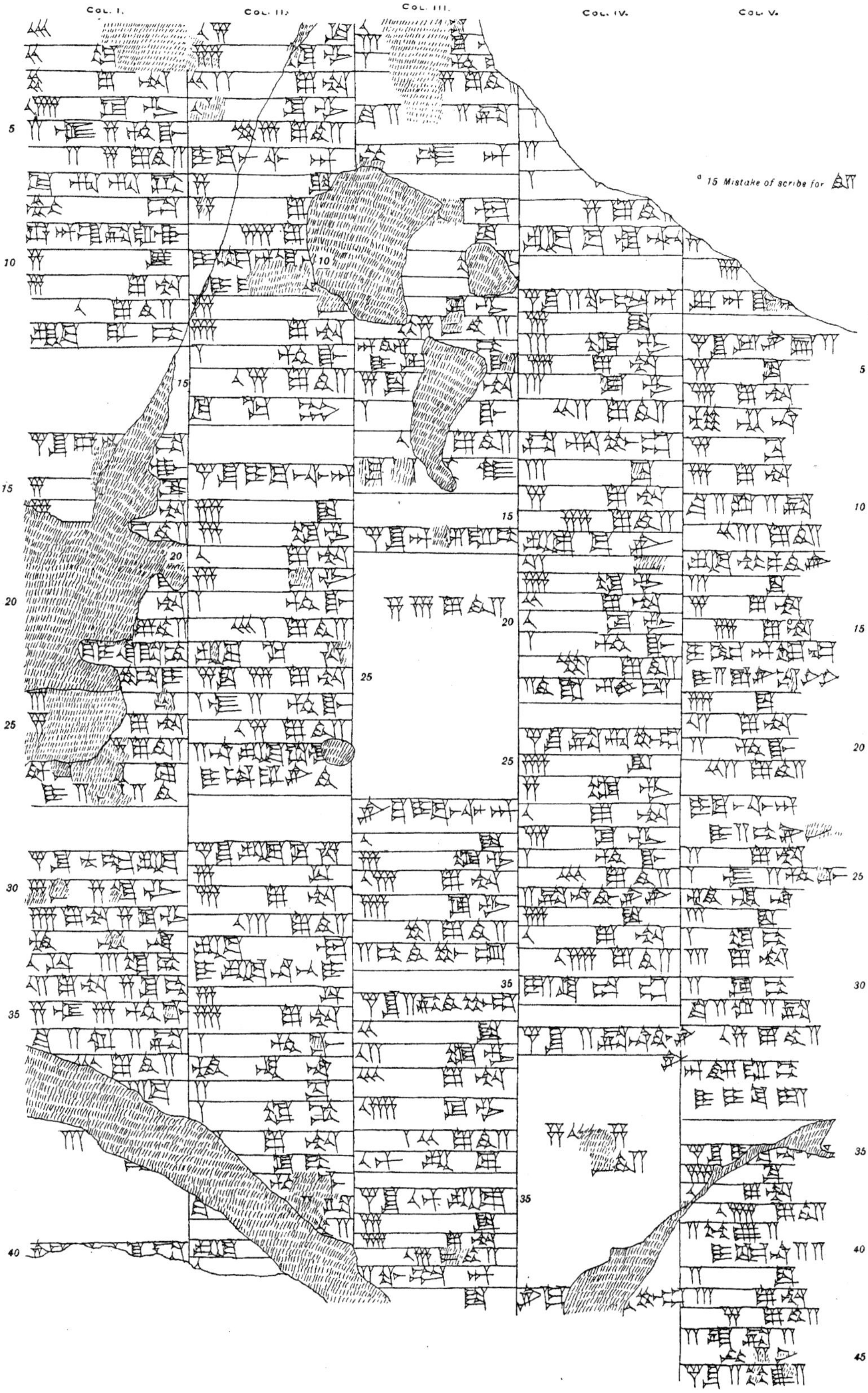

[a] 15 Mistake of scribe for [cuneiform sign]

4 REVERSE

Col. X — Col. IX. — Col. VIII. — Col. VII — Col. VI.

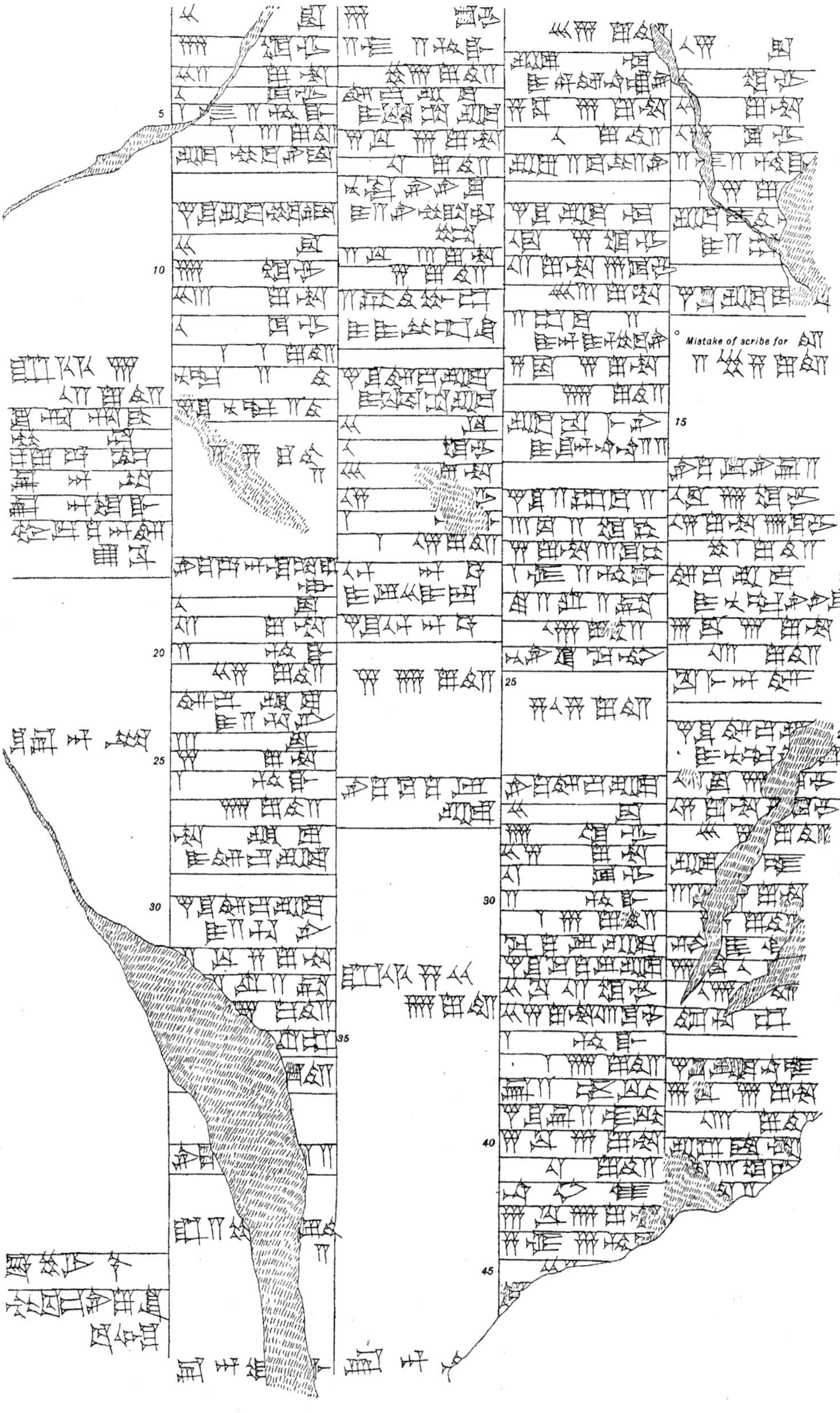

5 OBVERSE

COL. I — COL. II. — COL. III.

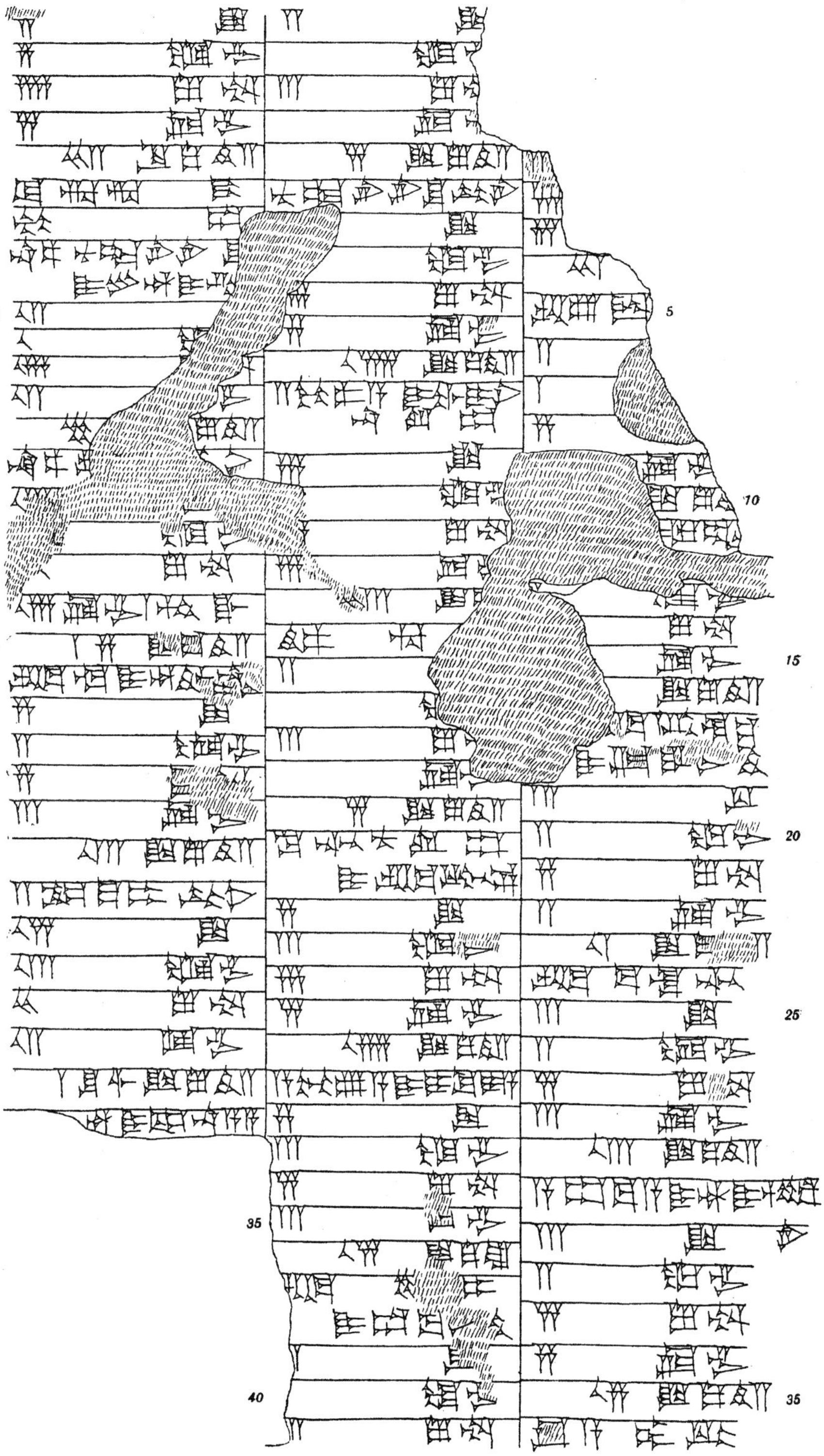

5 REVERSE

COL. VII. COL. VI. COL. V. COL. IV.

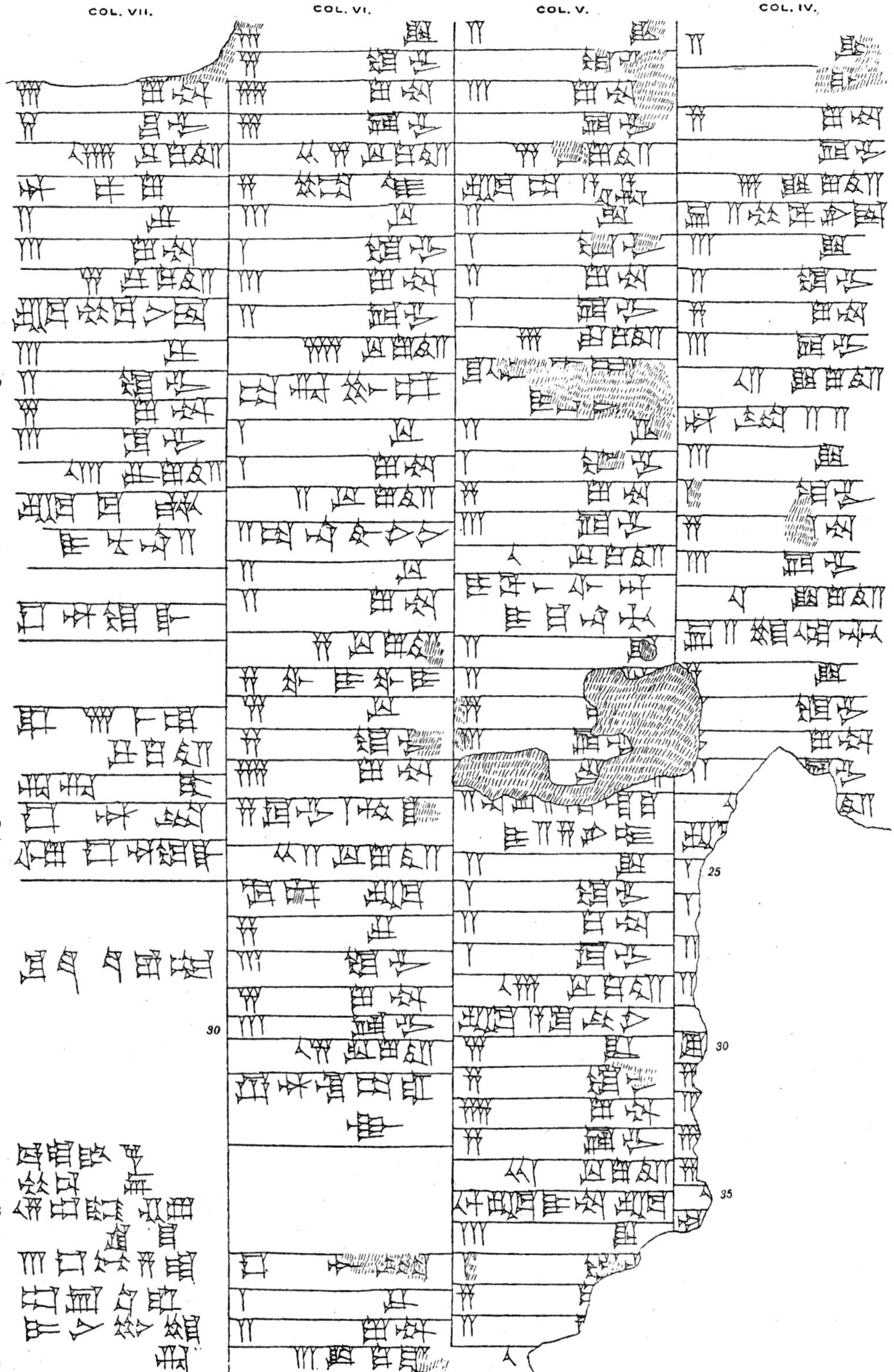

6 OBVERSE

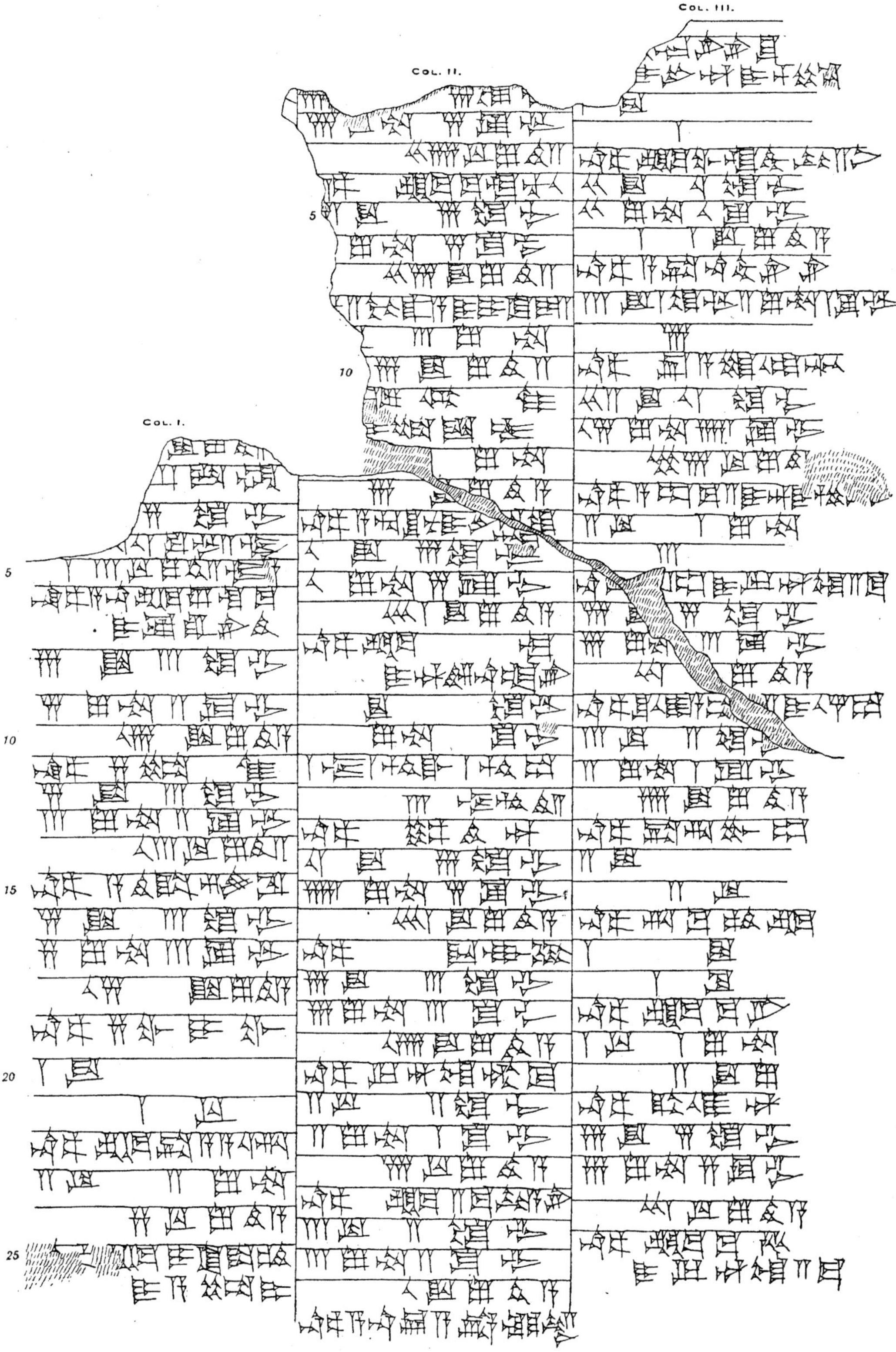

6 REVERSE

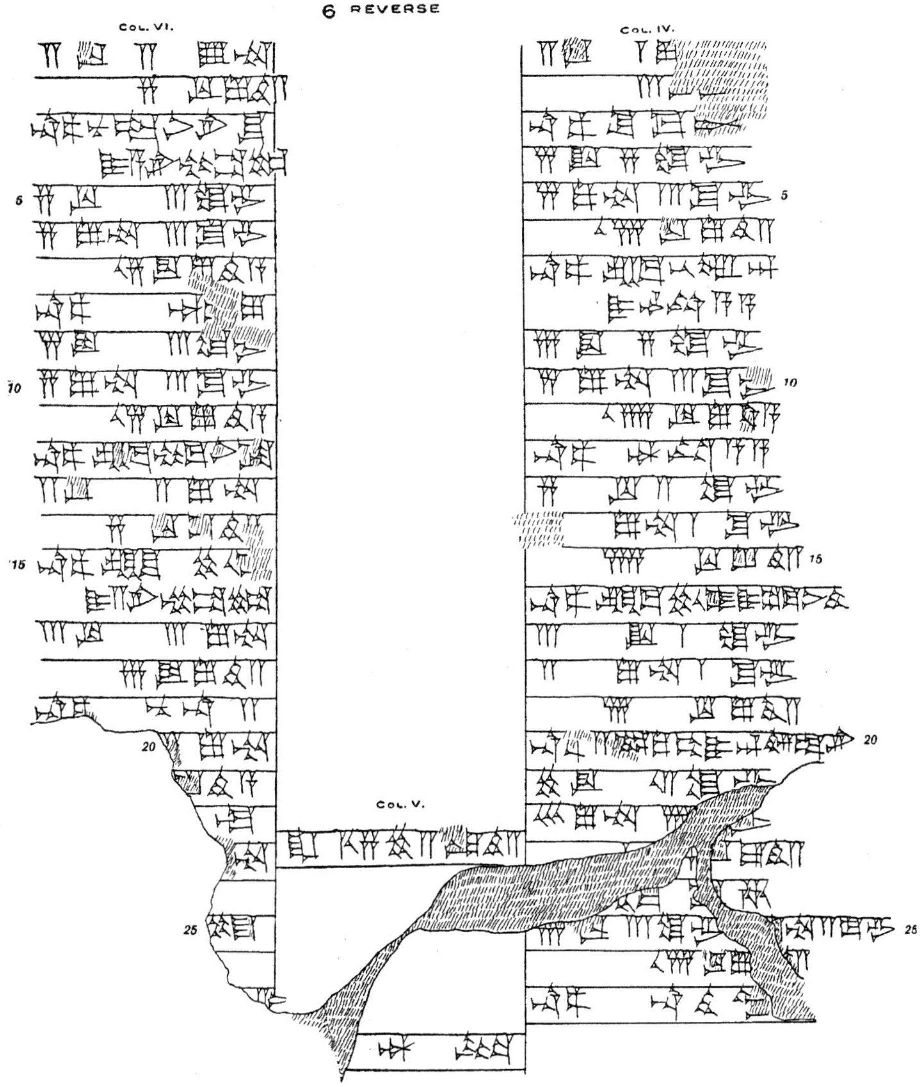

7

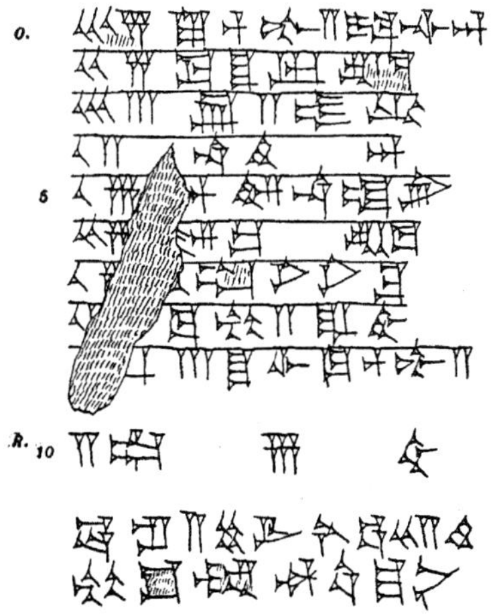

8

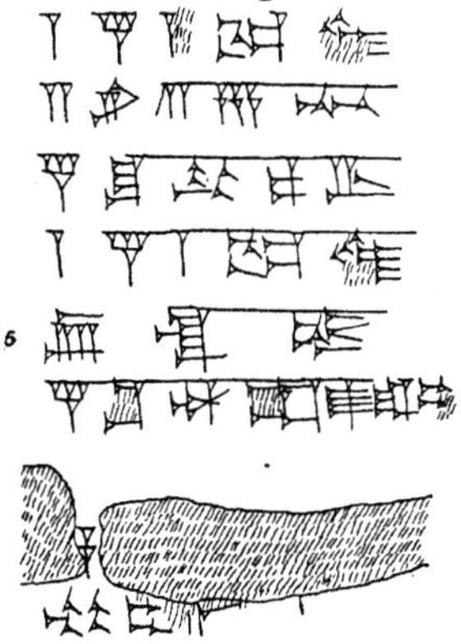

9

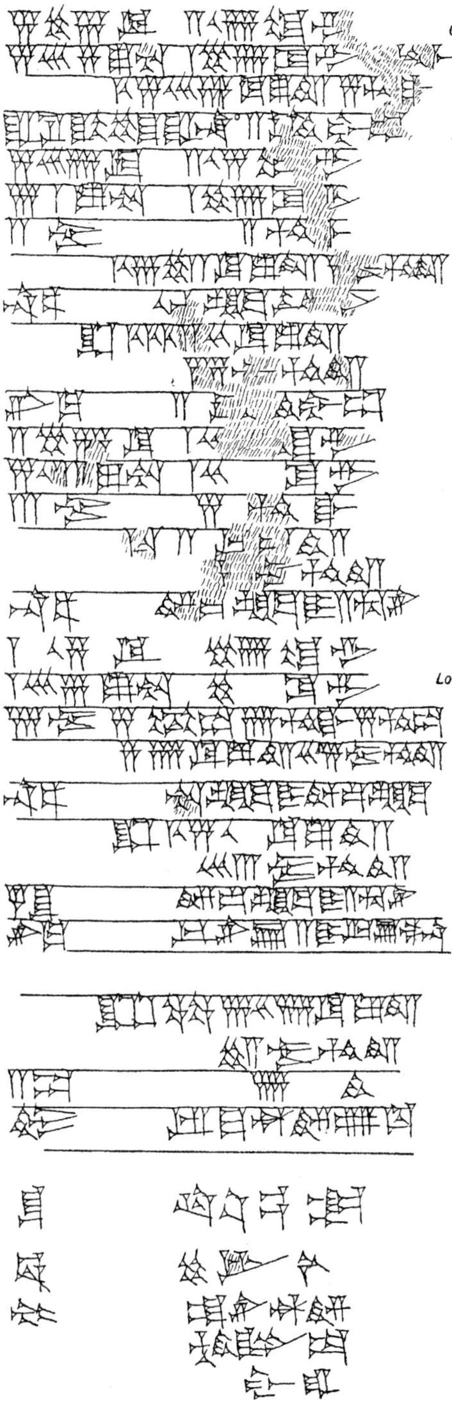

10

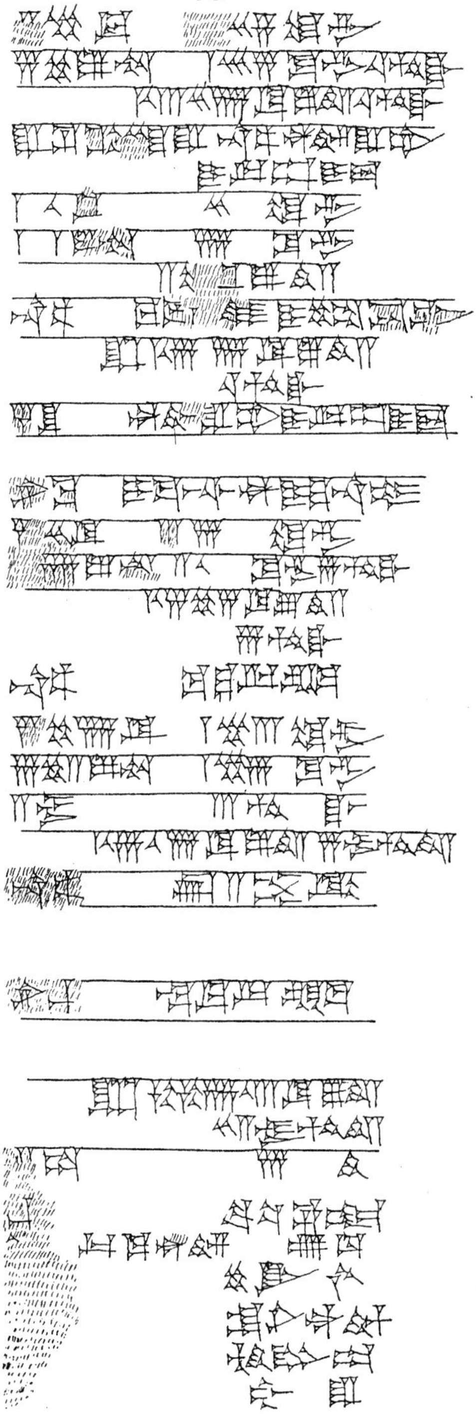

° [cuneiform sign] *omitted by scribe.*

11

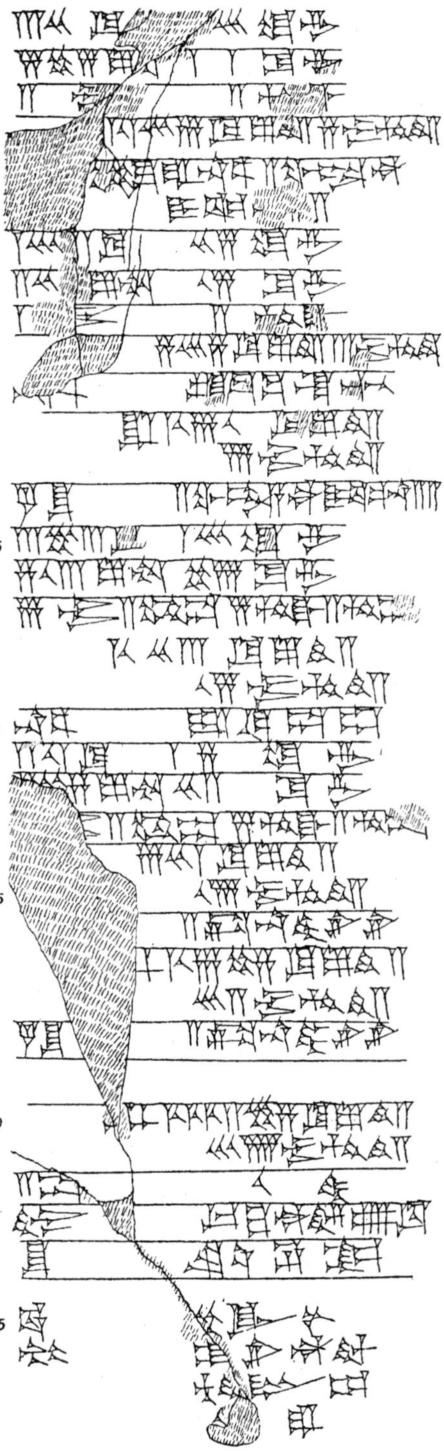

12

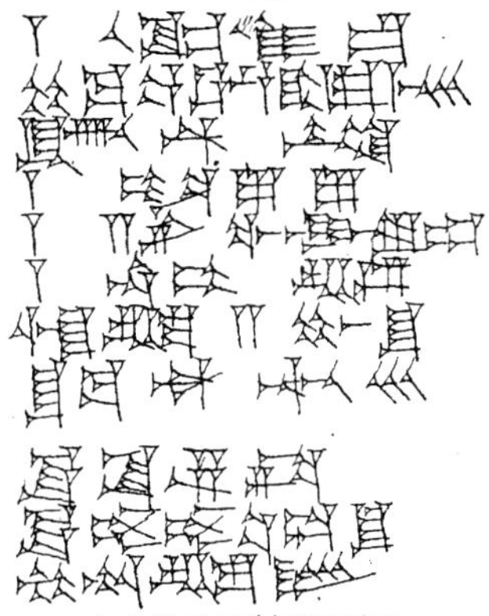

Indistinct seal impressions.

13

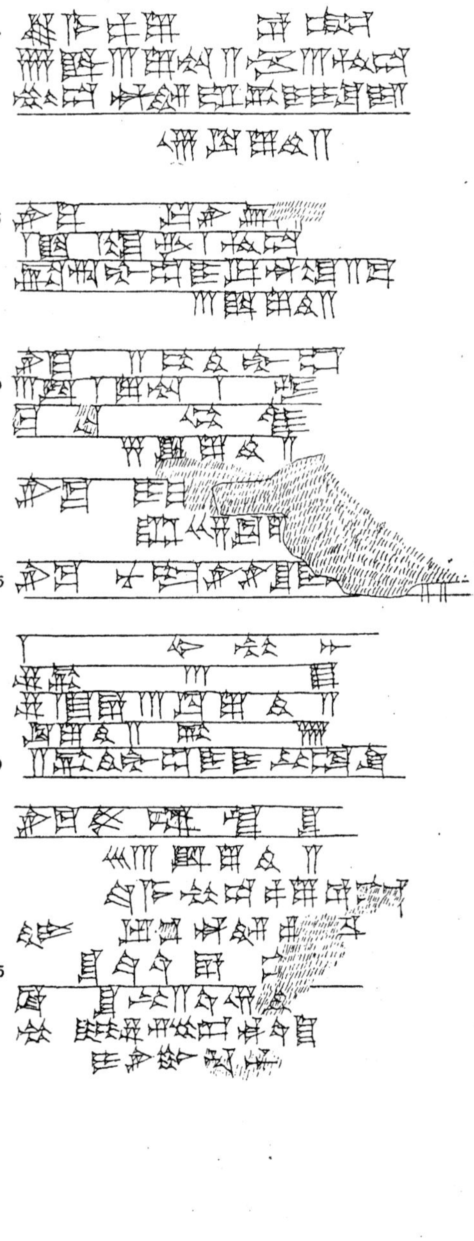

14

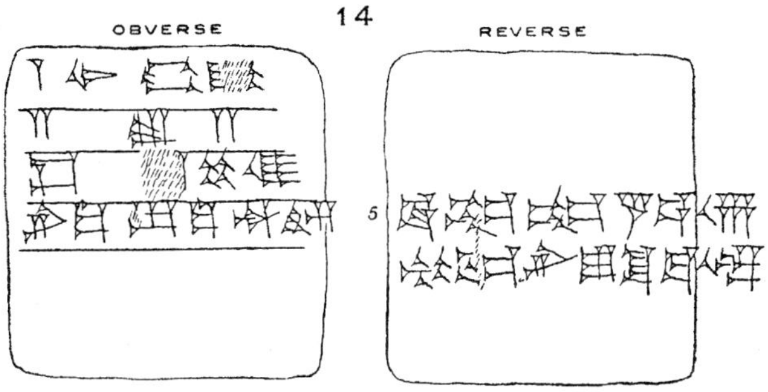

15

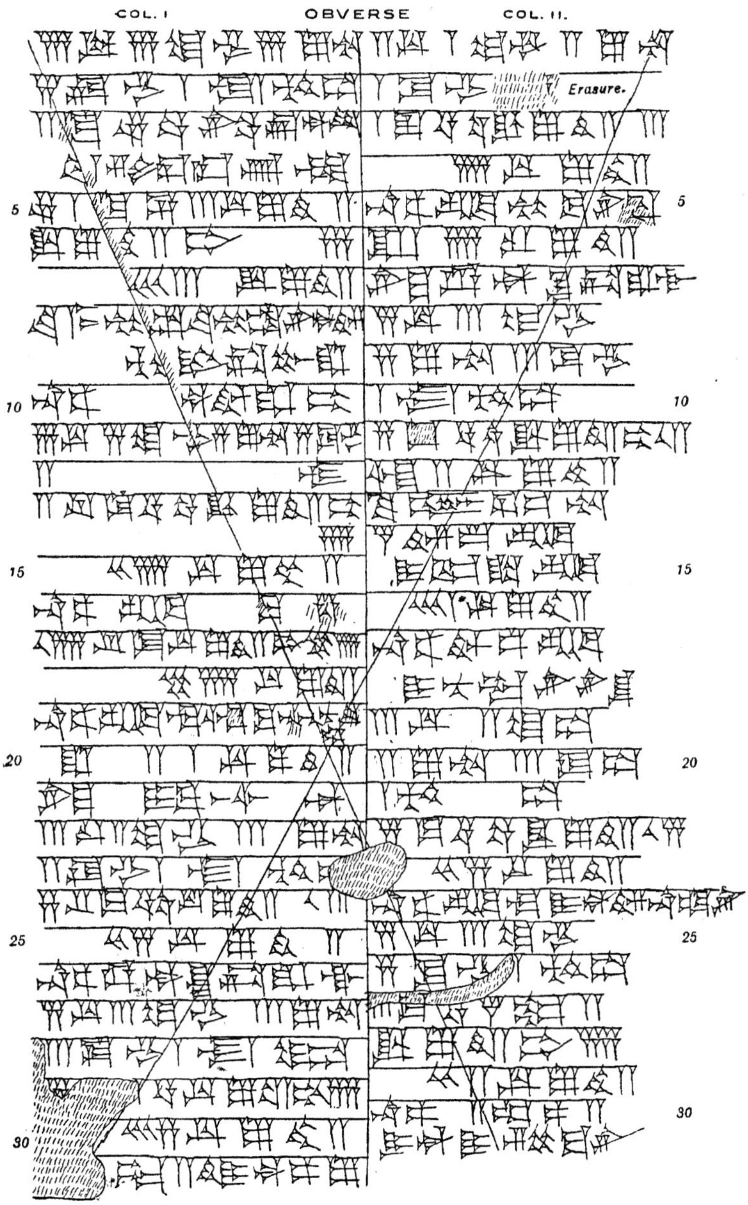

15

REVERSE

COL. IV. COL. III.

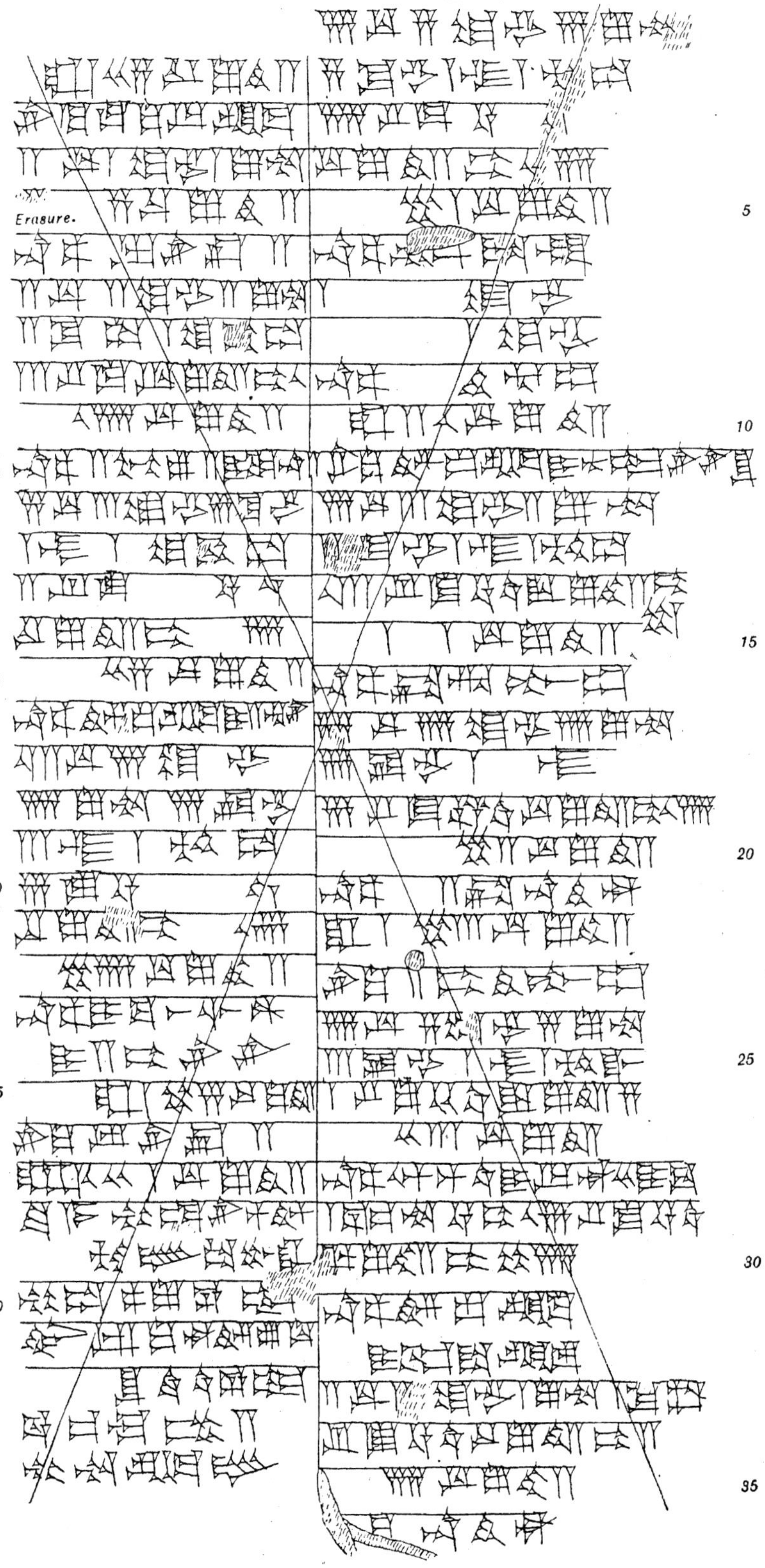

16

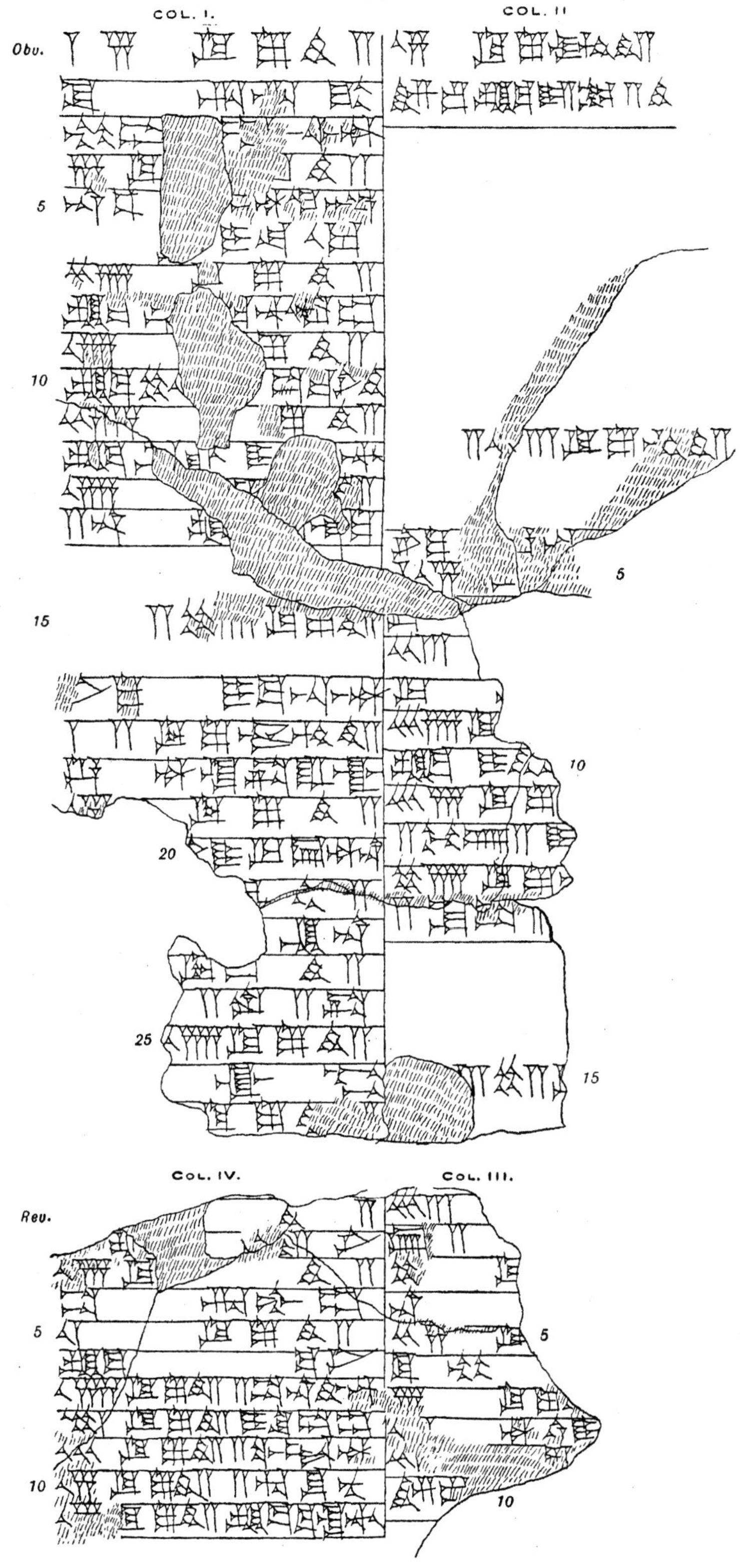

Col. IV. CONTINUED Col. III.

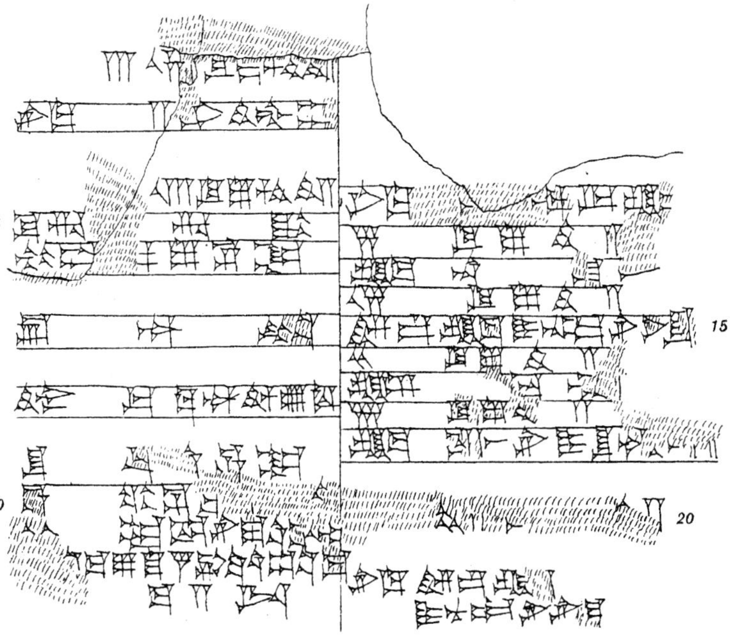

17

OBVERSE

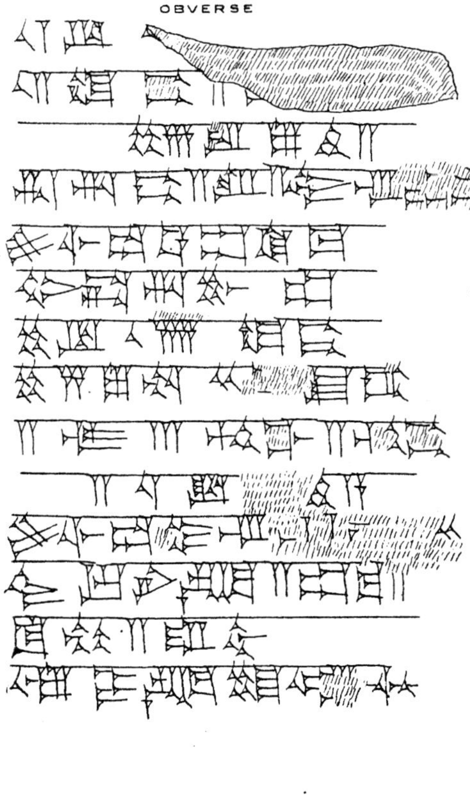

REVERSE

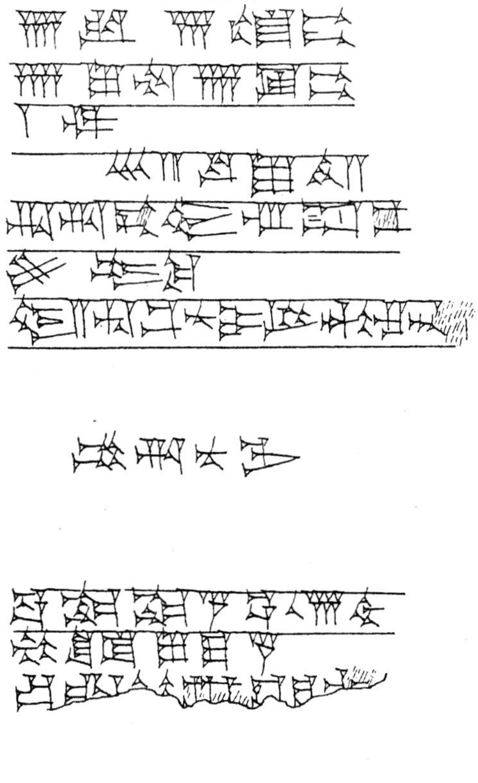

18

O.

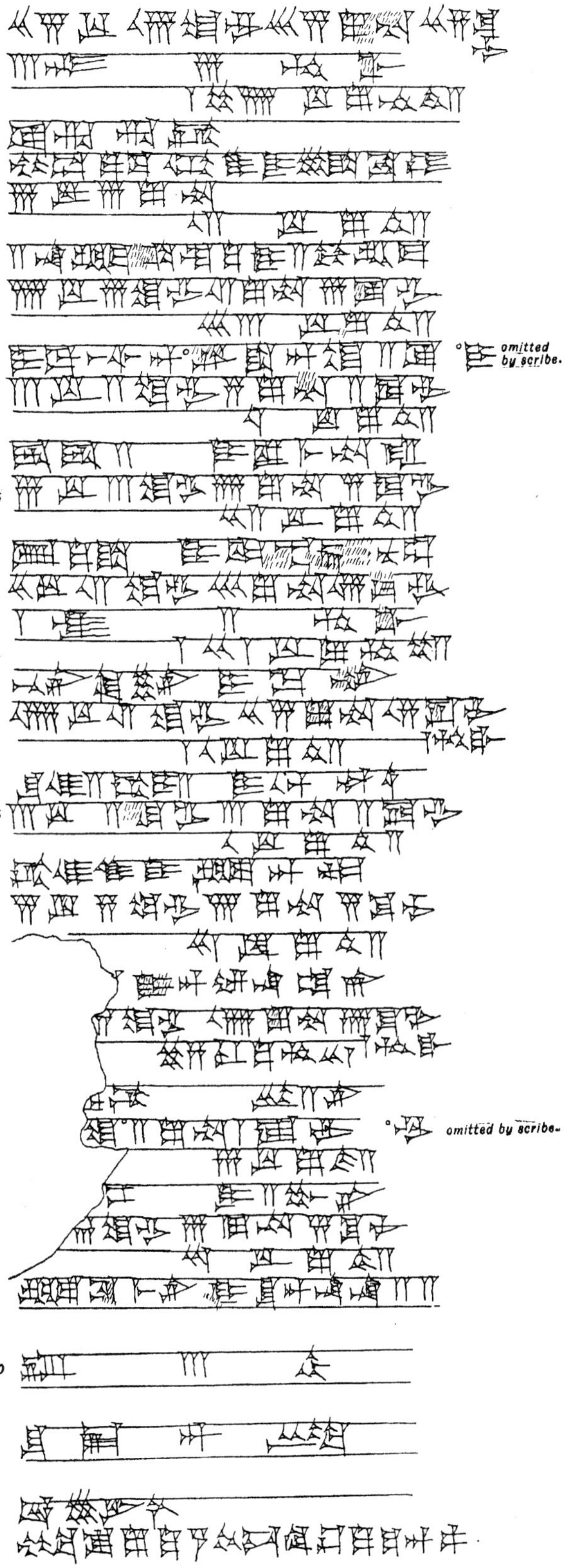

Lo. E.

R.

19

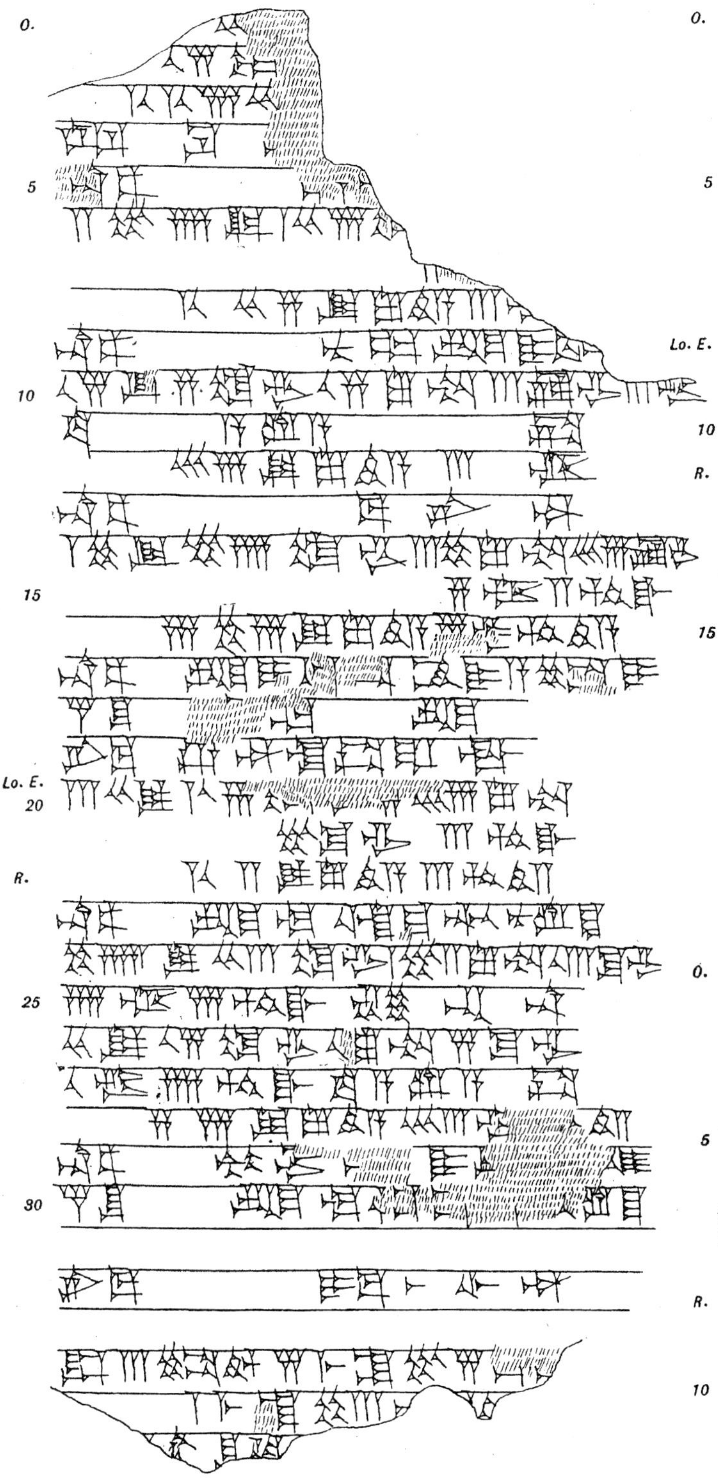

20

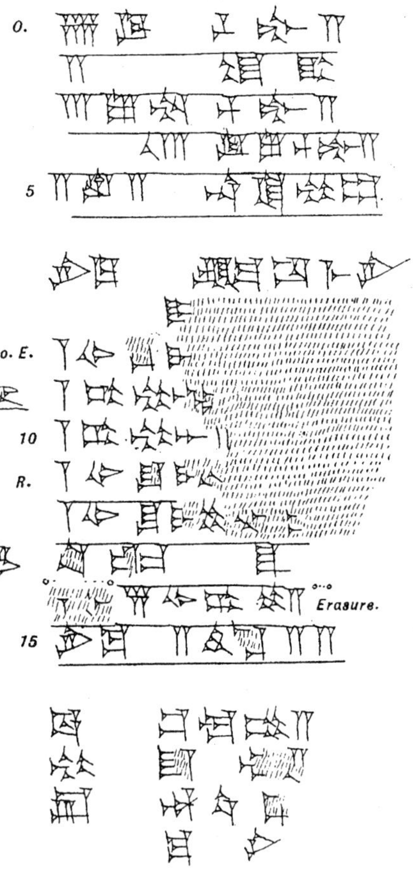

21

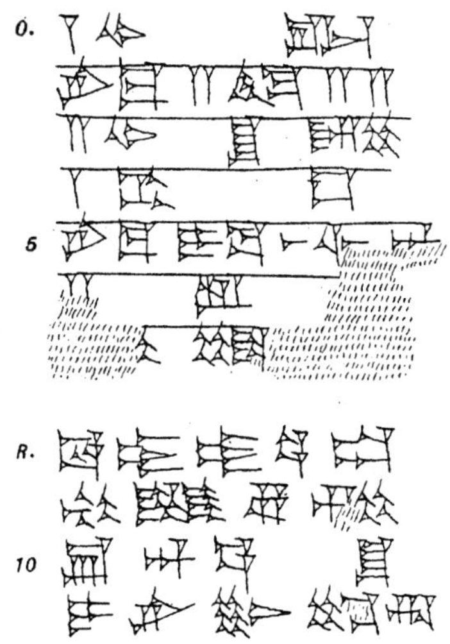

22

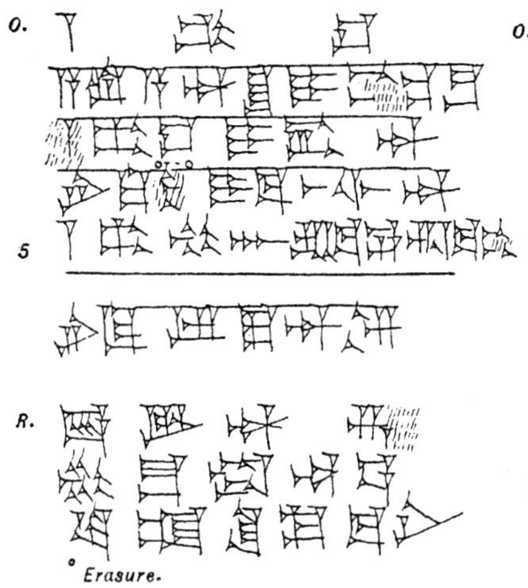

23

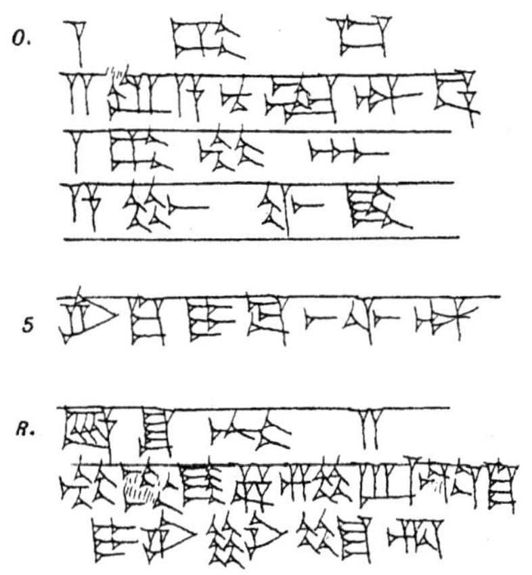

24

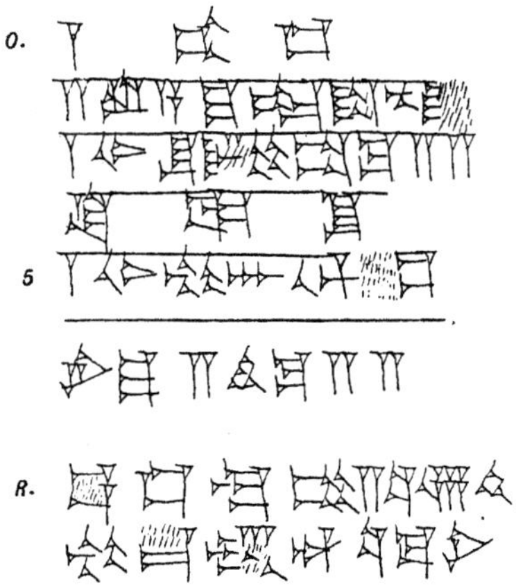

25

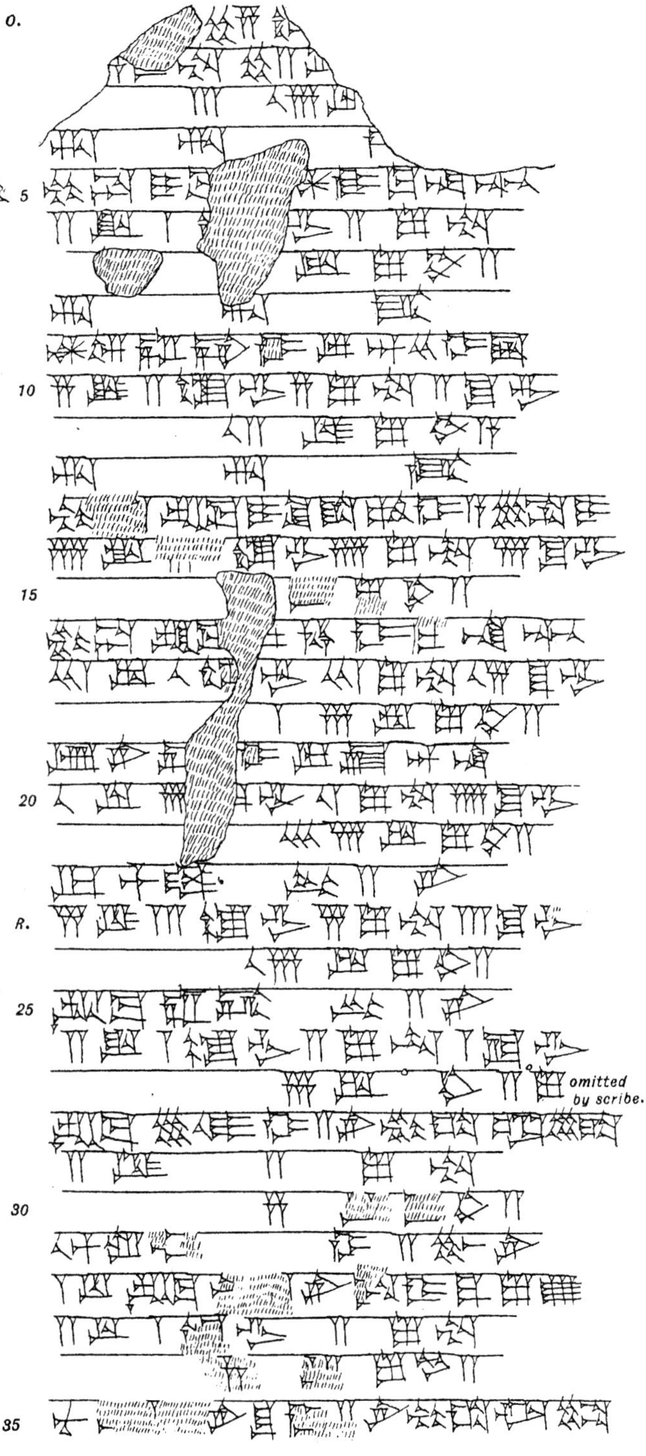

CONTINUED

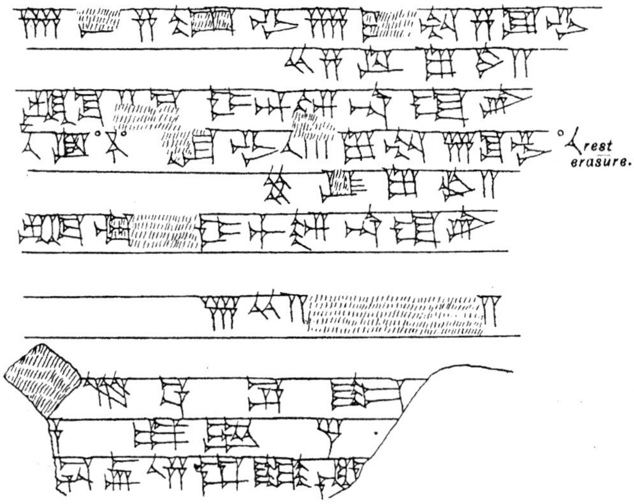

26

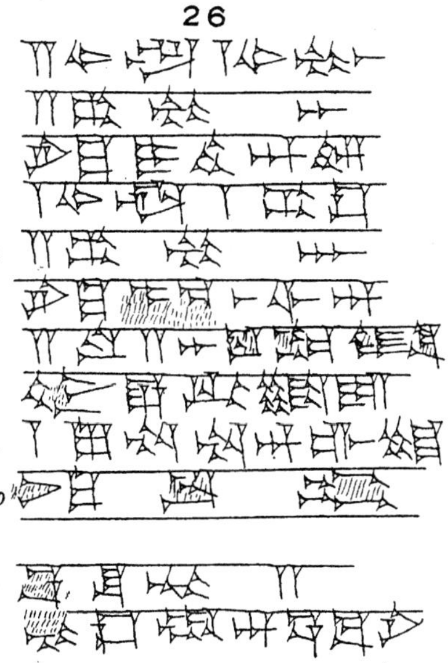

28

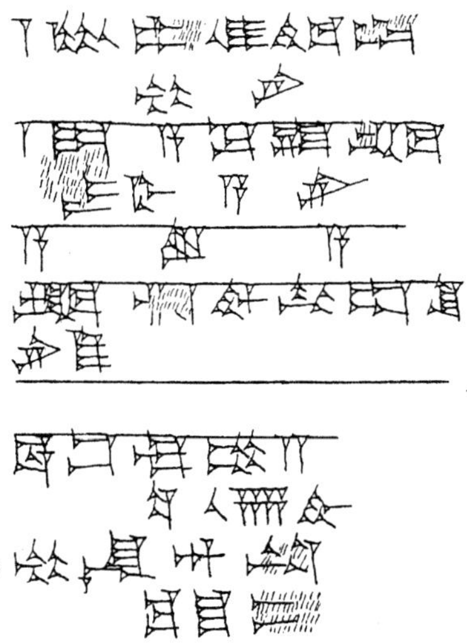

27

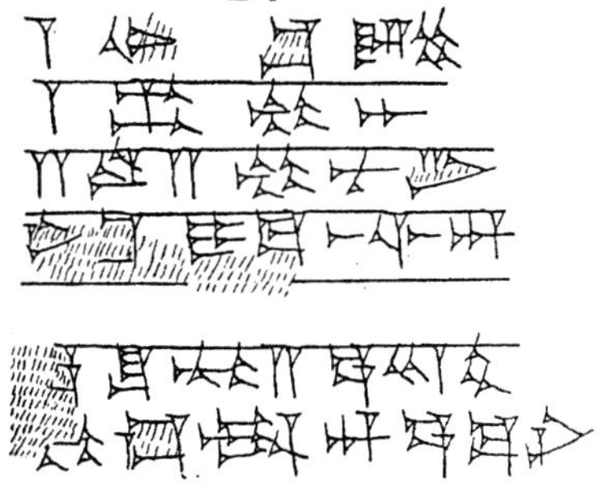

29

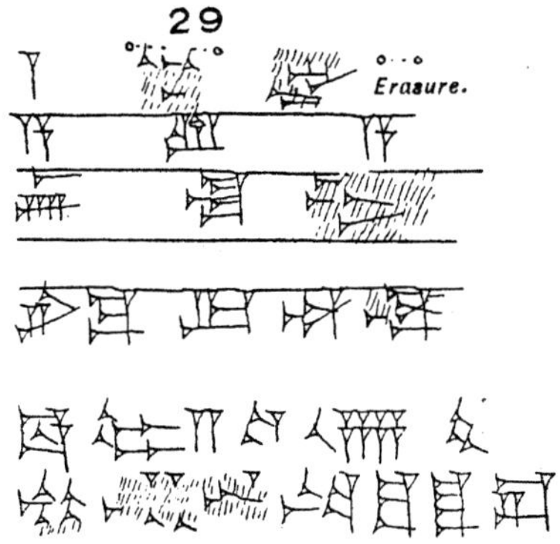

30

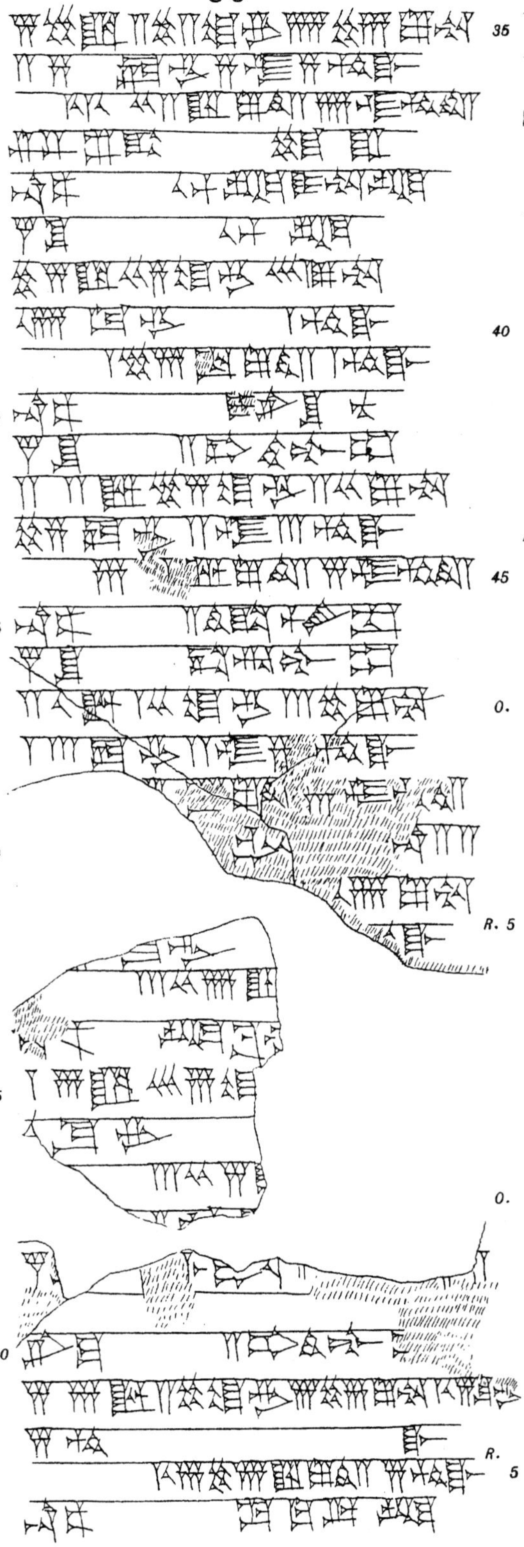

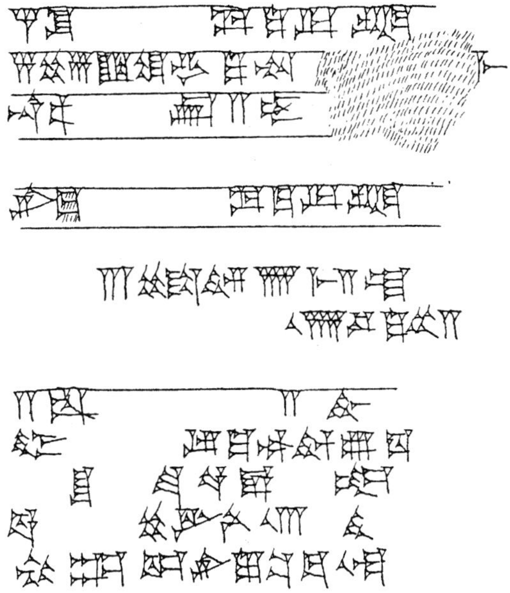

31

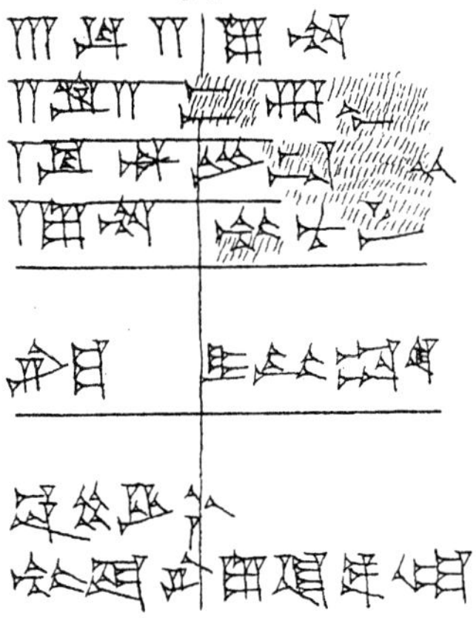

32

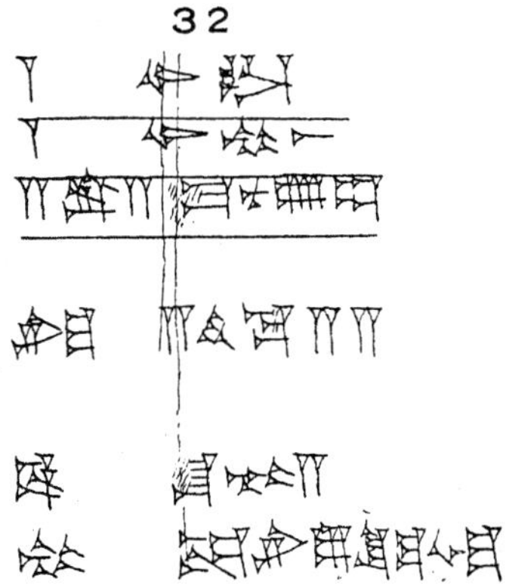

33

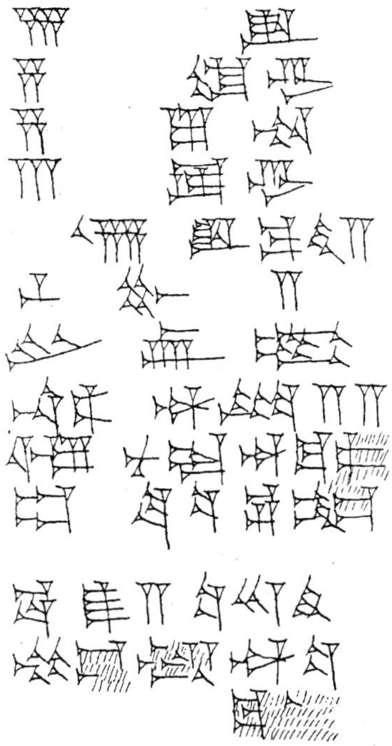

34

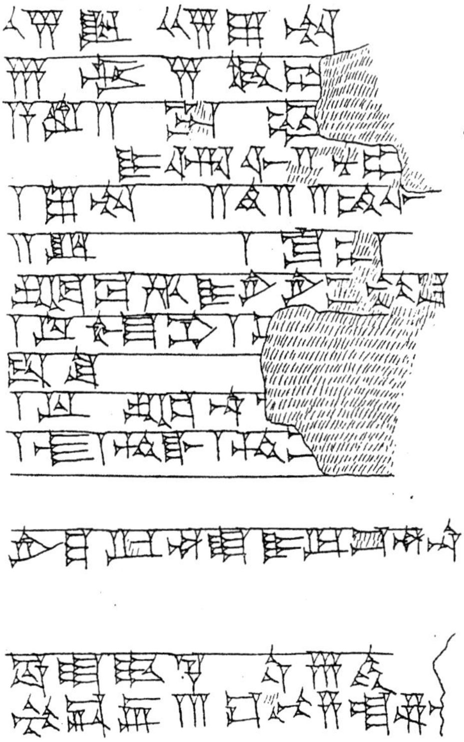

35

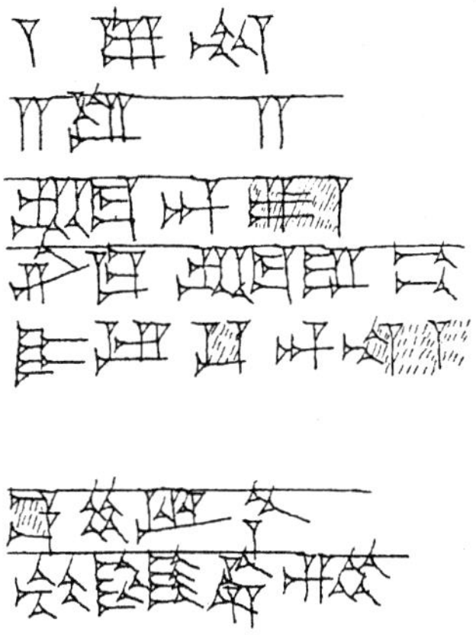

36

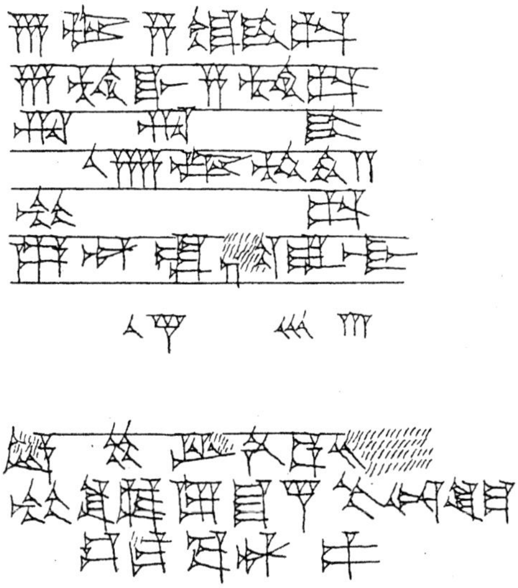

37

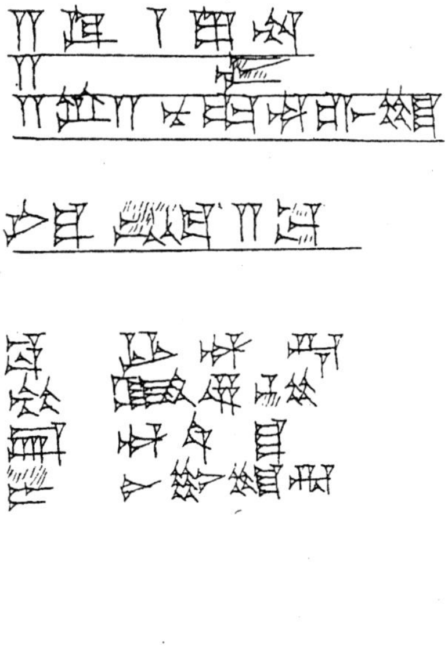

PLATE XXV

38

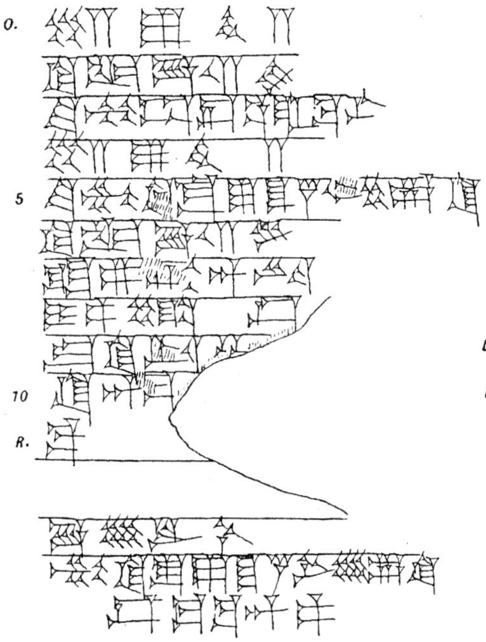

40

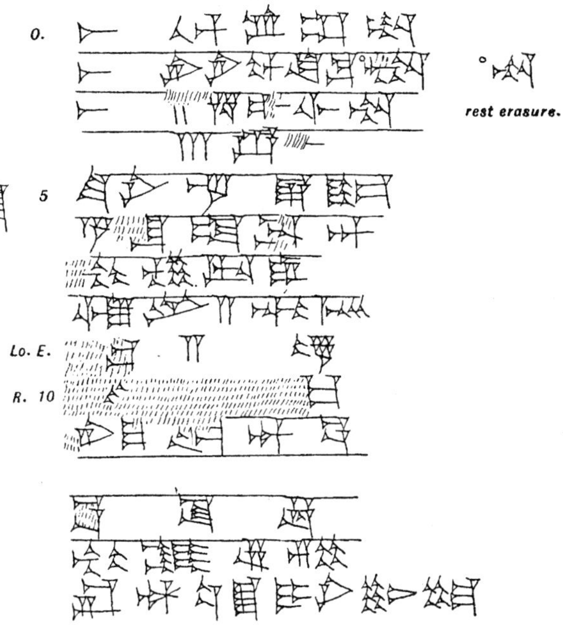

39

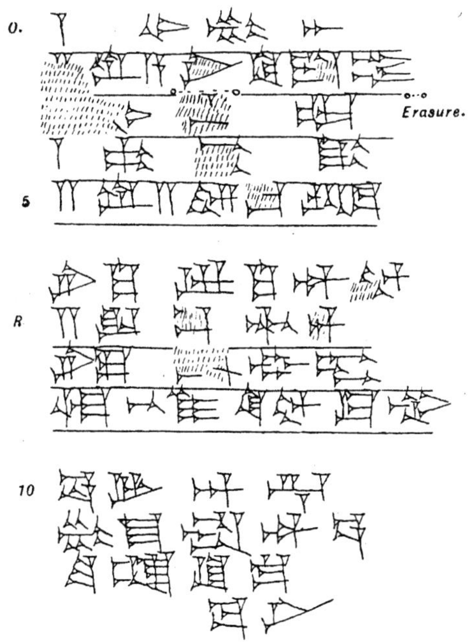

41

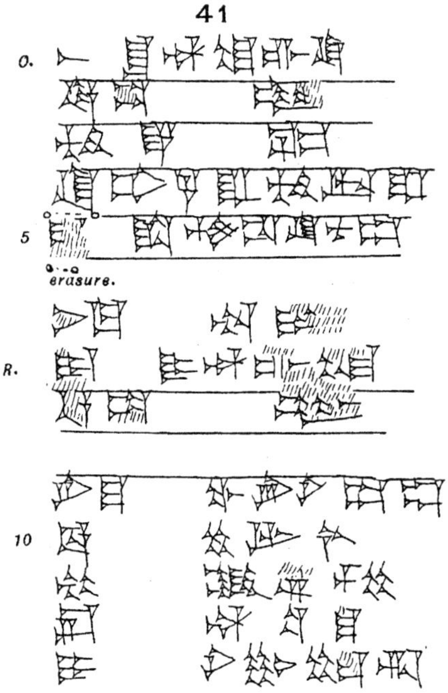

42

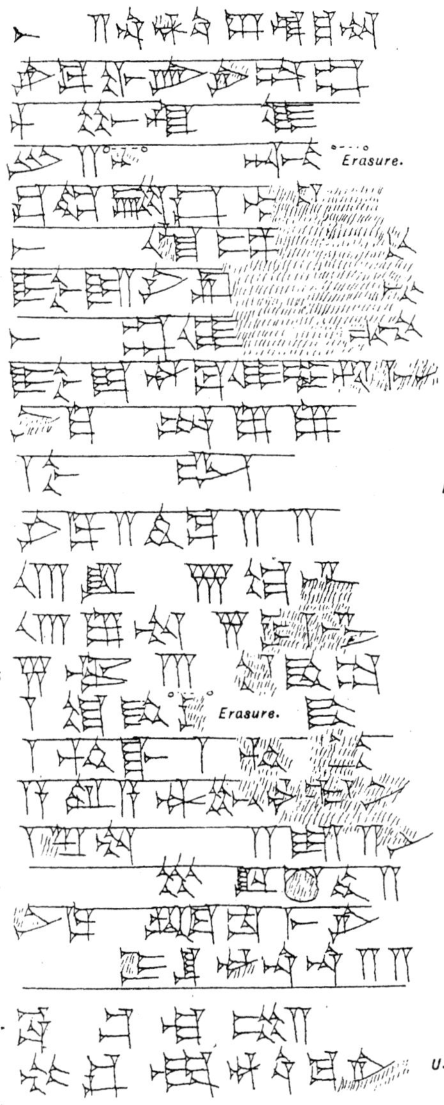

O. Lo. E. R. U. E.

44

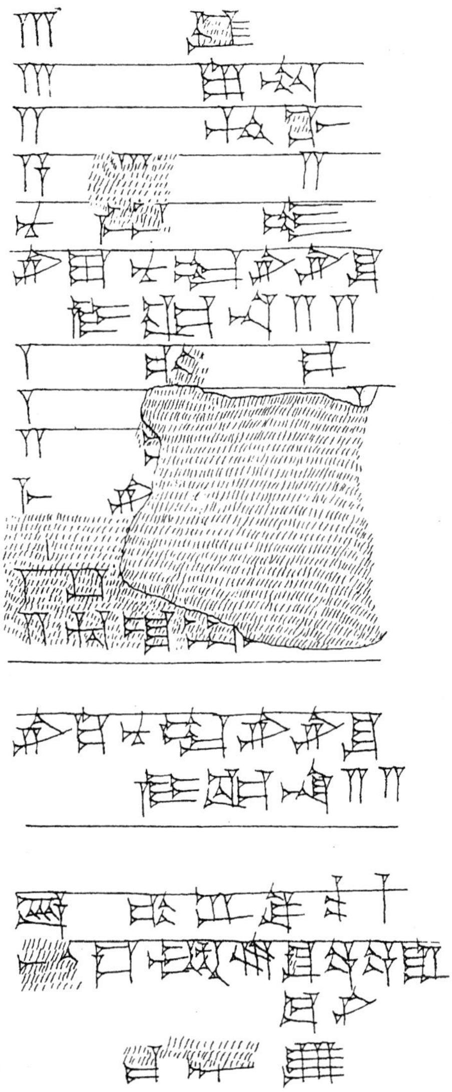

O. Lo. E. R. U. E.

43

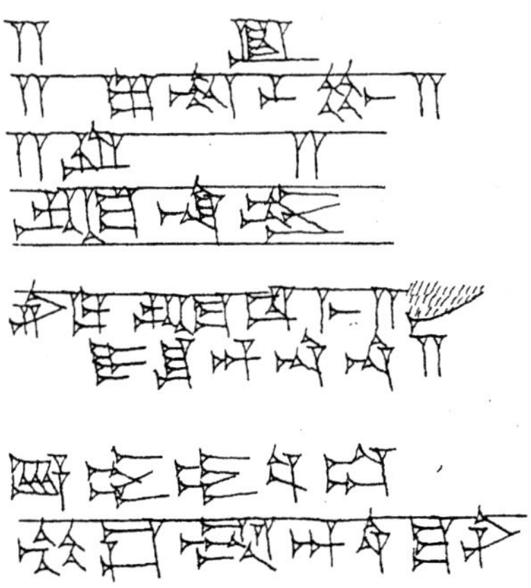

O. R.

45

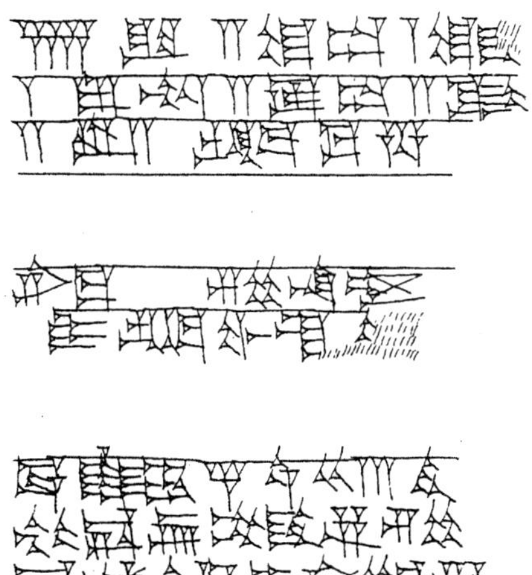

O. R.

46

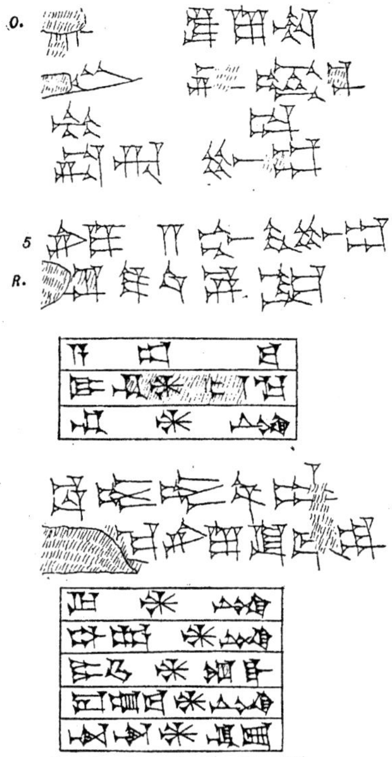

Contains also seals 50c, 52a, 53b

47

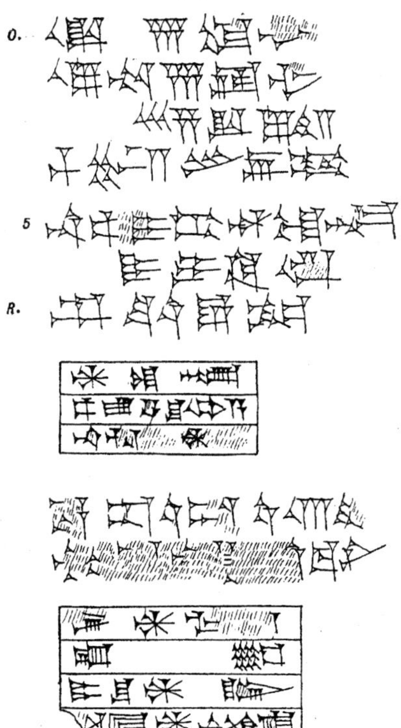

Contains also Seals 46b, 50a, 51b, 52a, 52b

48

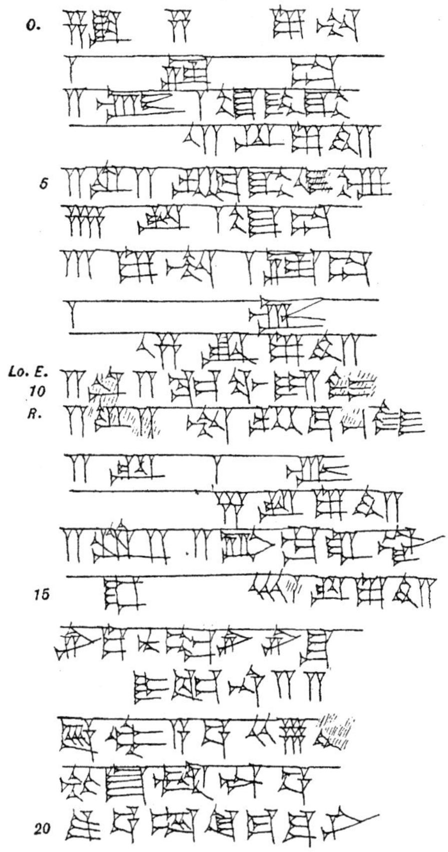

49

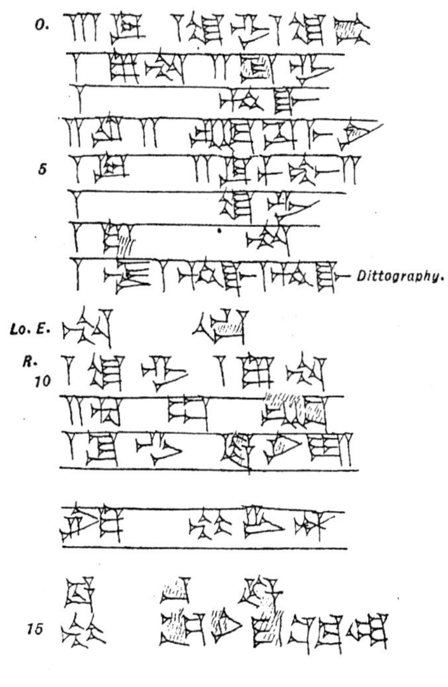

50

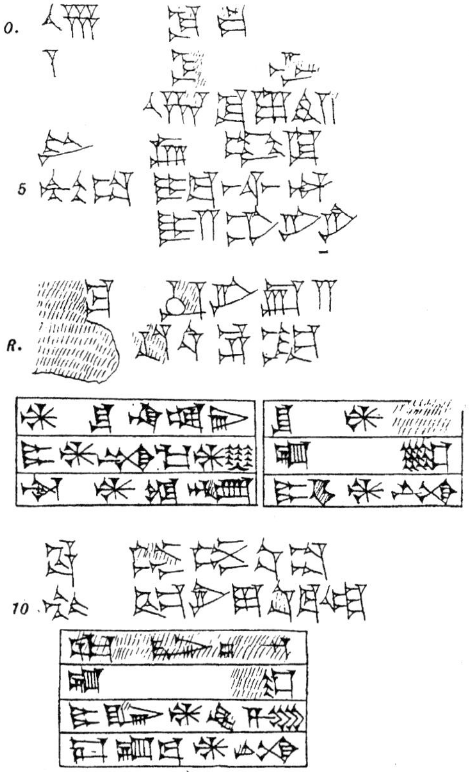

Contains also seals 46a, 46b, 52a.

51

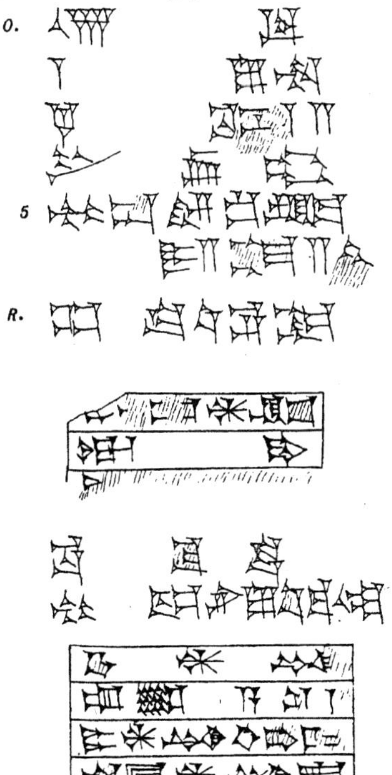

Contains also Seals 46a, 46b, 52a, 52b

52

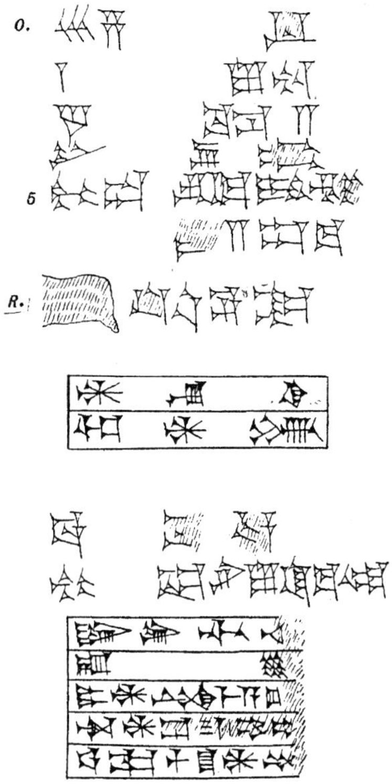

Contains also seals 46b, 51b, also indistinct impressions.

53

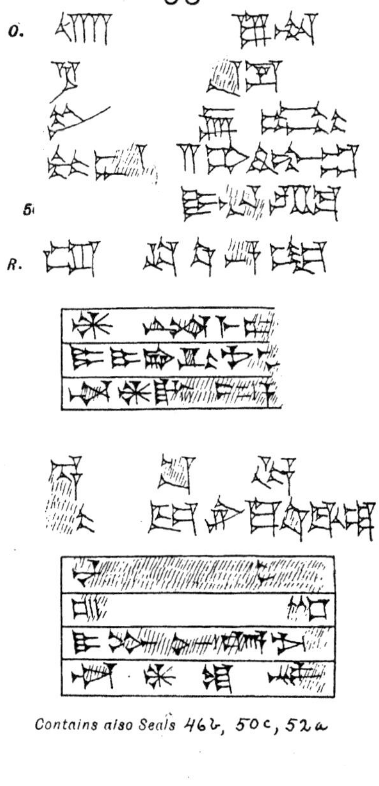

Contains also Seals 46b, 50c, 52a

54

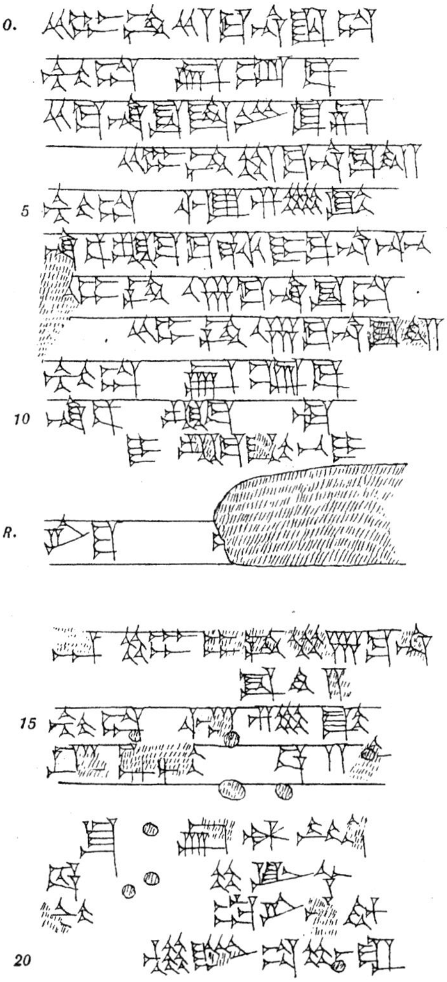

55

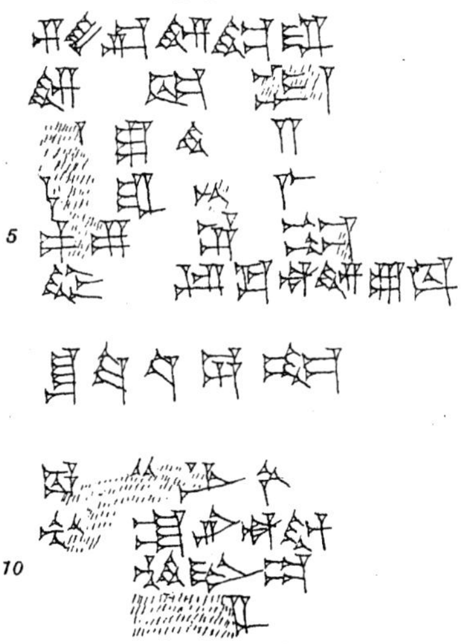

56

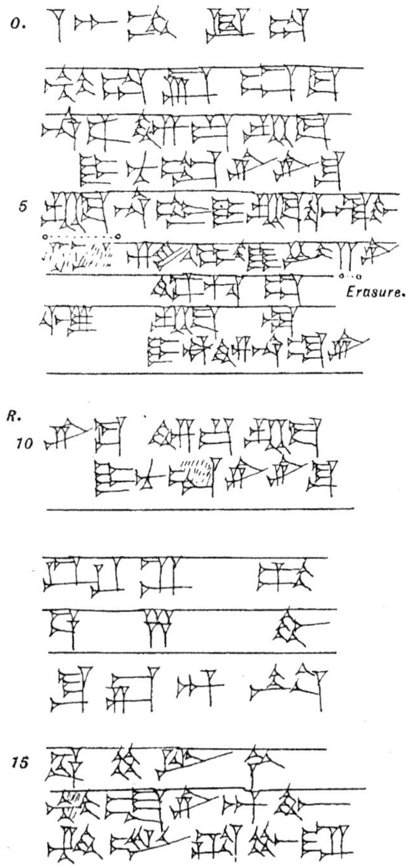

57

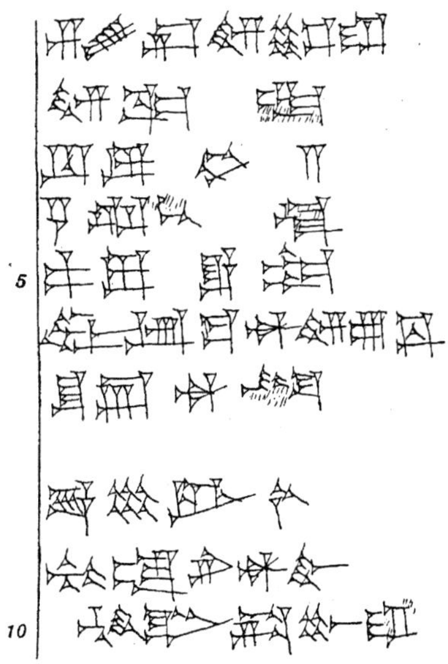

58

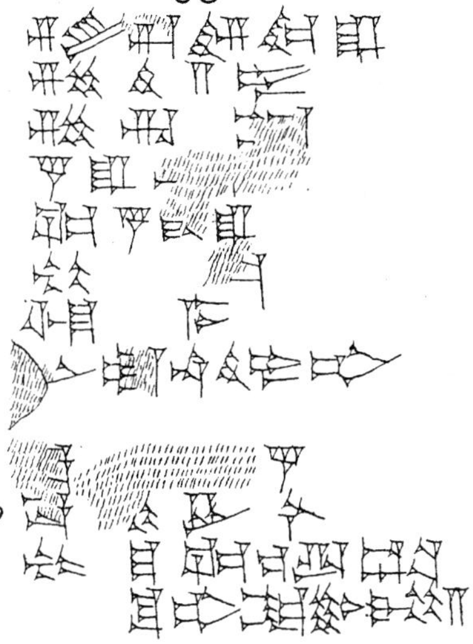

59

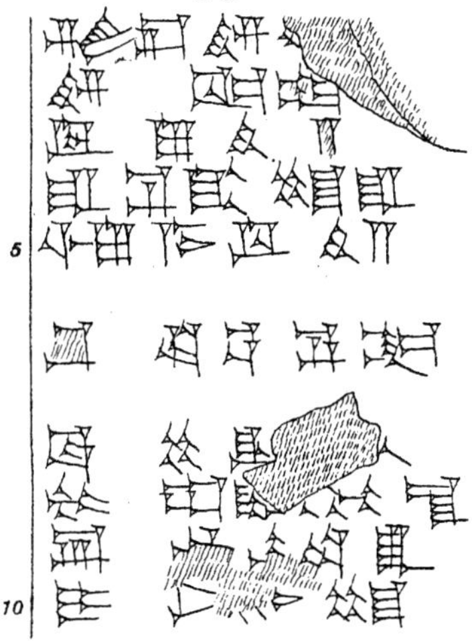

60

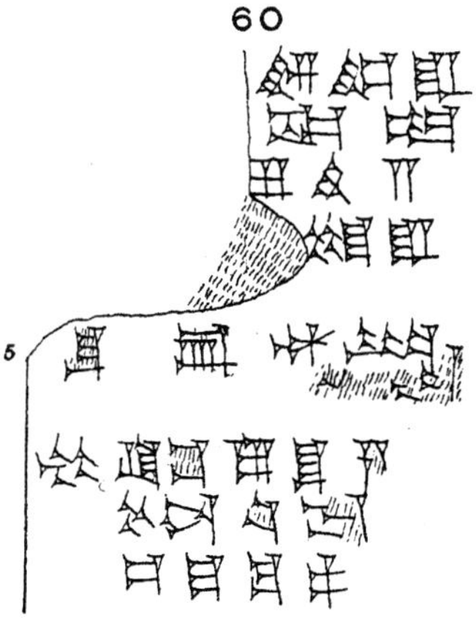

Erasure.

61

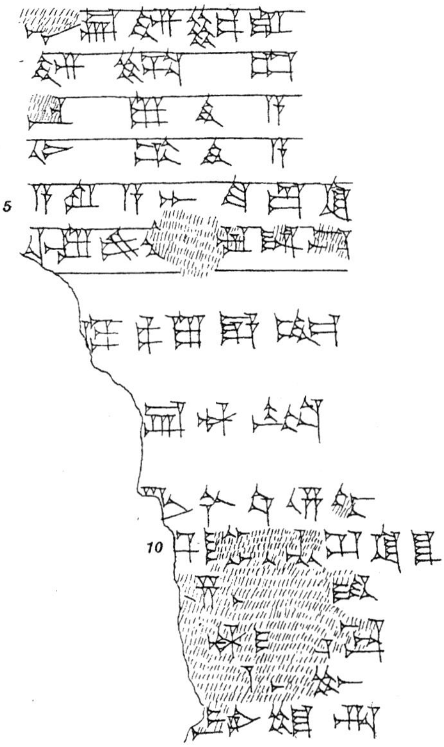

62

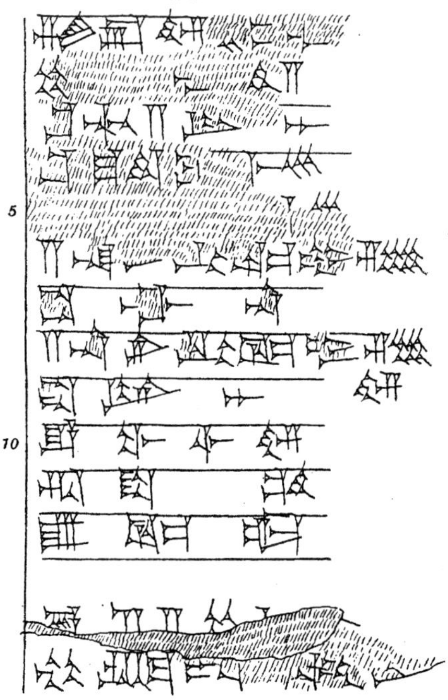

63

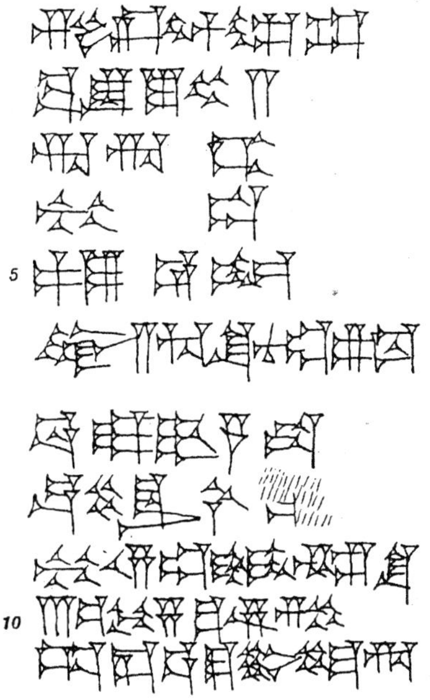

64

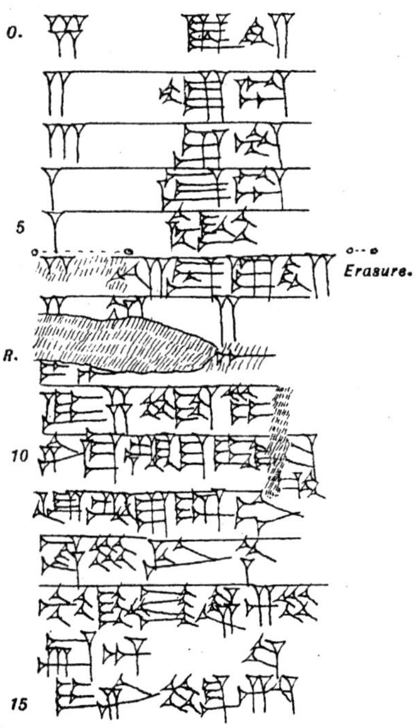

65

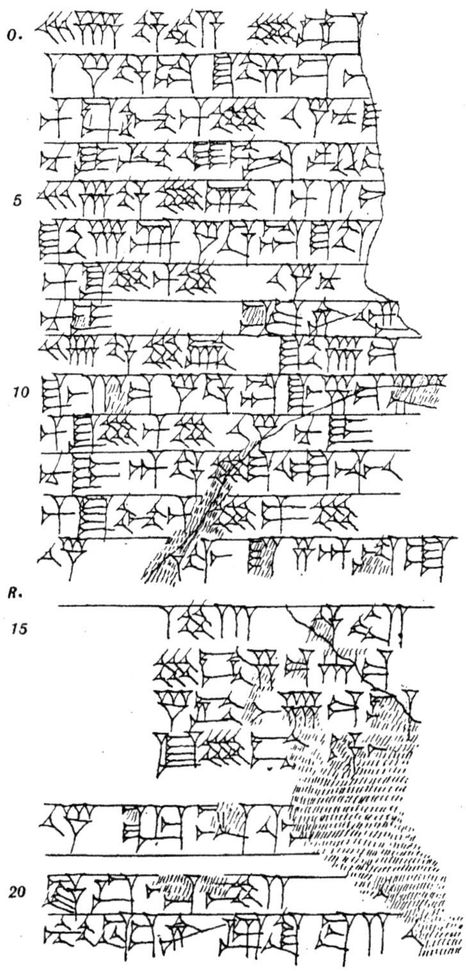

66

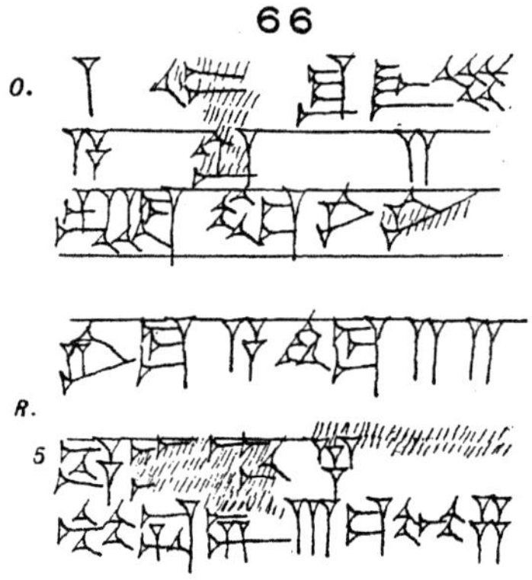

67

O.

R. 5

10

U. E.

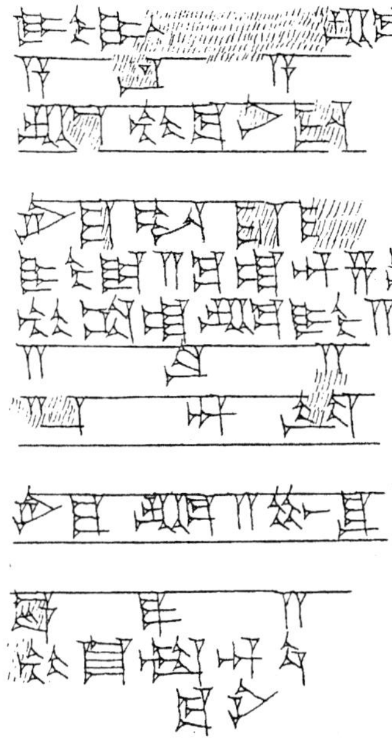

68

O.

R.

5

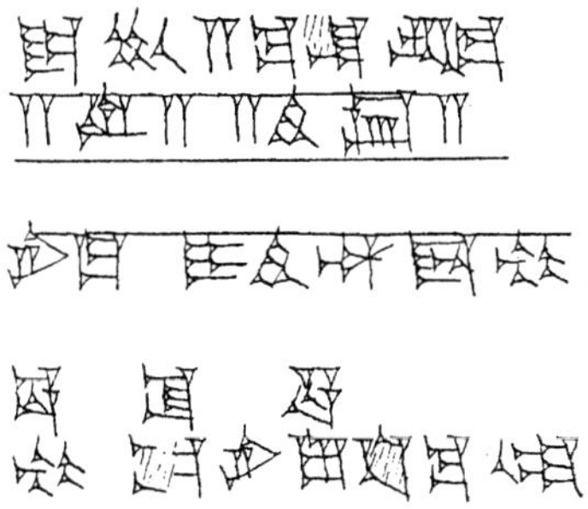

69

O.

5

R.

10

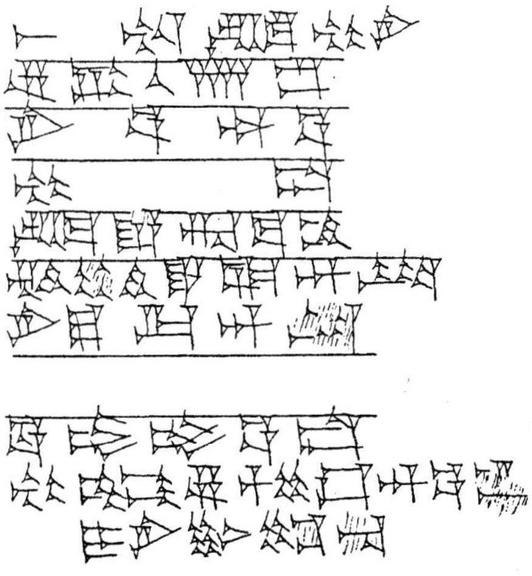

70

O.

5

R. 10

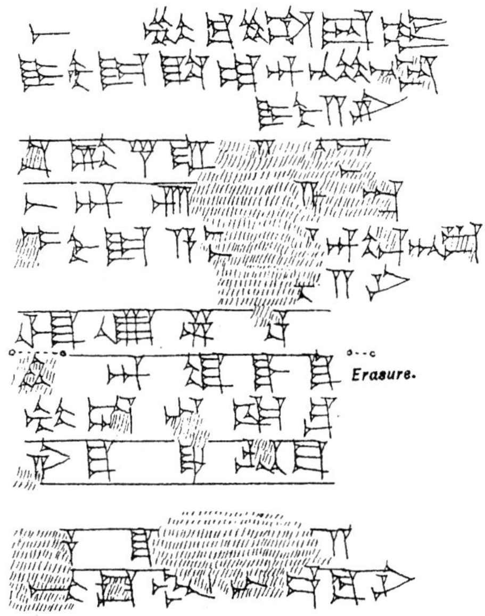

71

O.

5

R.

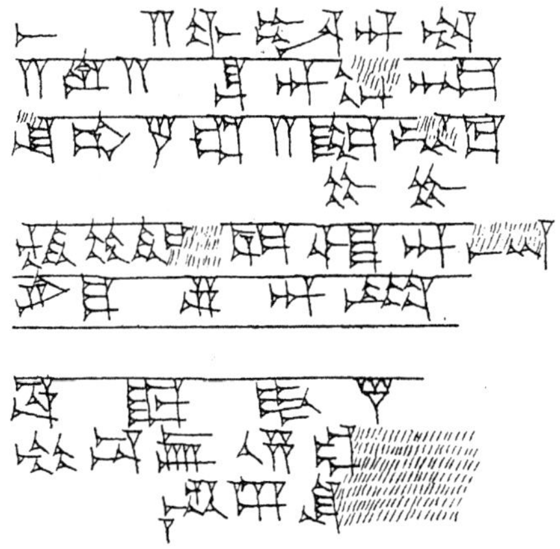

72

O.

5

Lo. E.

R.

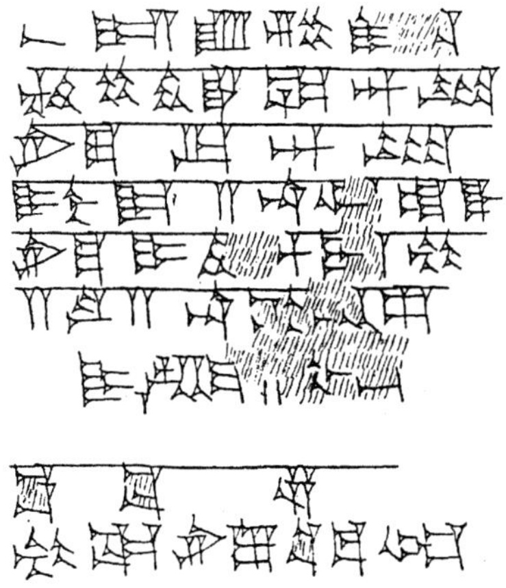

73

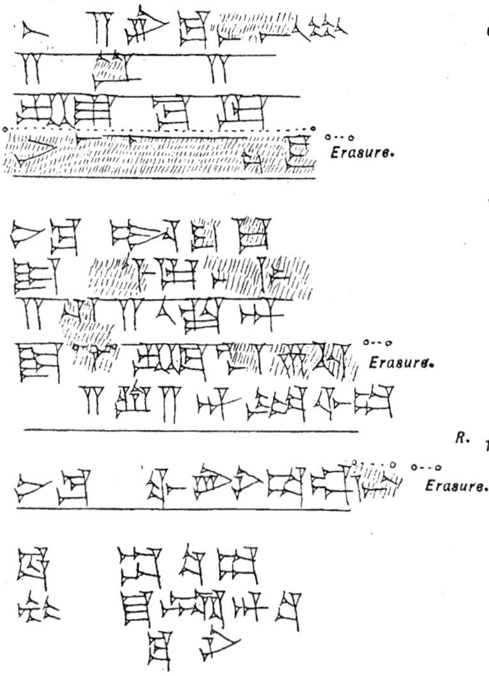

74

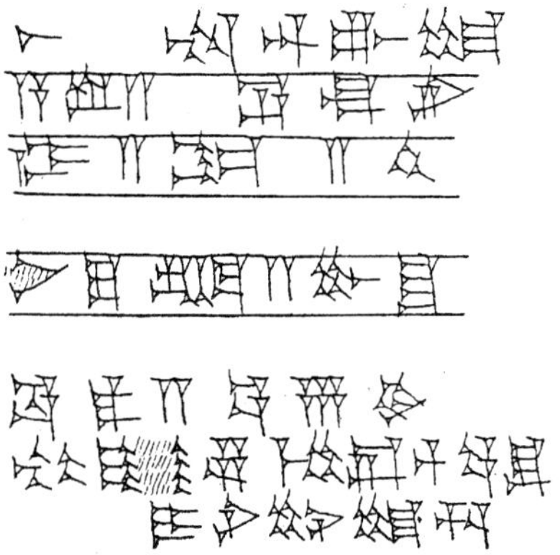

75

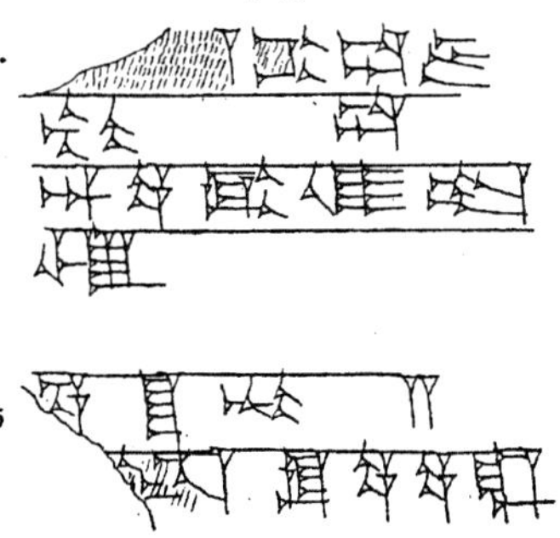

76

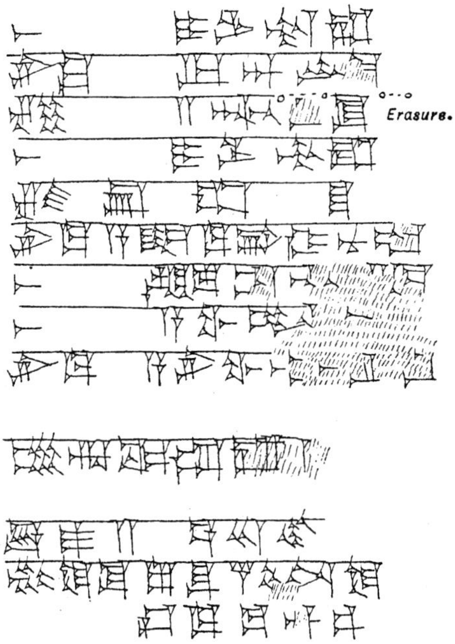

77

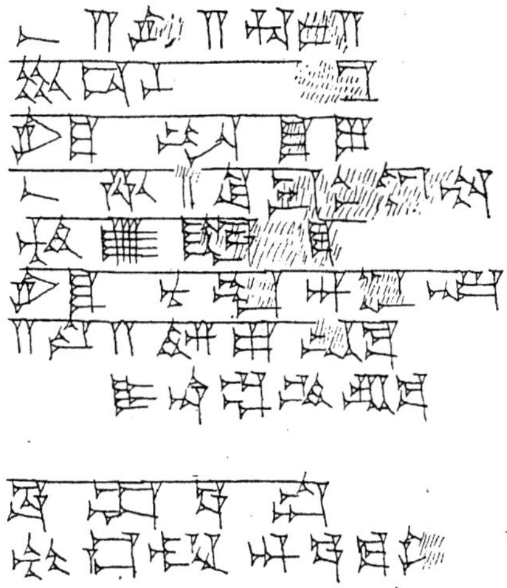

78

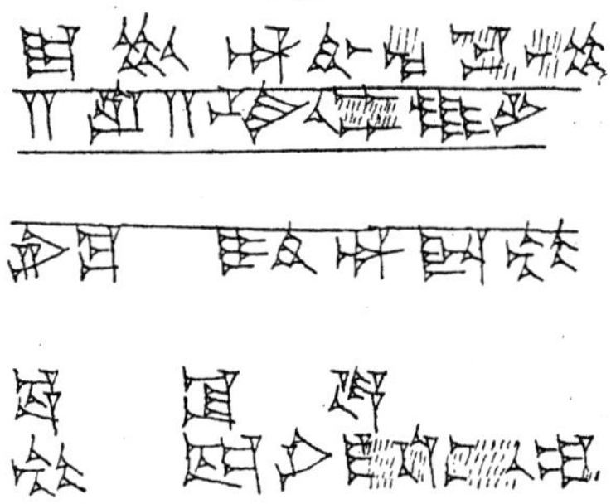

79

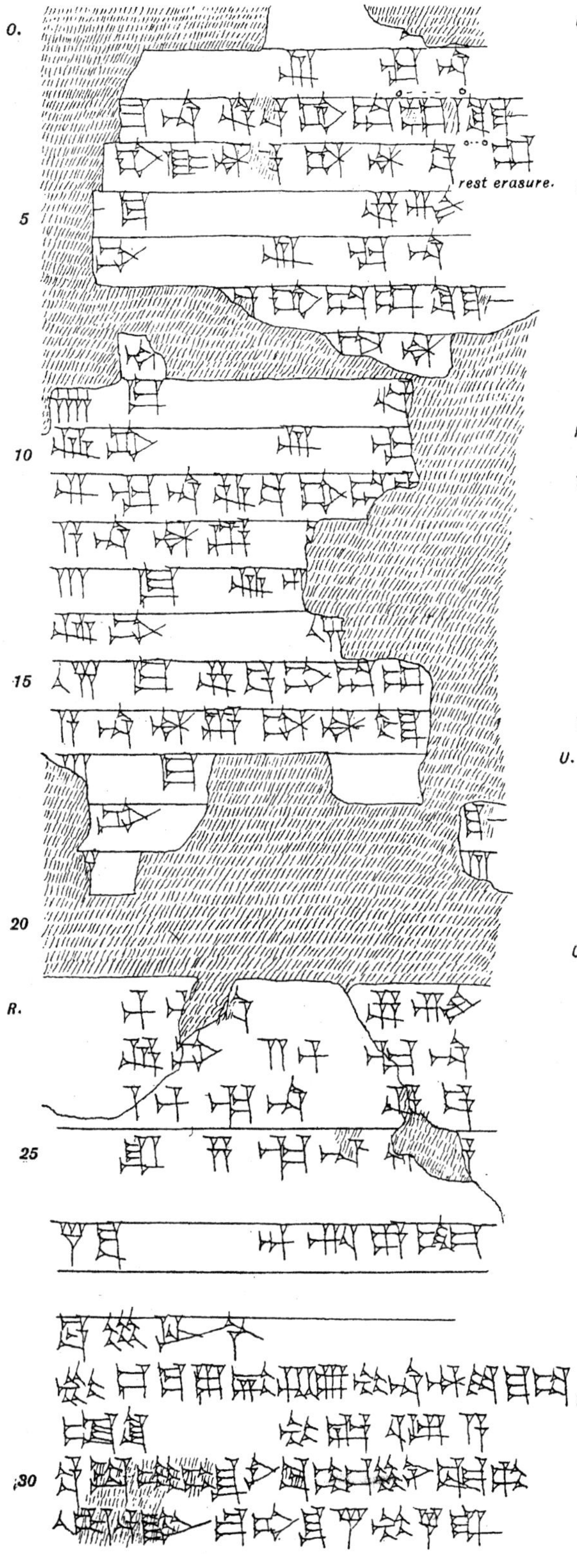
O.
rest erasure.
5
10
15
20
R.
25
30

80

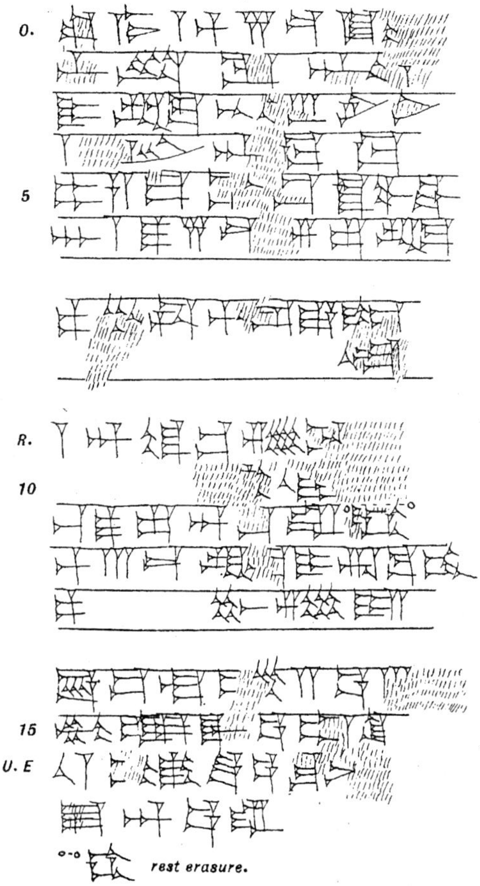
O.
5
R.
10
15
U. E
rest erasure.

81

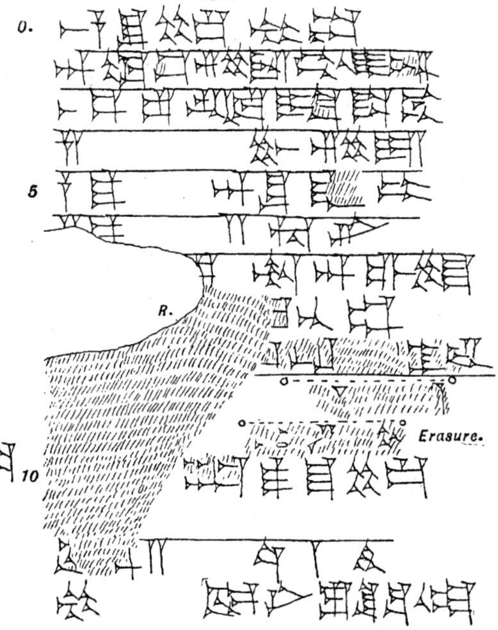
O.
5
R.
Erasure.
10

82

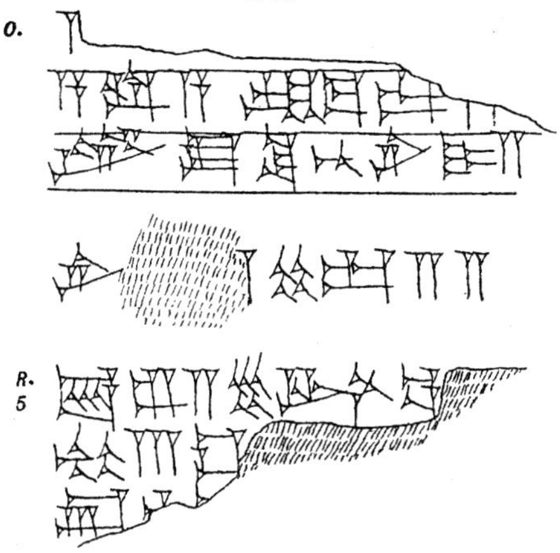

85

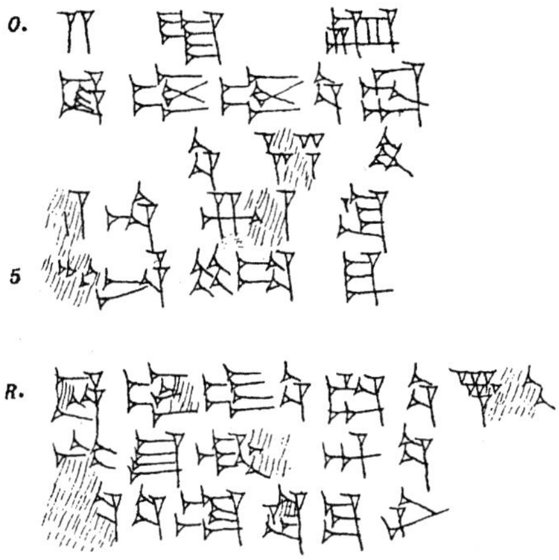

83

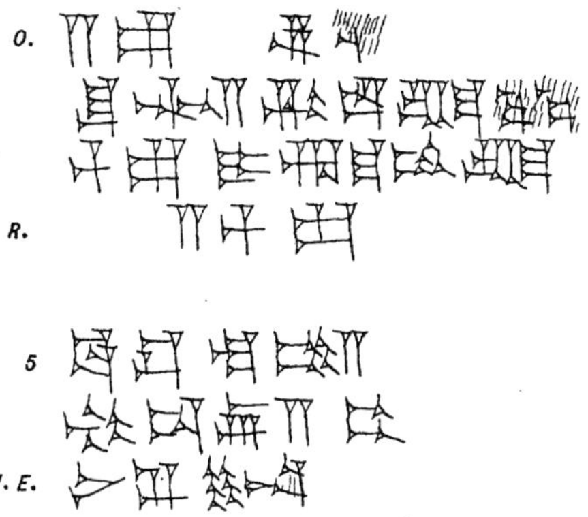

86

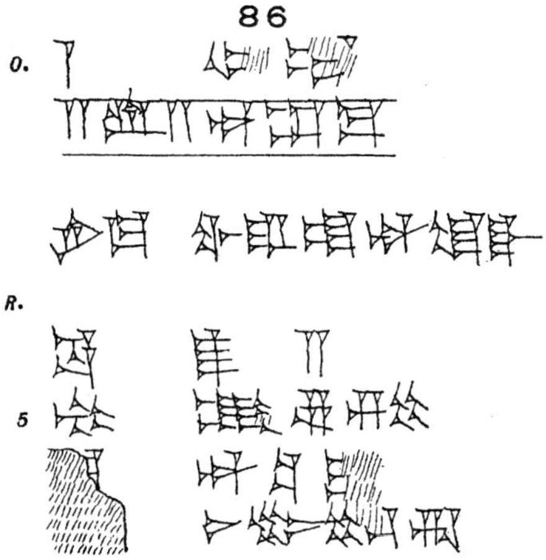

84

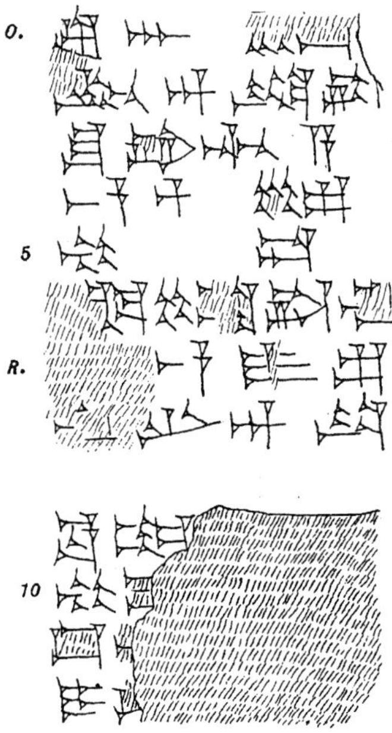

87

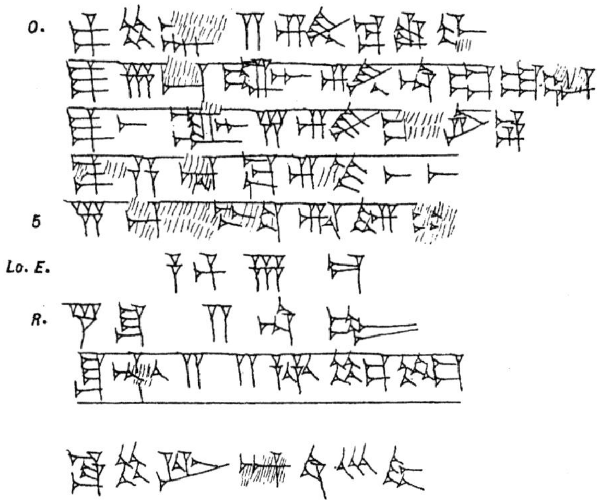

88

O.

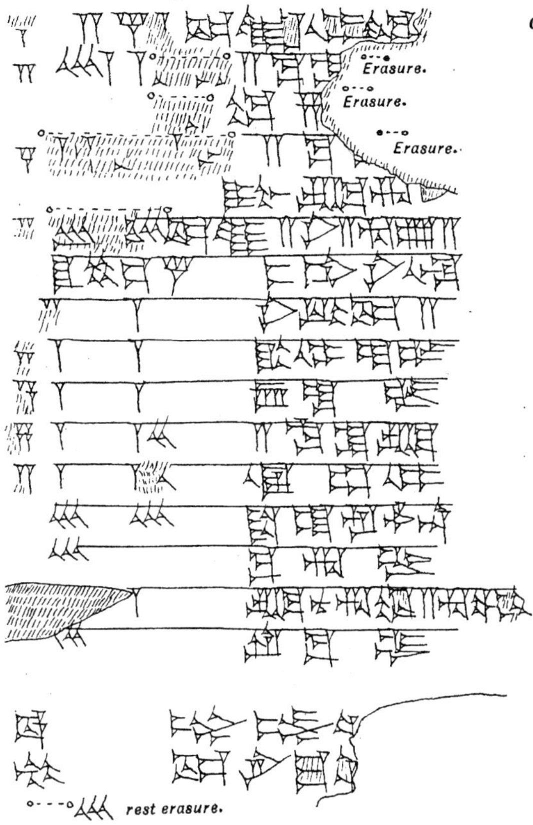

R.

89

O.

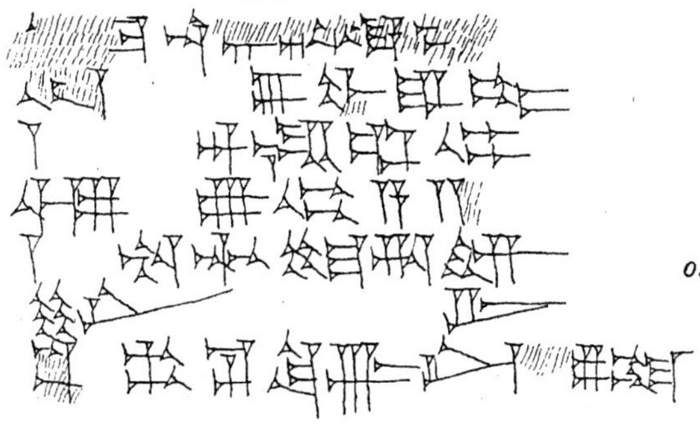

90

O.

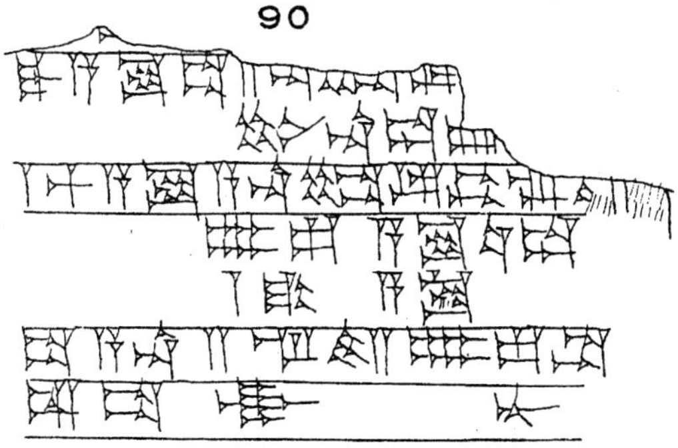

91

O.

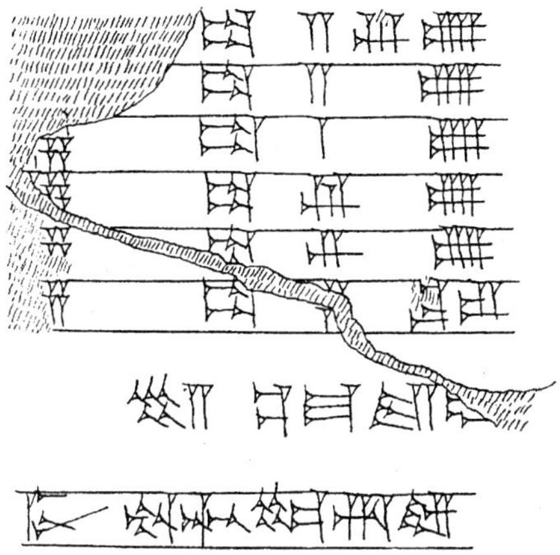

92

O.

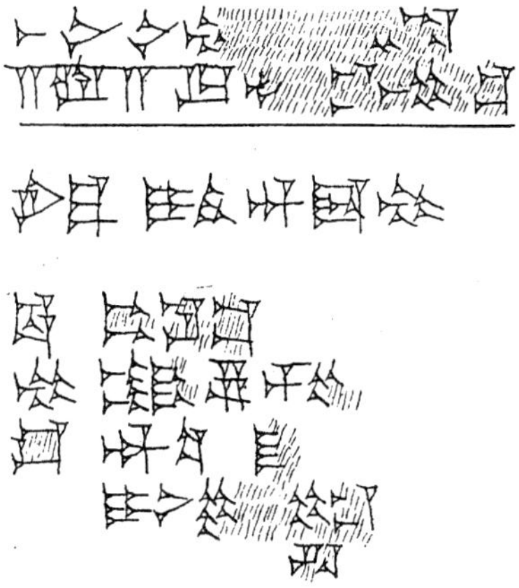

R.

93

O.

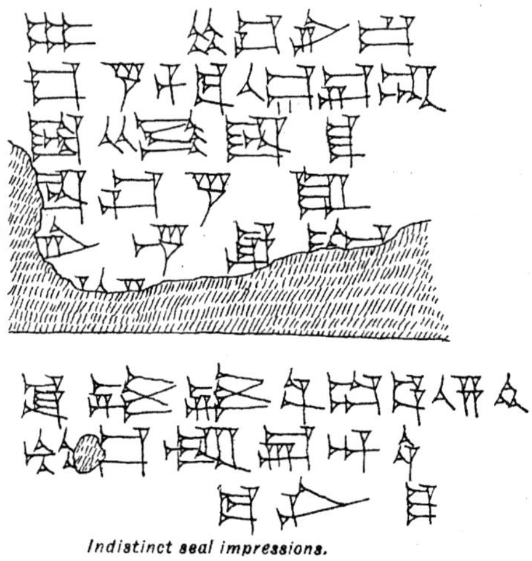

R.

Indistinct seal impressions.

94

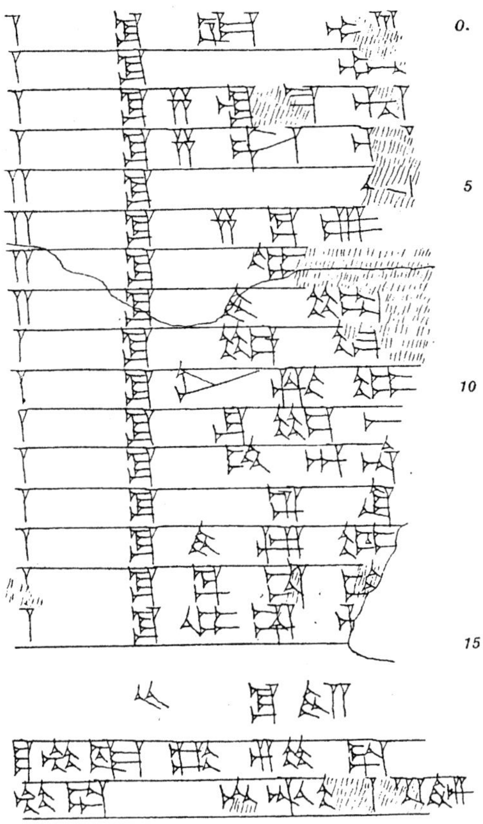

96

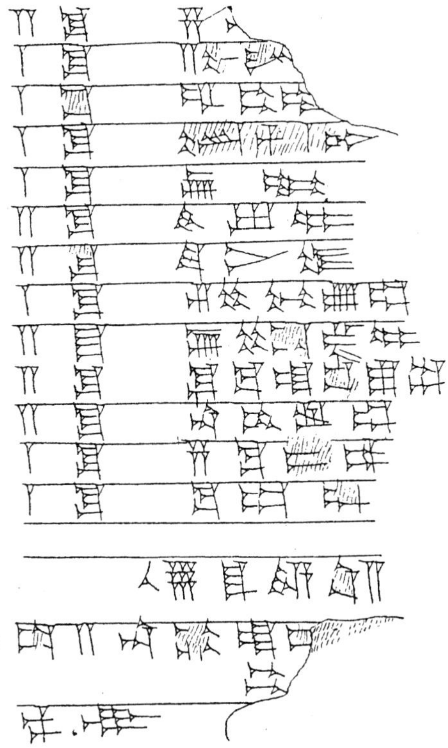

95

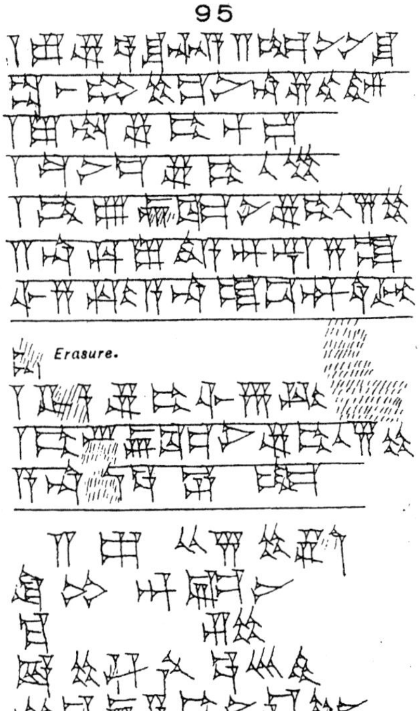

97

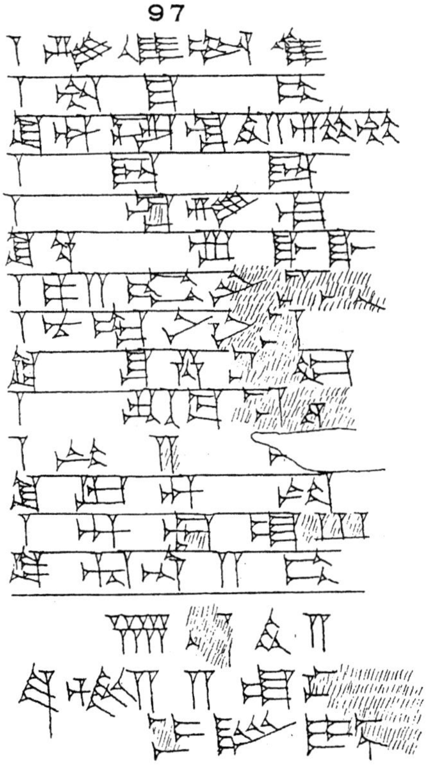

98 OBVERSE

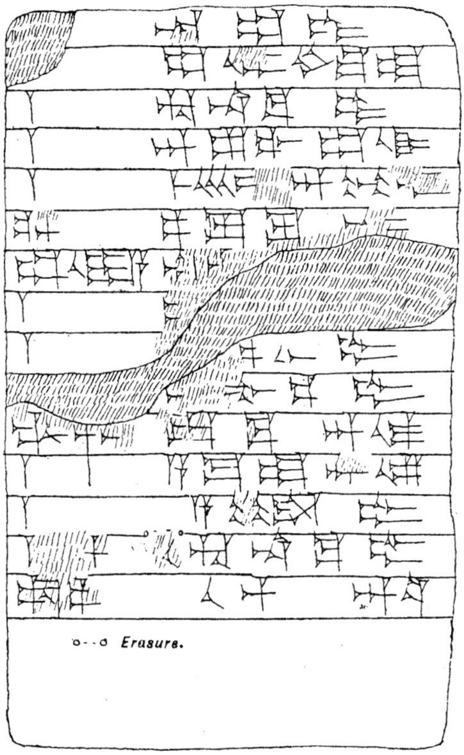

98 REVERSE

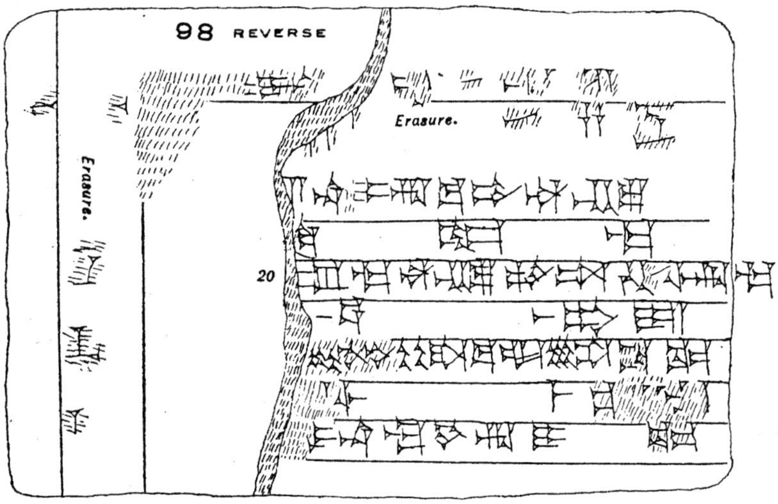

100

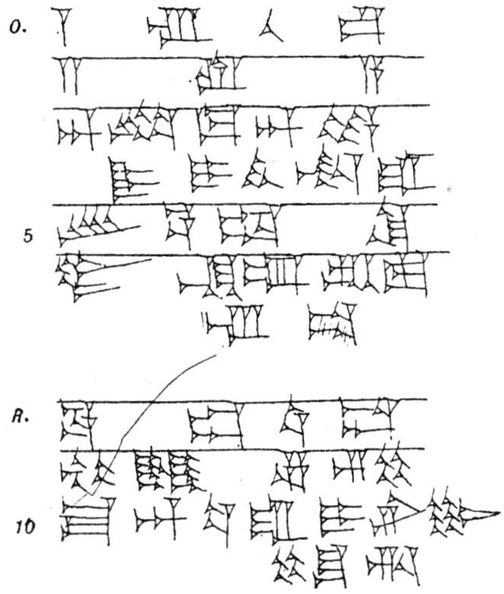

99

101

Indistinct seal impressions.

102

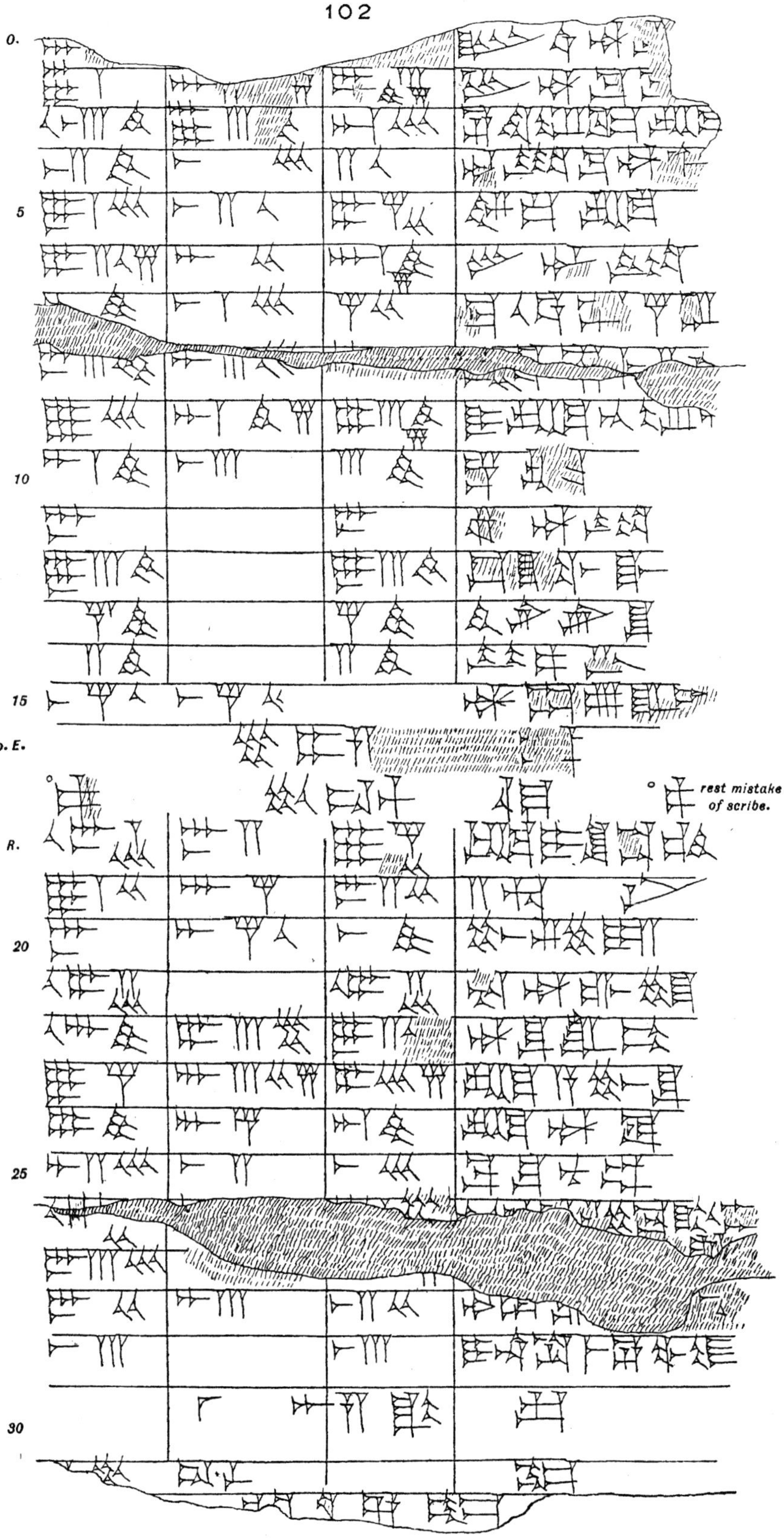

103

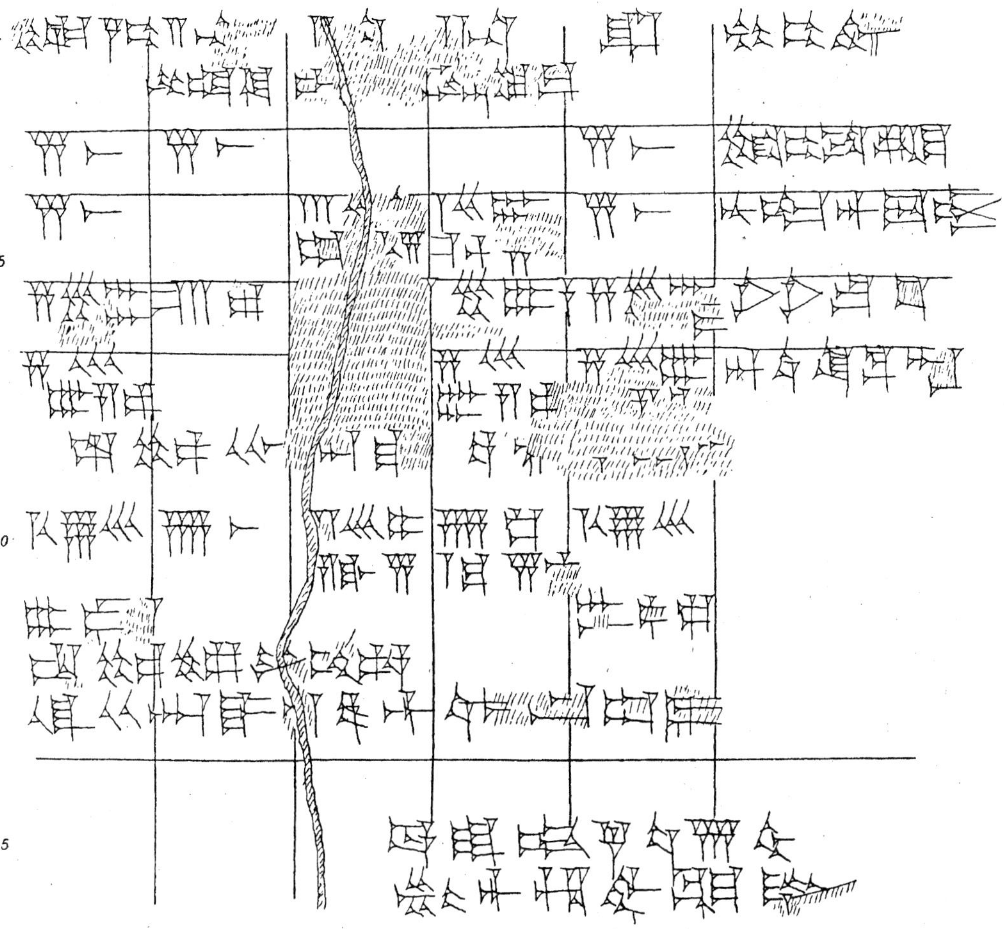

104 TABLET

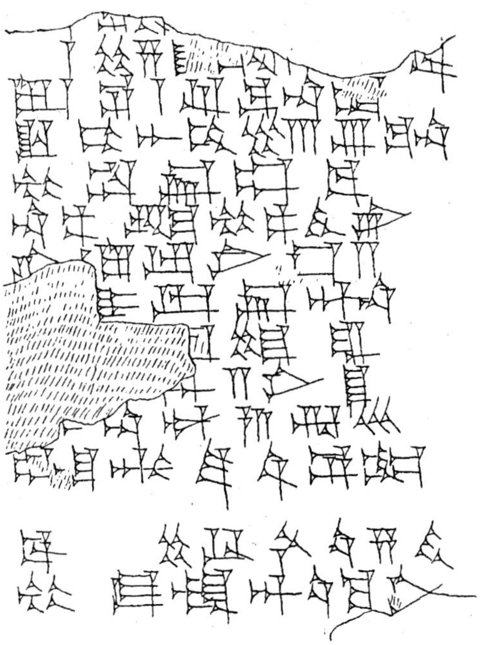

104 CASE

105

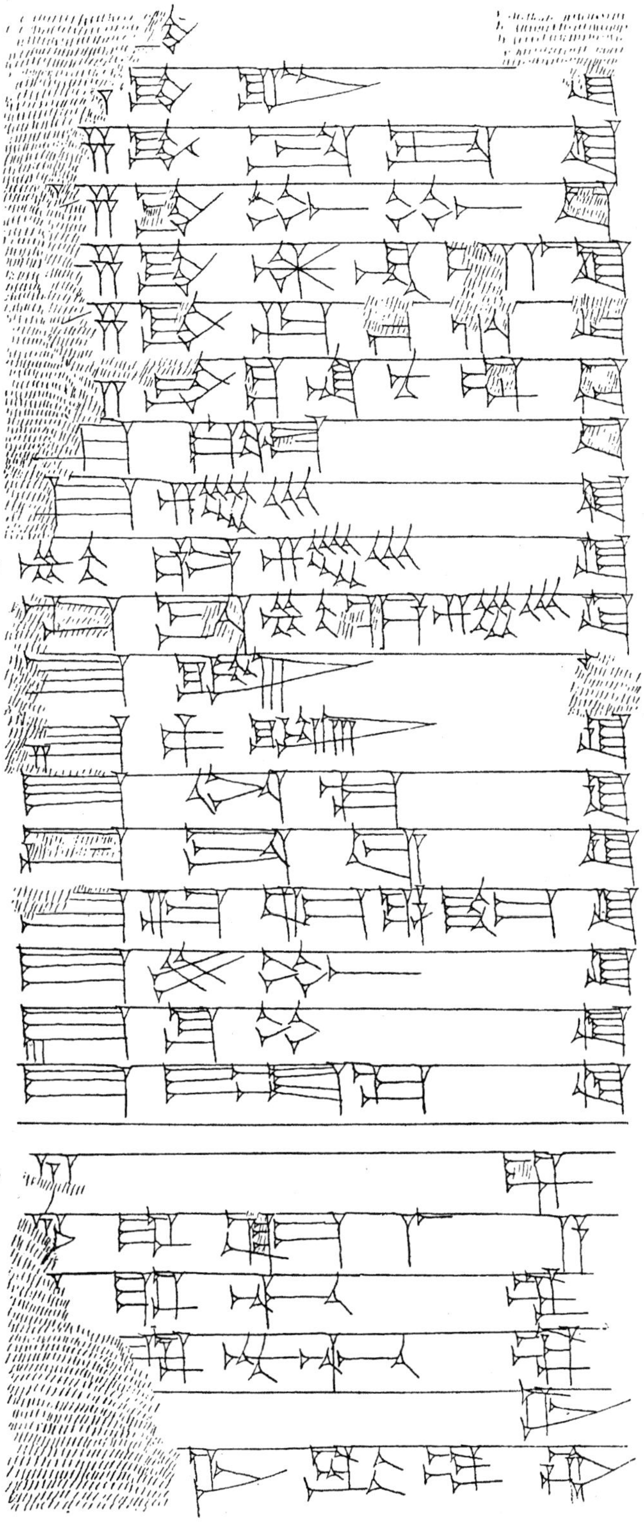

106

OBVERSE | REVERSE

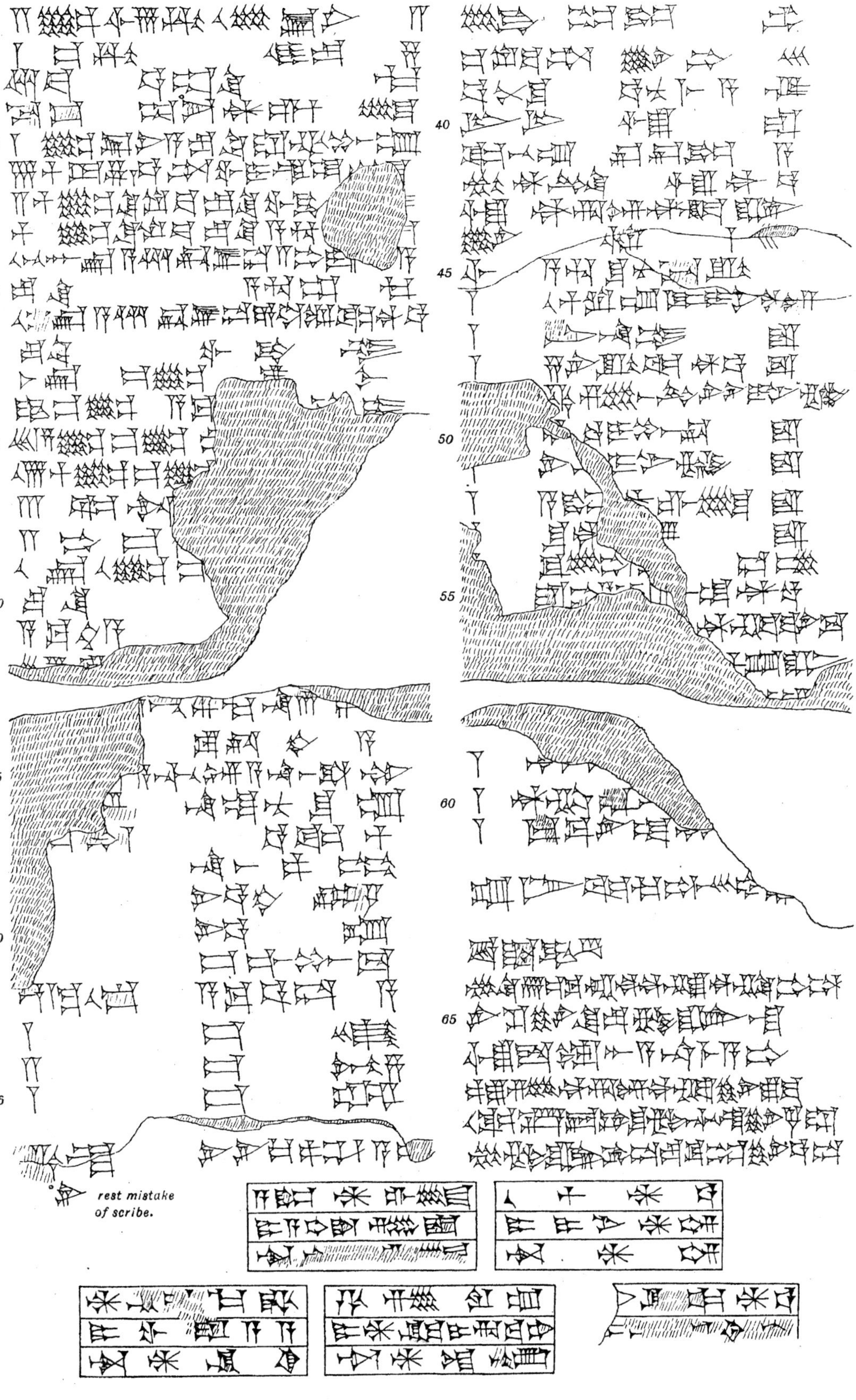

107

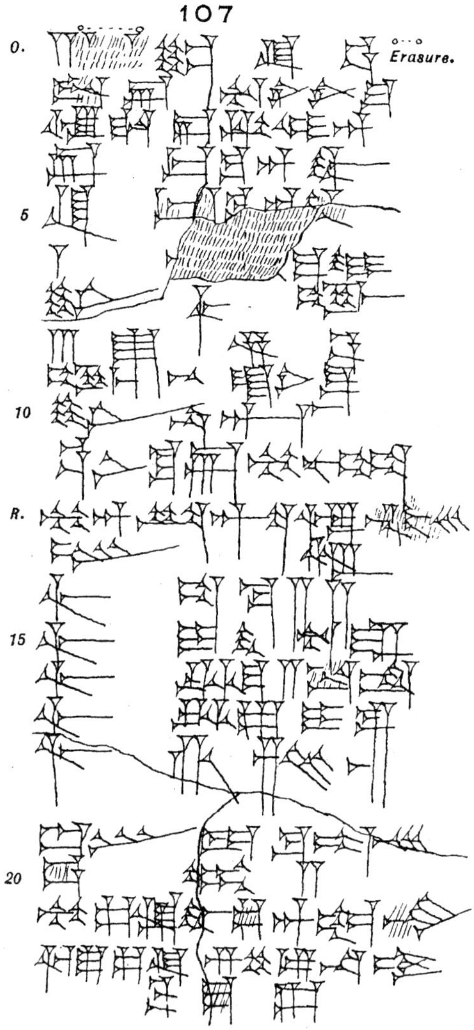

108

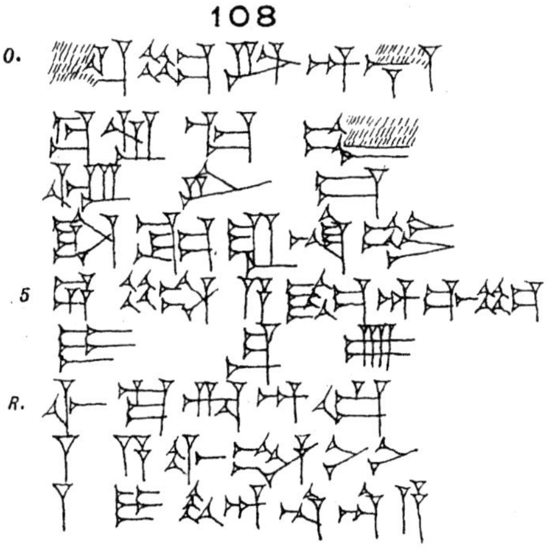

Indistinct seal impressions.

109

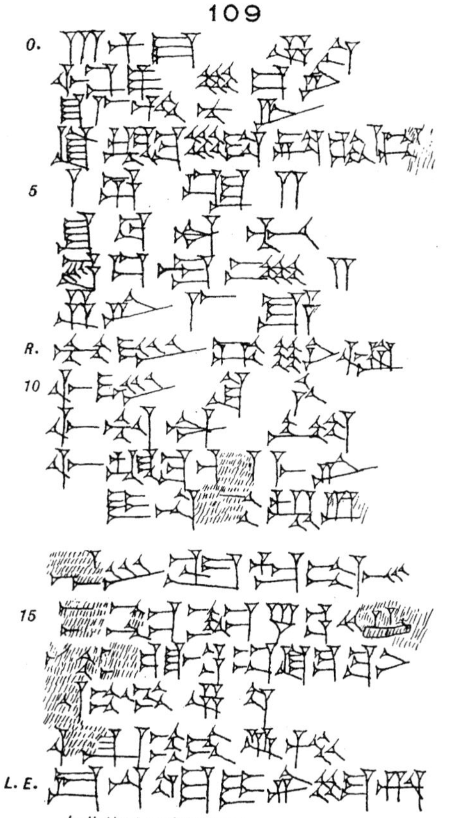

Indistinct seal impressions.

110

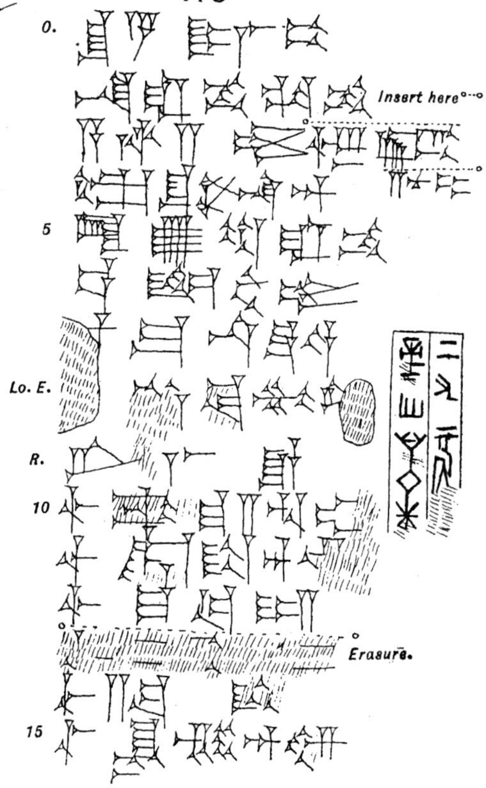

111

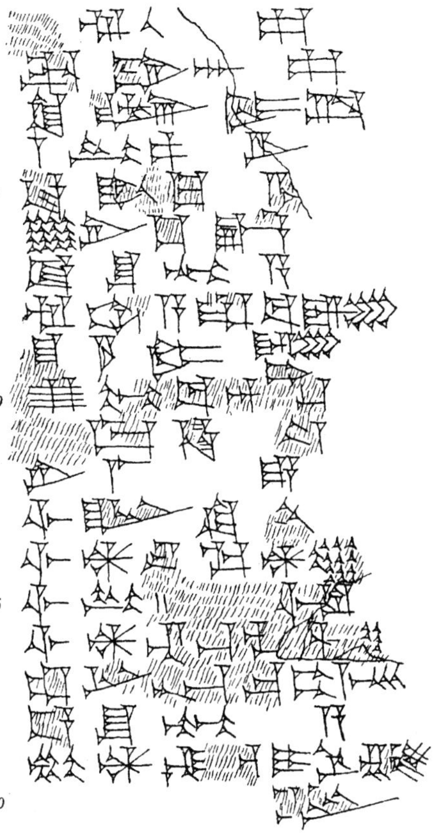

112

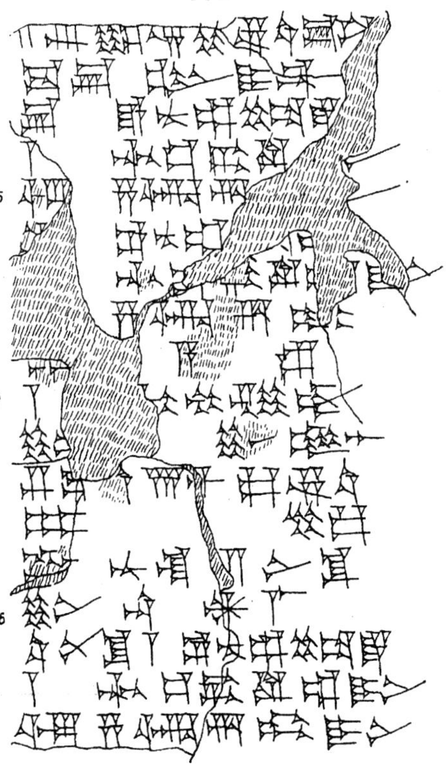

Indistinct seal impressions.

113

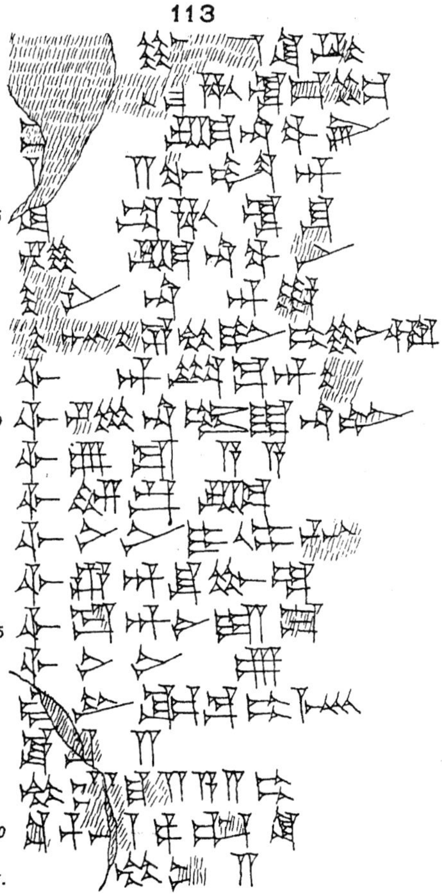

Indistinct seal impressions.

114

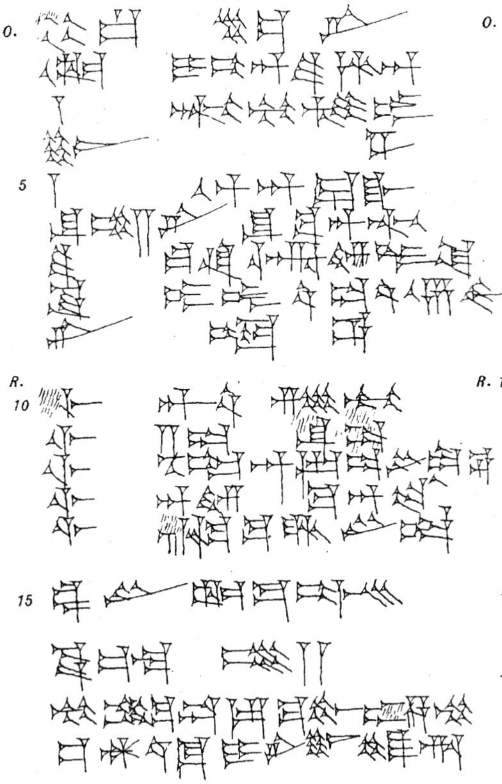

Indistinct seal impressions.

116

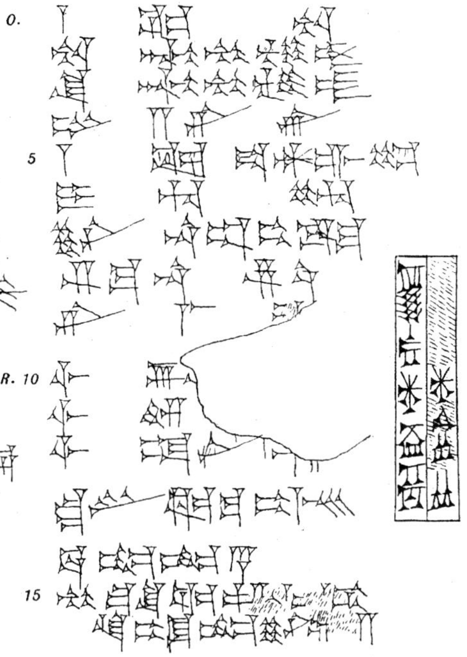

117

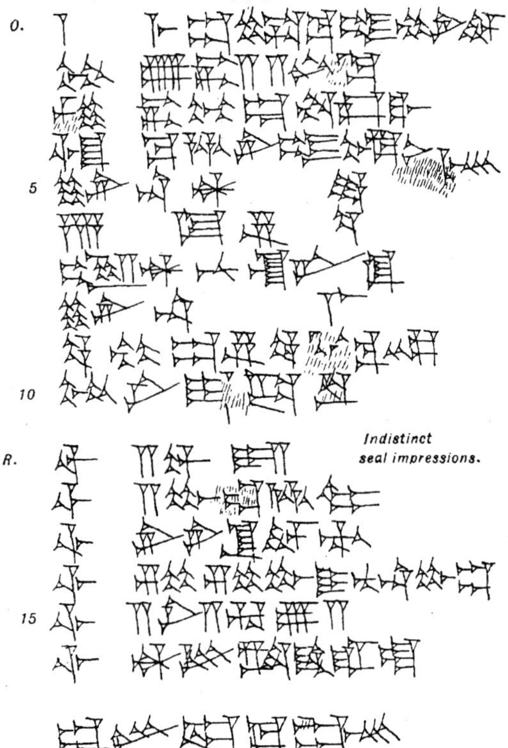

Indistinct seal impressions.

115

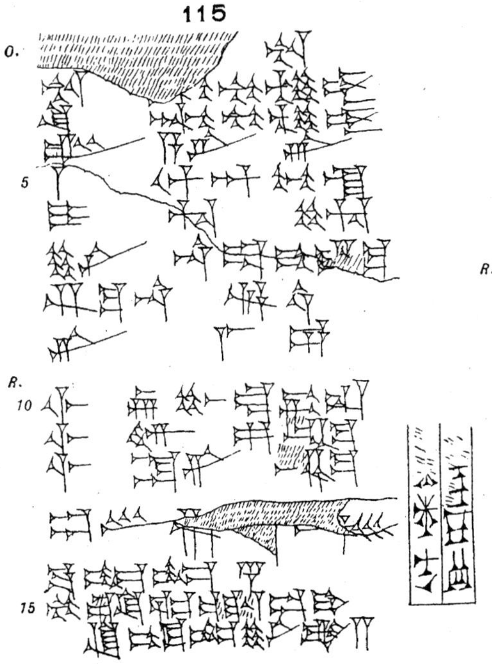

118

O.

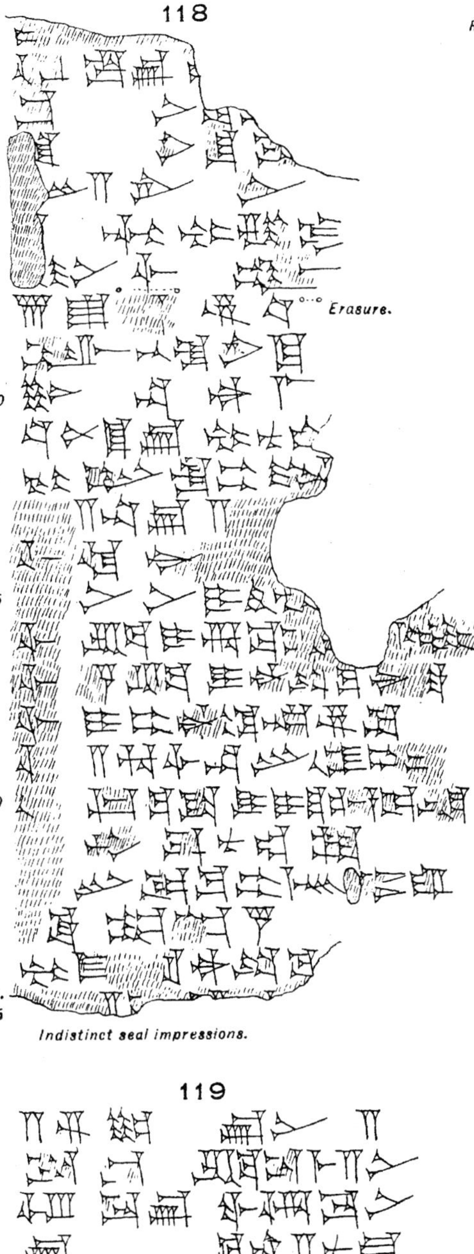

Lo. E.

R.

U. E.

Indistinct seal impressions.

119

O.

R.

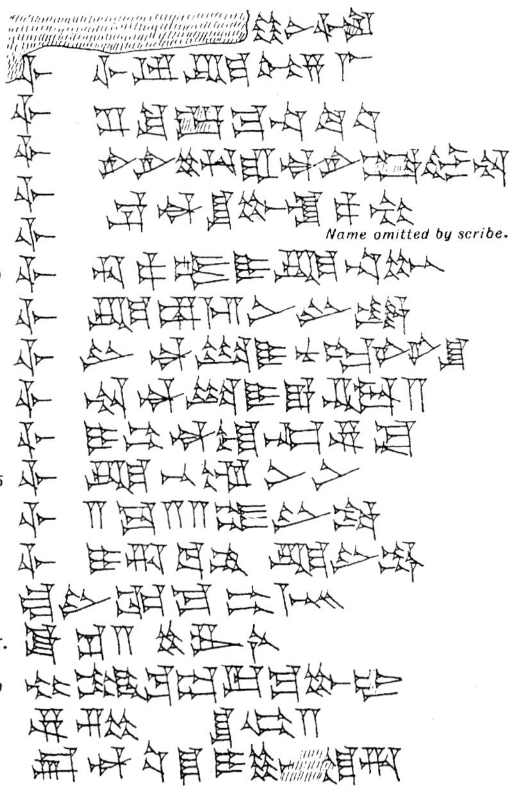

U. E.

Indistinct seal impressions.

120

O.

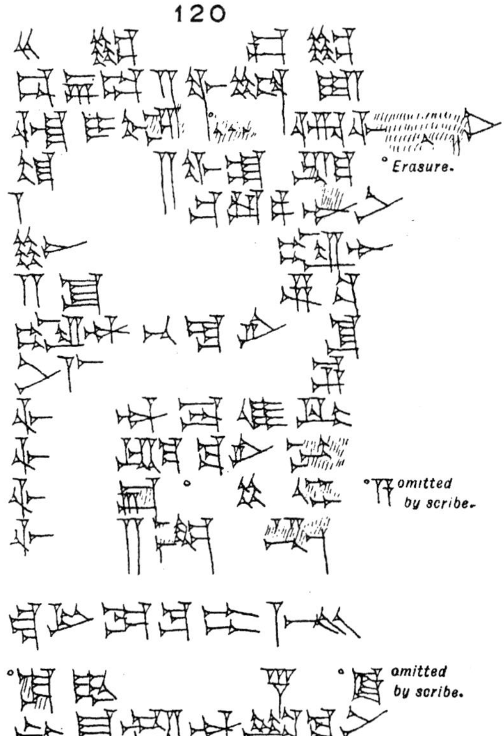

R.

Indistinct seal impressions.

121 CASE

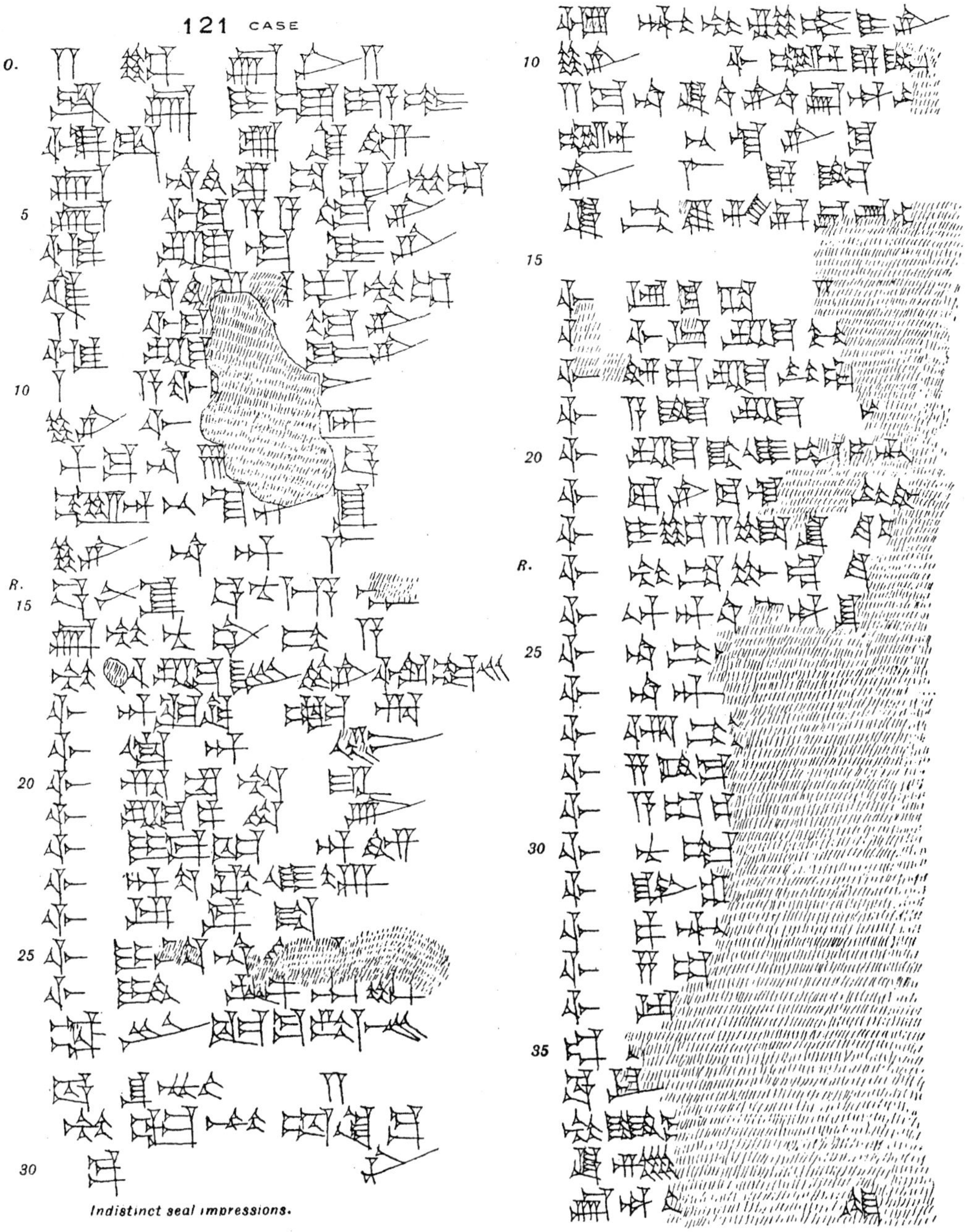

Indistinct seal impressions.

122

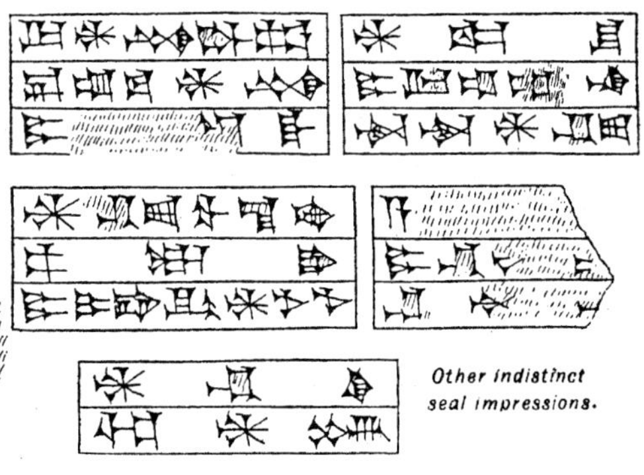

Other indistinct seal impressions.

123

O.

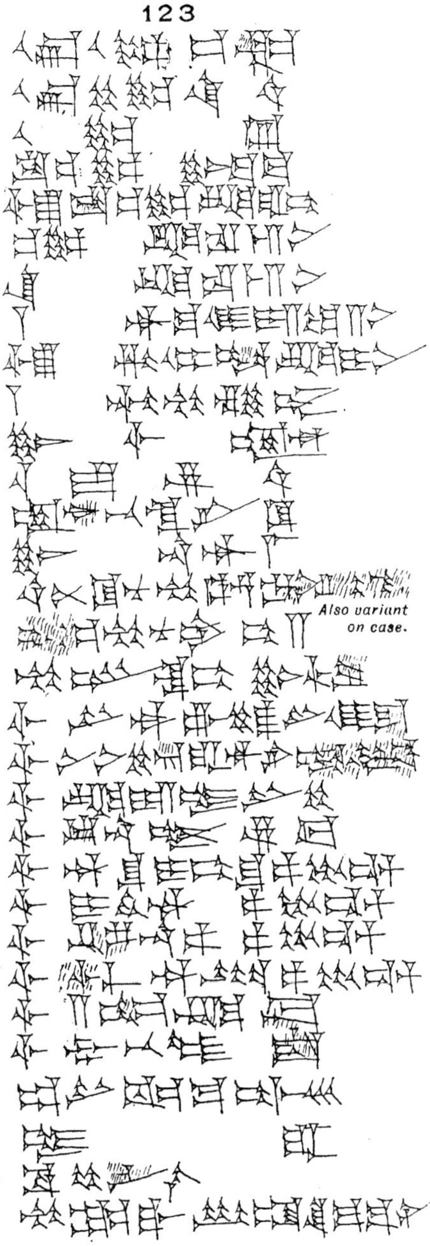

Also variant on case.

R.

124

O.

R.

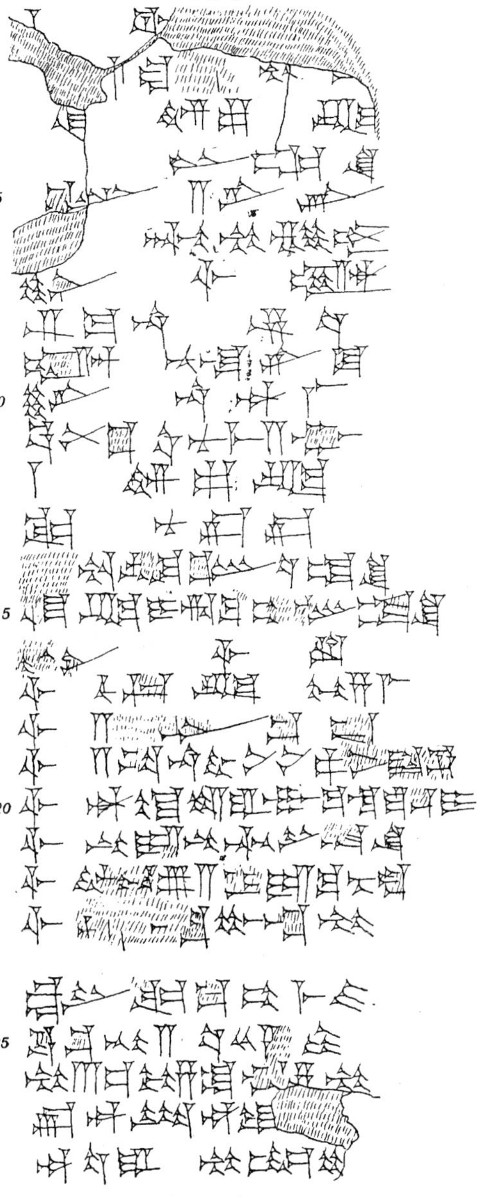

Indistinct seal impressions.

Line 15 The case reads

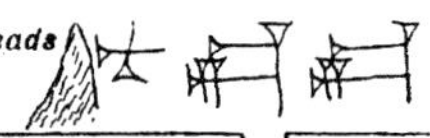

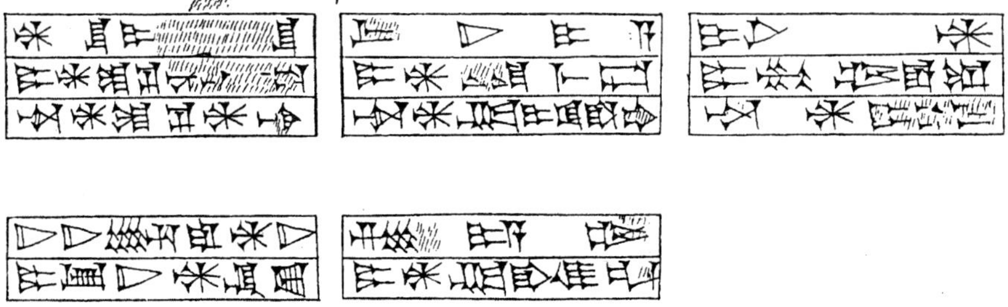

125

CASE

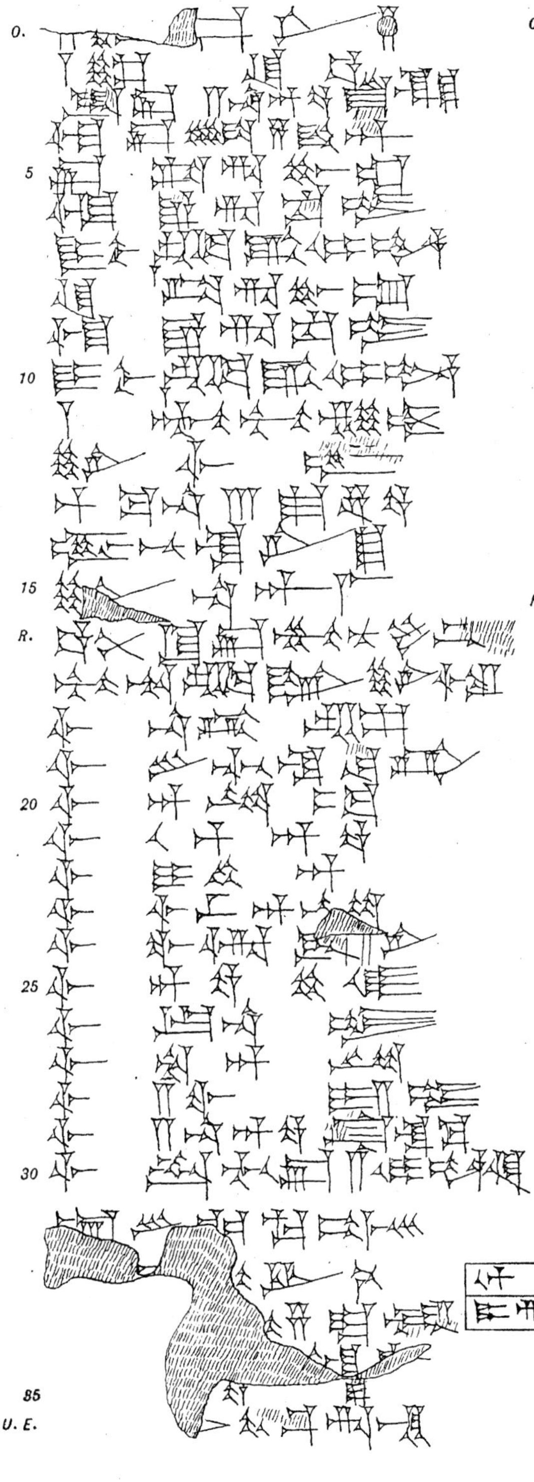

TABLET

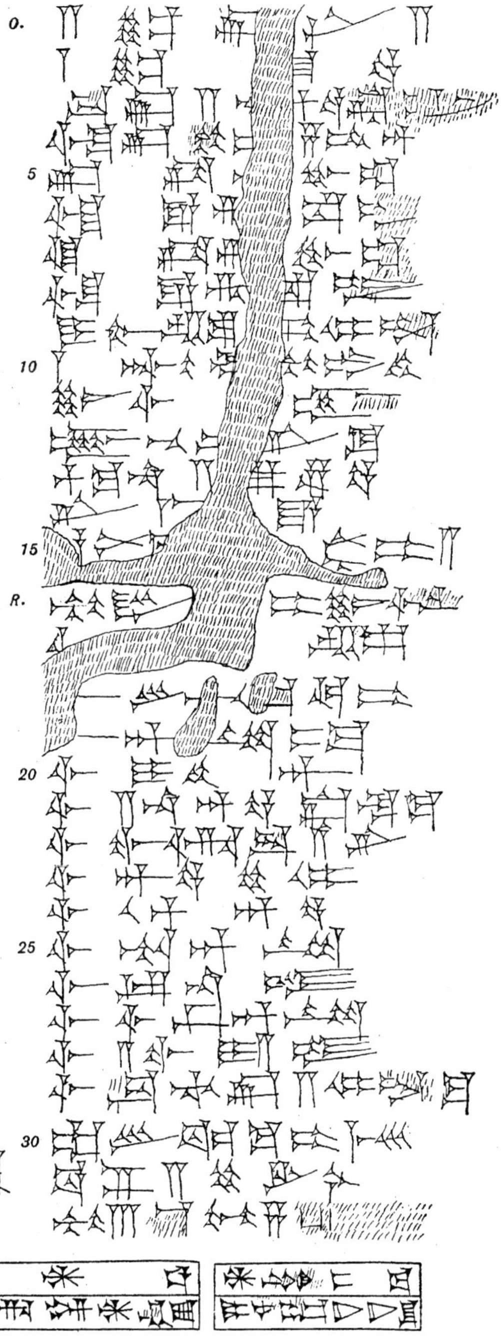

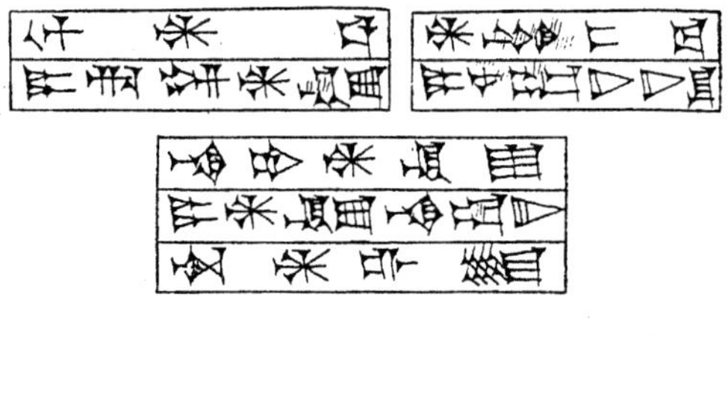

85
U. E.

126

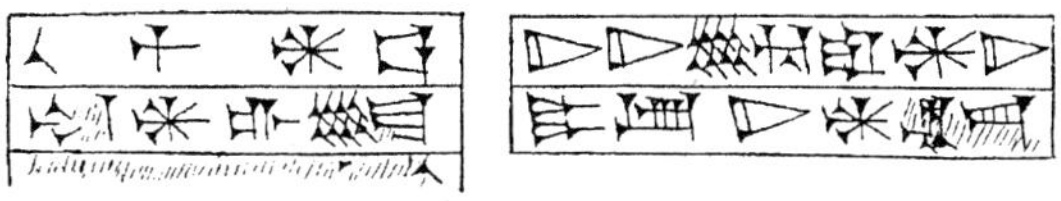

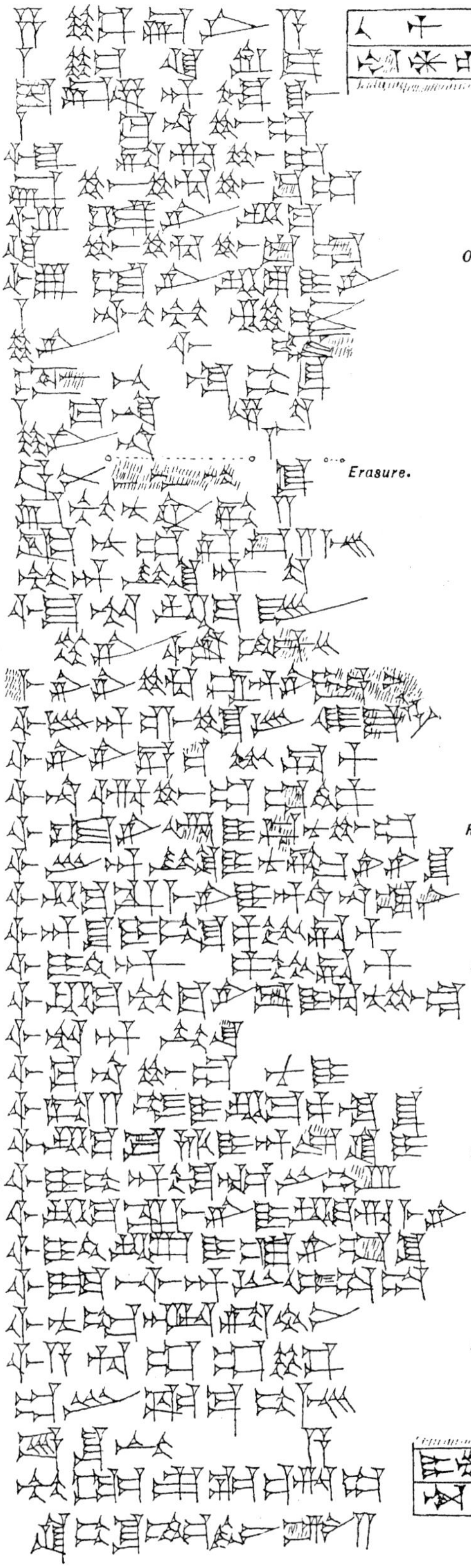

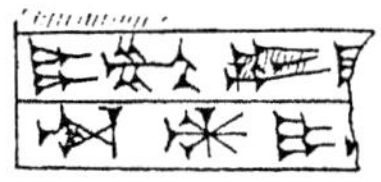

127

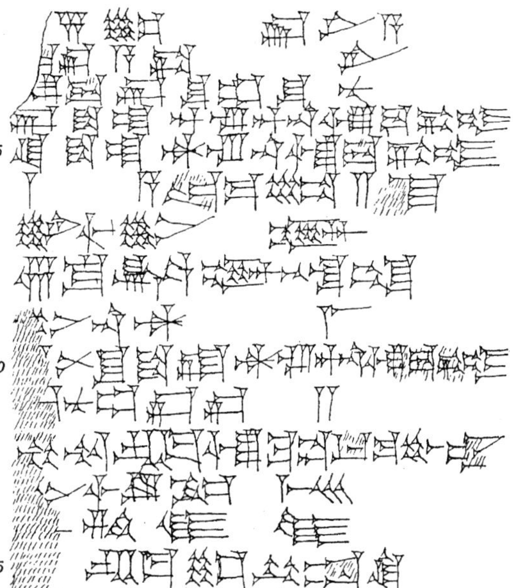

Indistinct seal impressions.

128

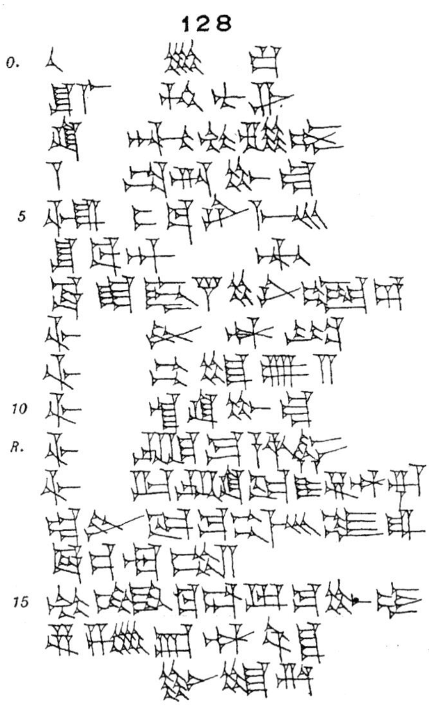

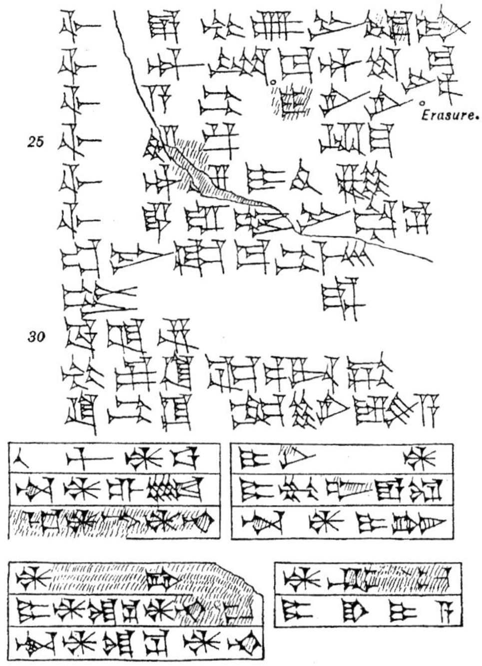

Indistinct seal impressions.

129

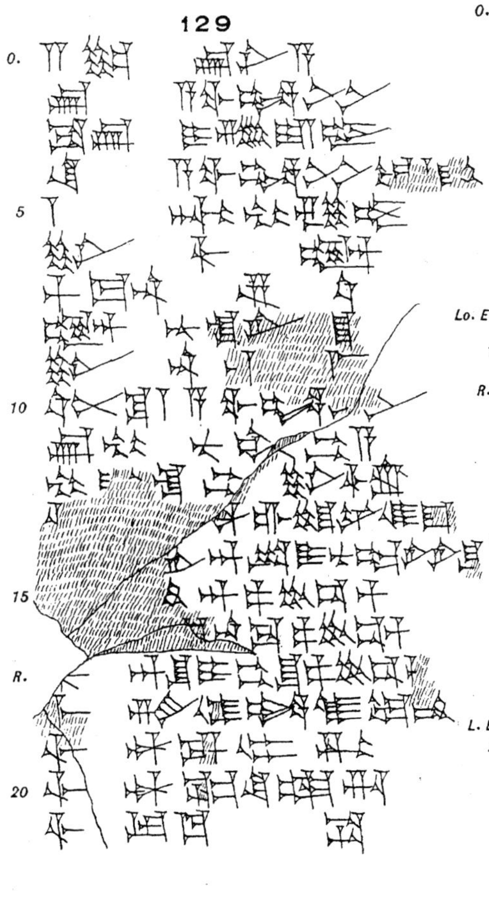

130

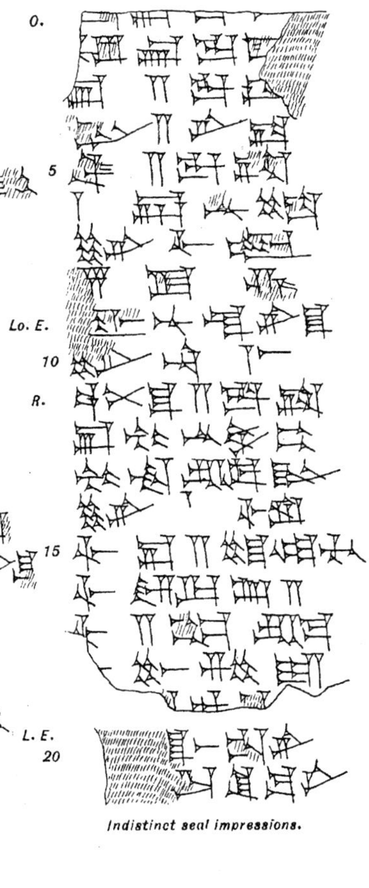

Indistinct seal impressions.

131

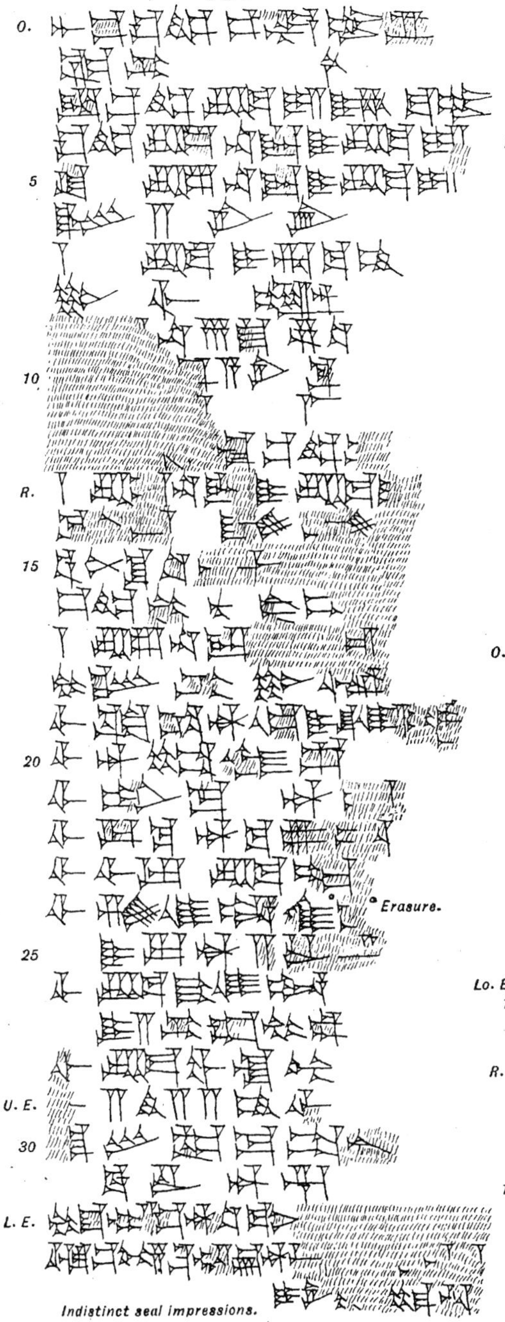

132

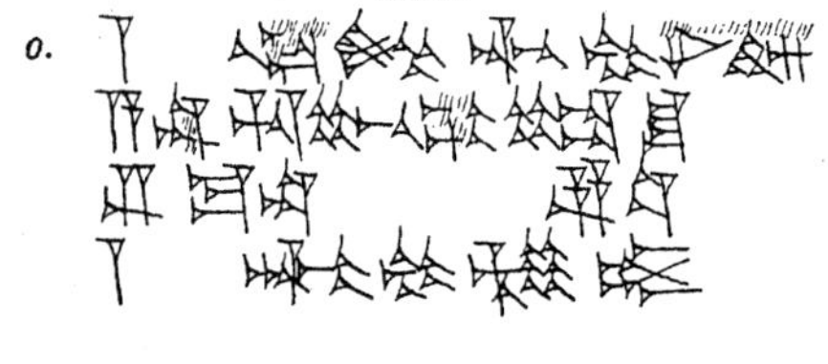

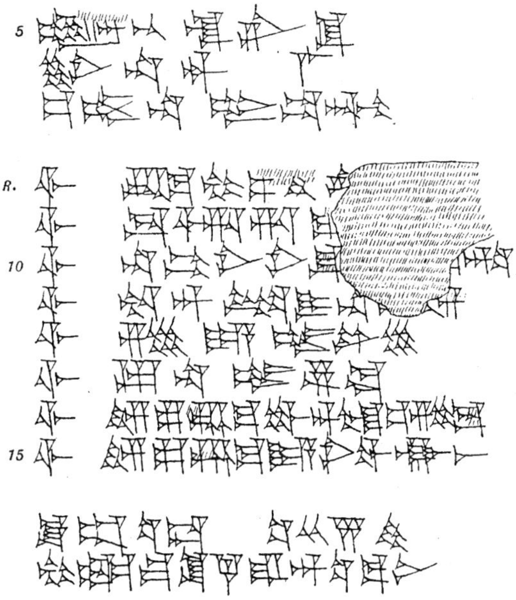

133

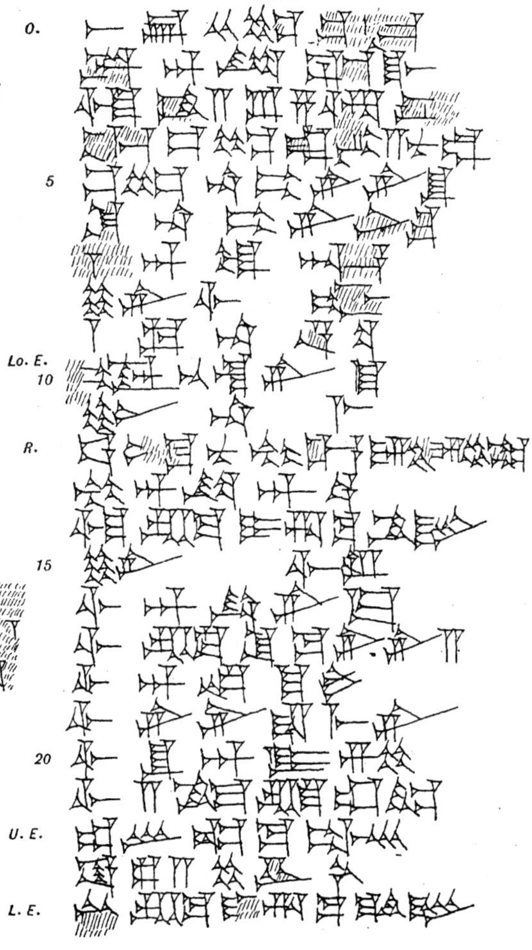

134

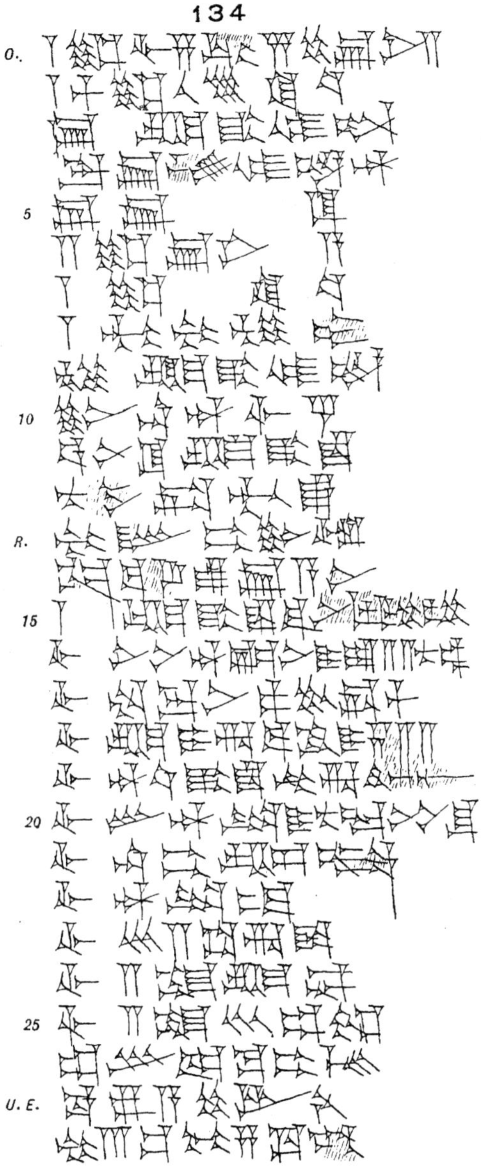

Indistinct seal impressions.

135

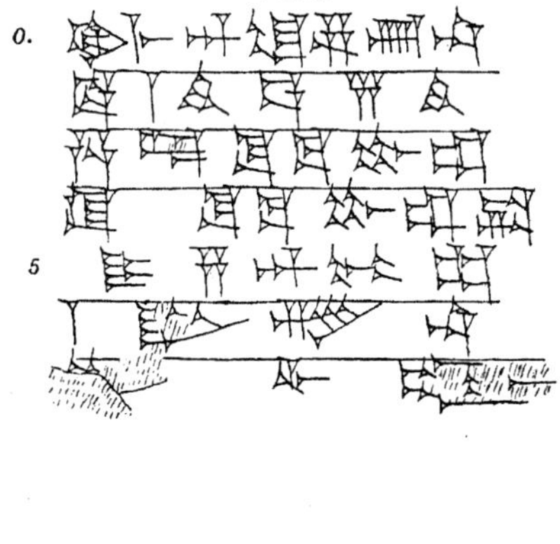

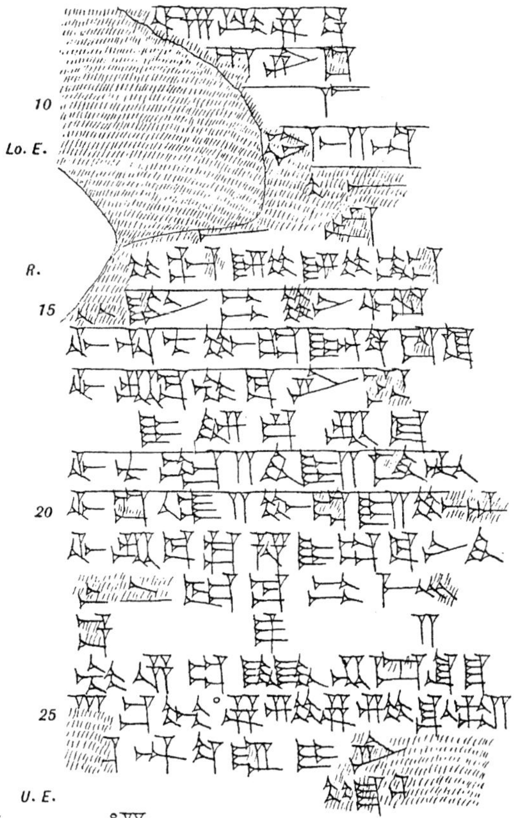

omitted by scribe.

Indistinct seal impressions.

136

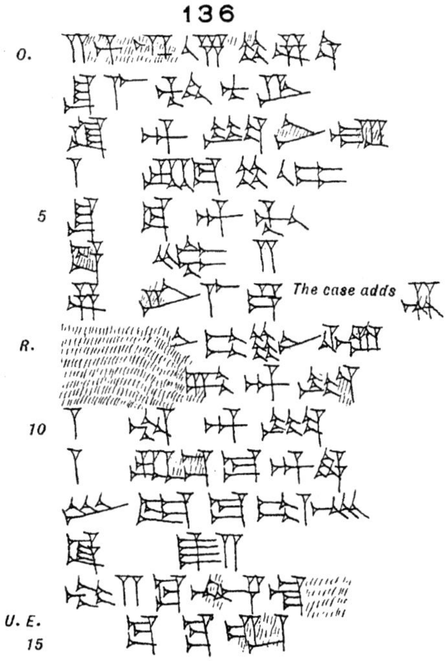

Indistinct seal impressions on case.

137

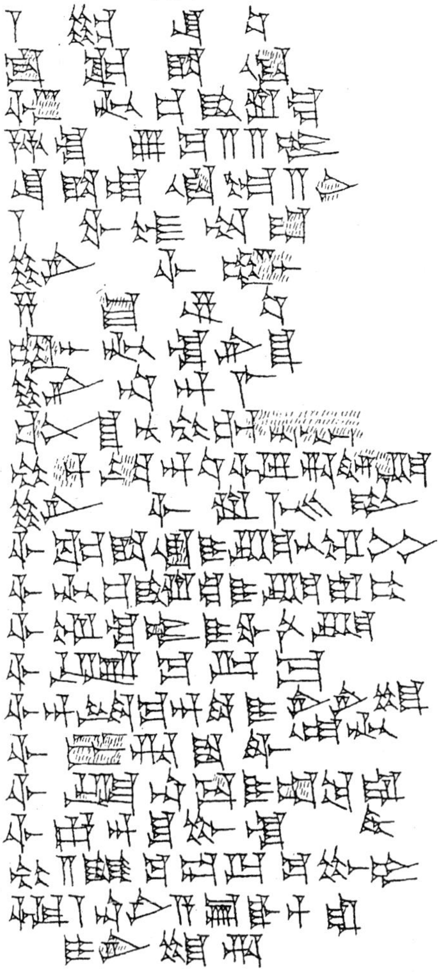

138

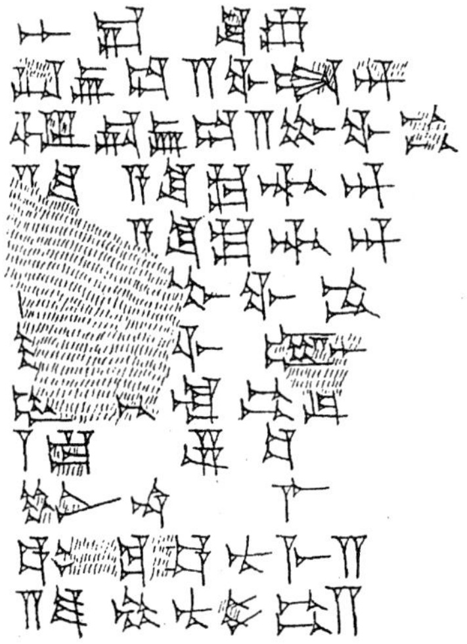

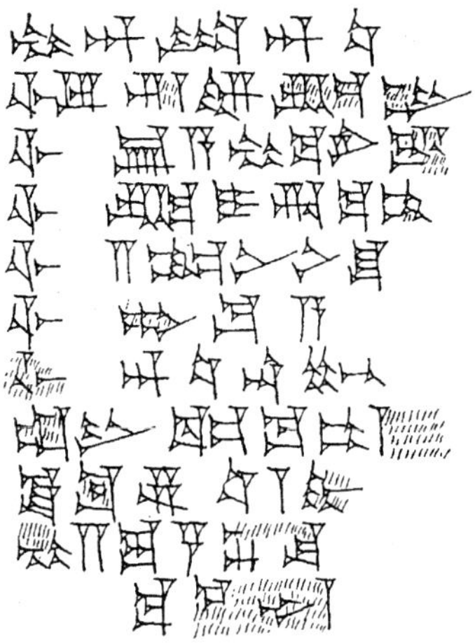

139

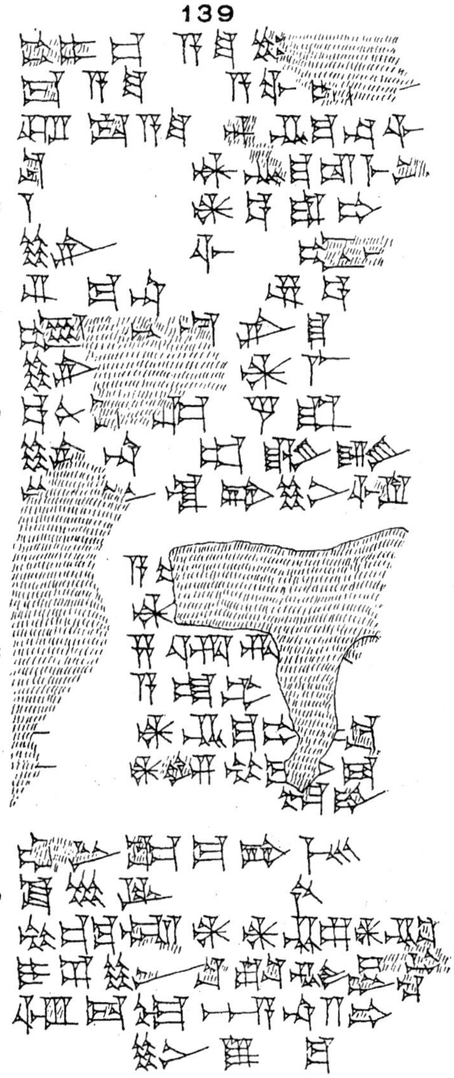

Indistinct seal impressions.

140

O.

R.

U.E.

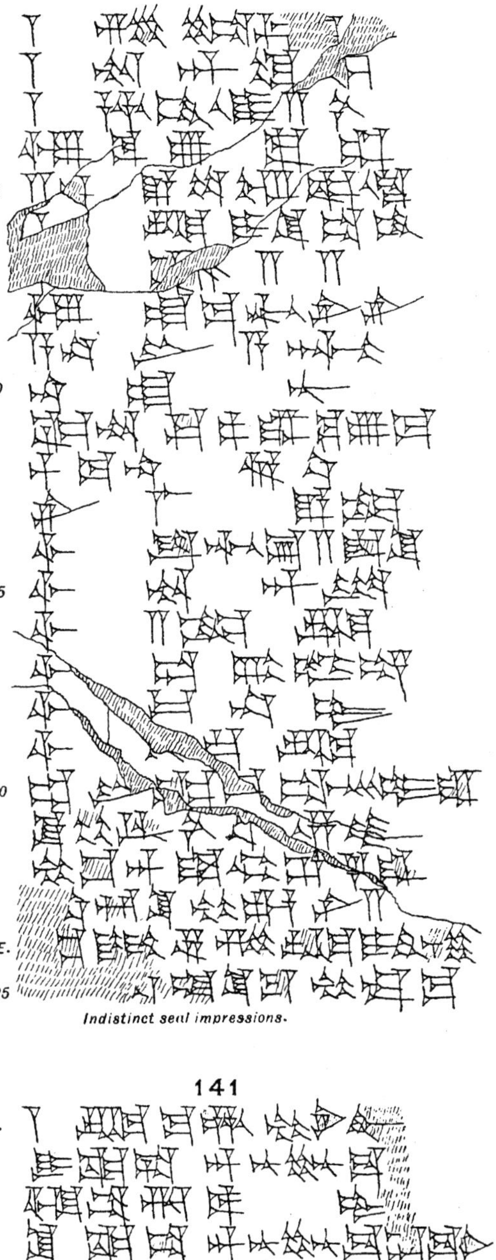

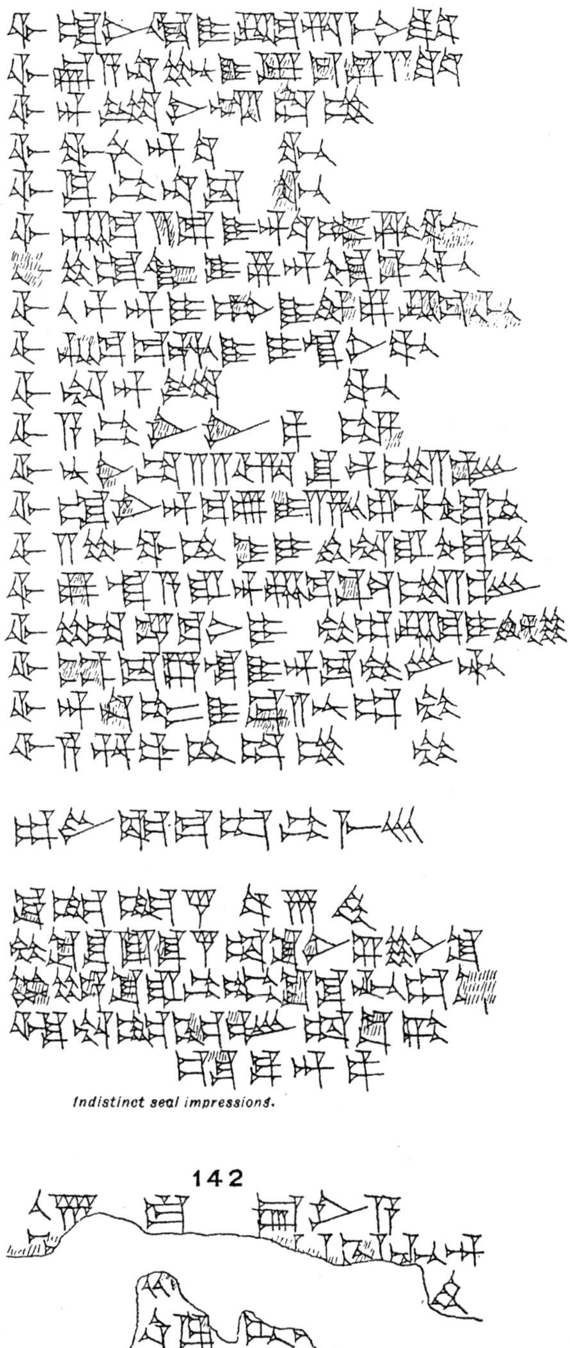

R

Indistinct seal impressions.

Indistinct seal impressions.

141

O.

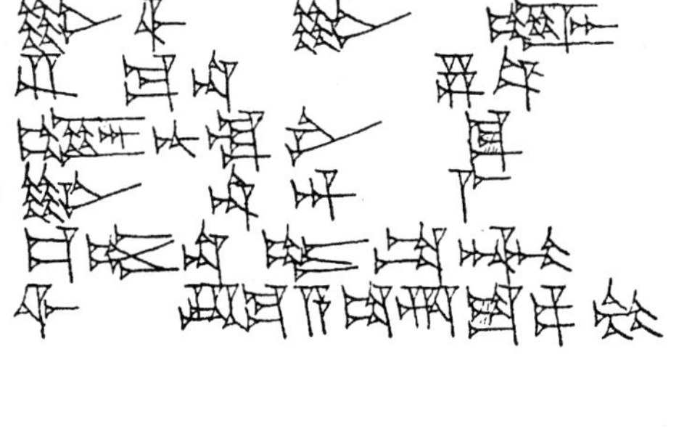

142

O.

R.

U.E.

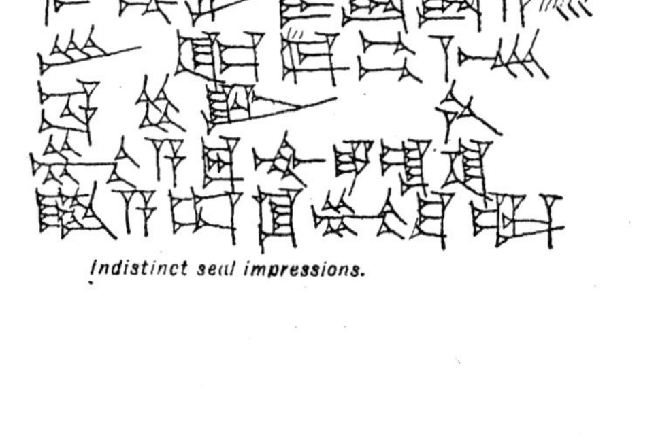

Indistinct seal impressions.

143

TABLET

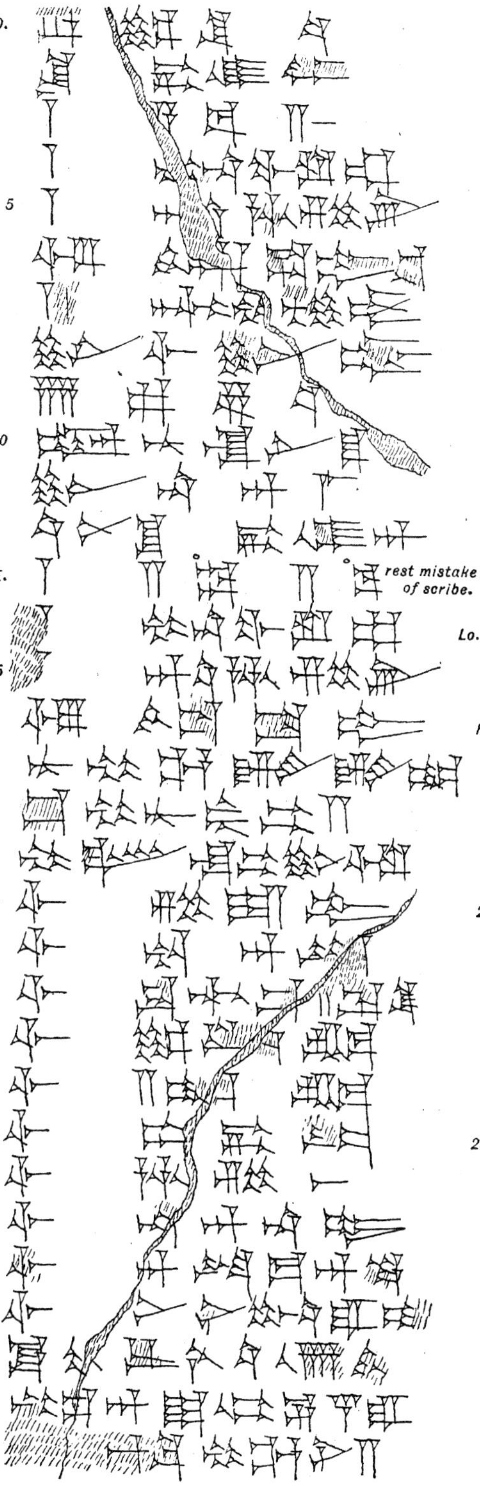

CASE

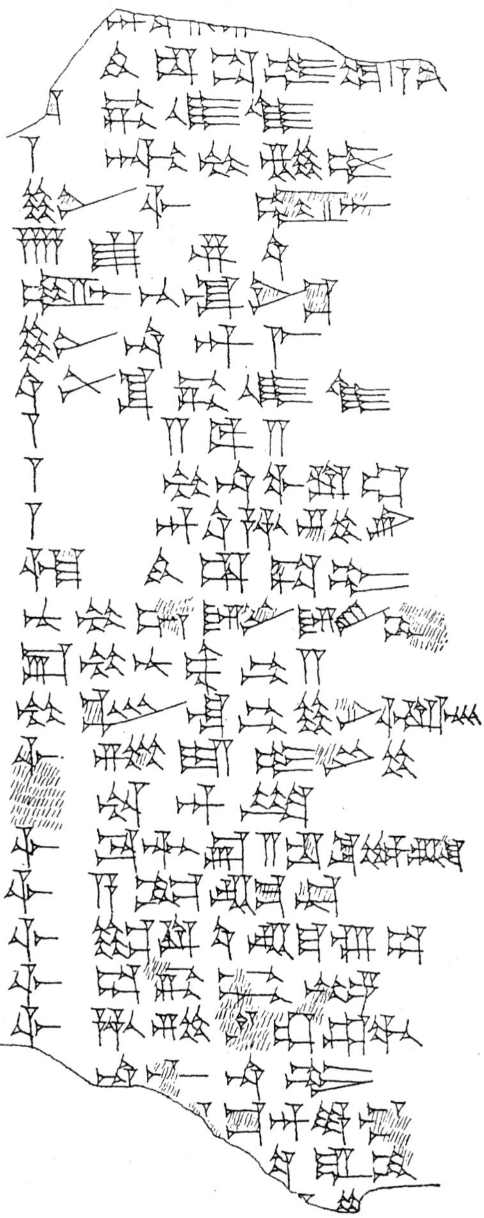

Indistinct seal impressions.

144

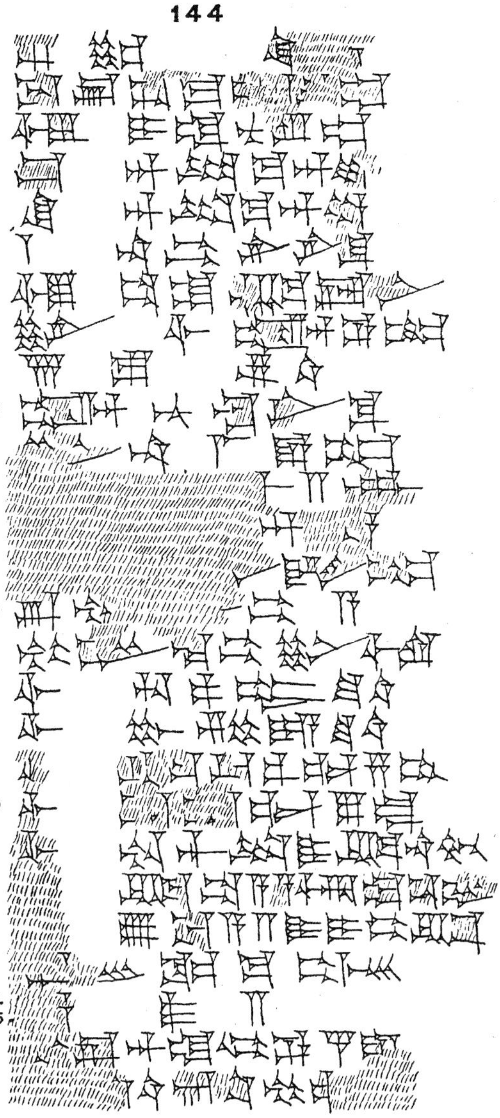

Indistinct seal impressions.

145

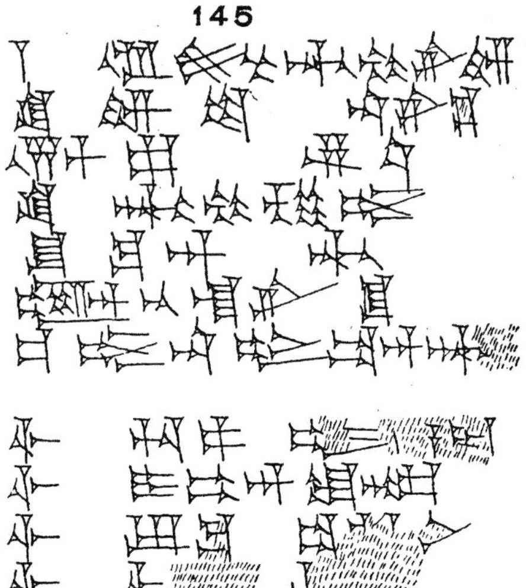

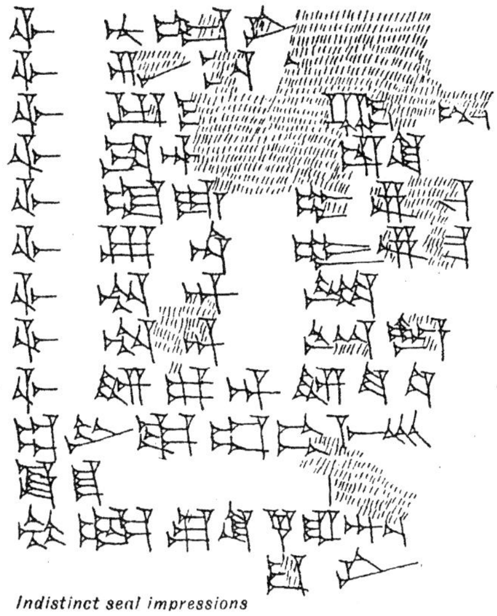

Indistinct seal impressions

146

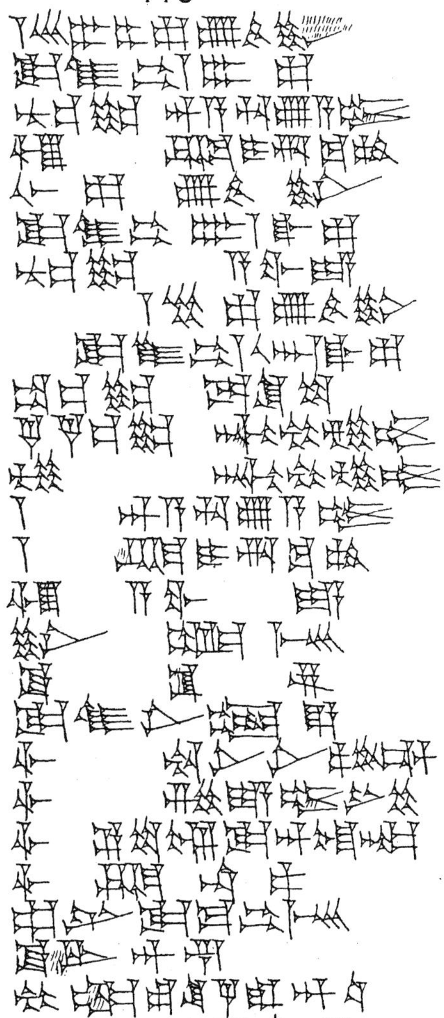

Indistinct seal impressions

147

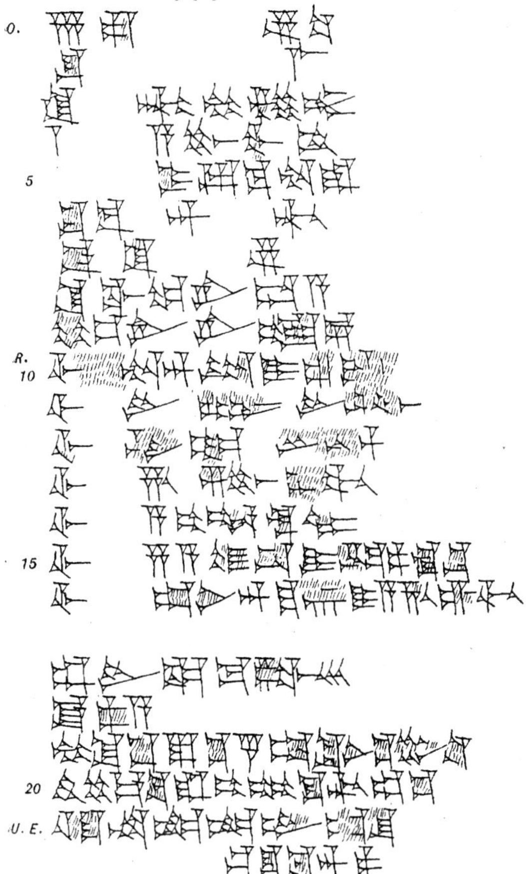

Indistinct seal impressions

148

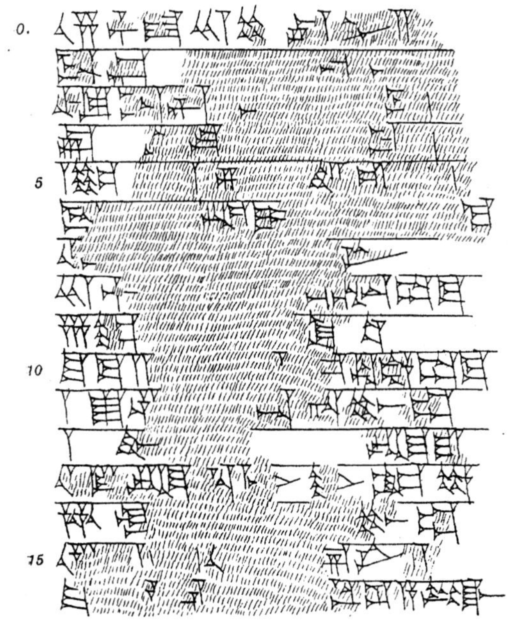

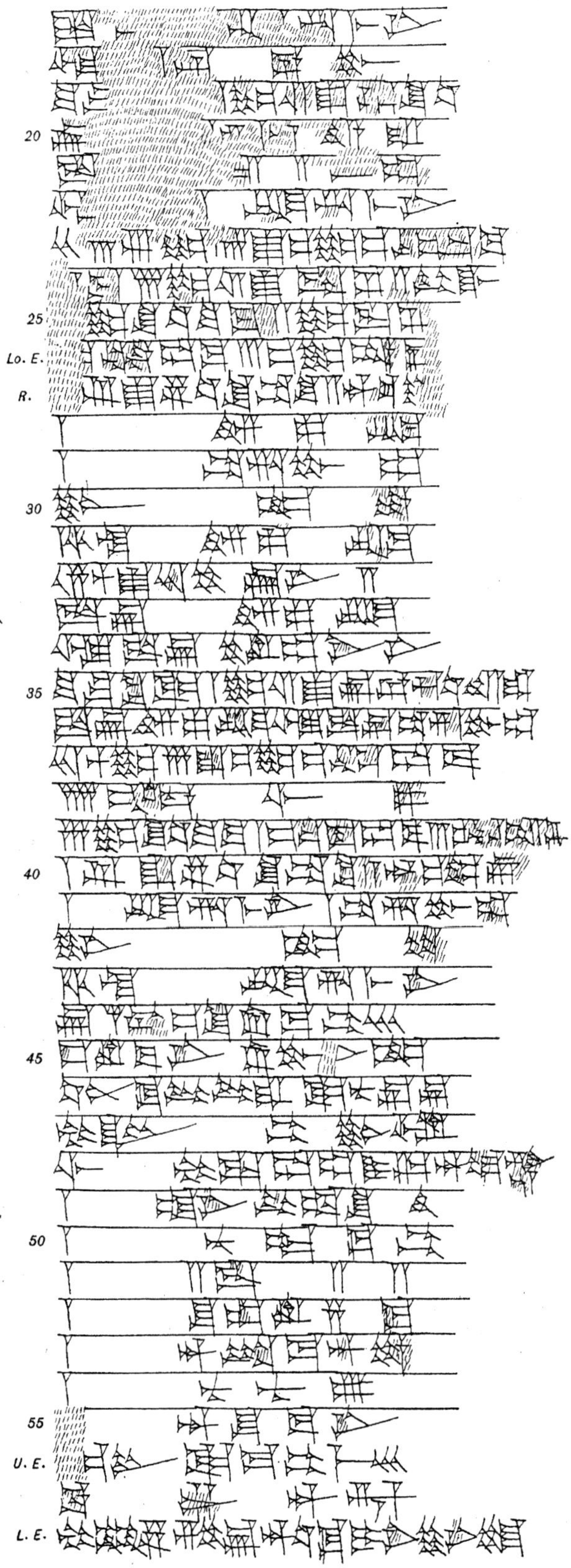

150

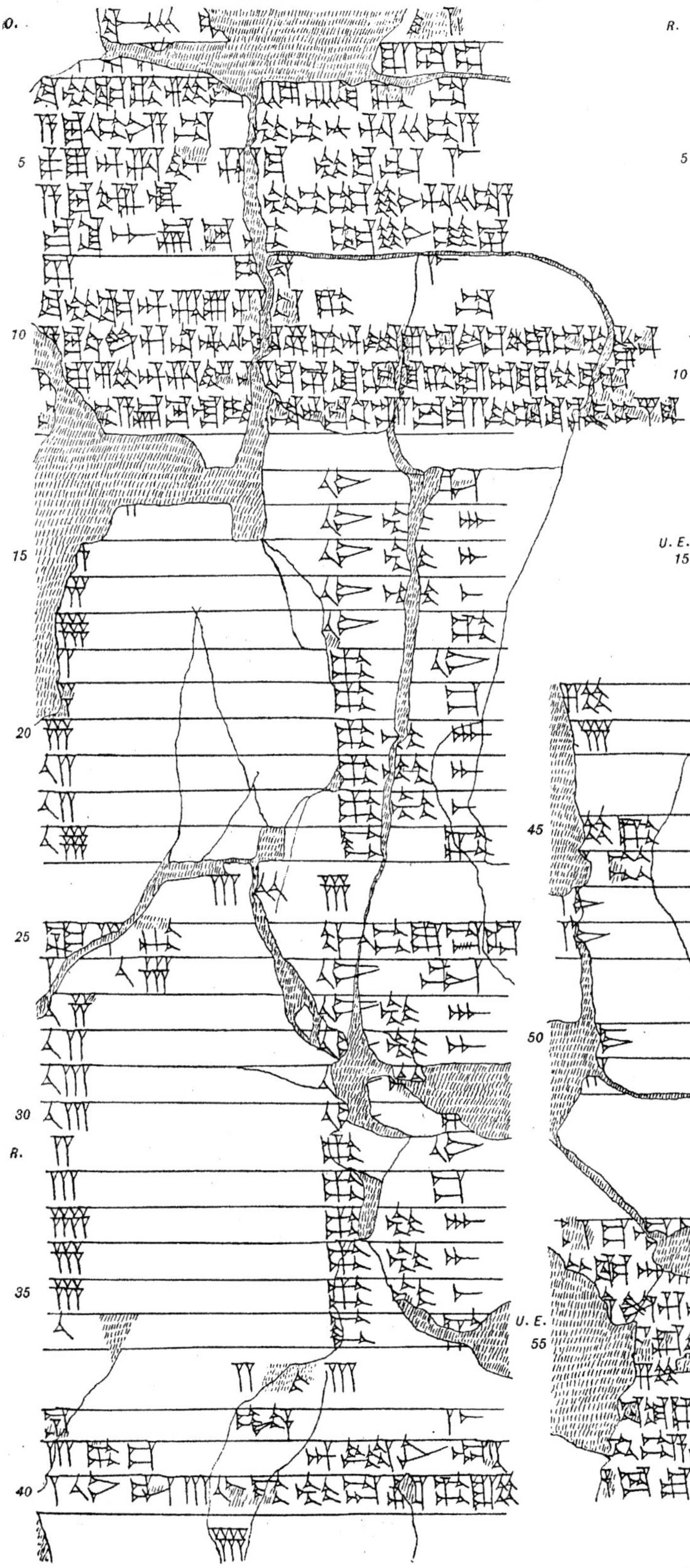

149

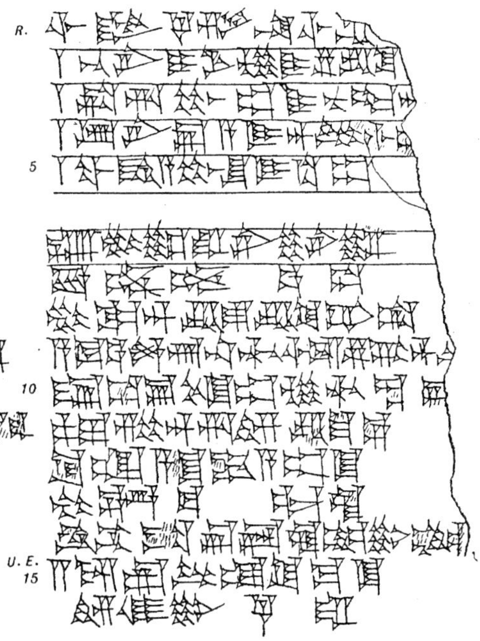

Indistinct seal impressions

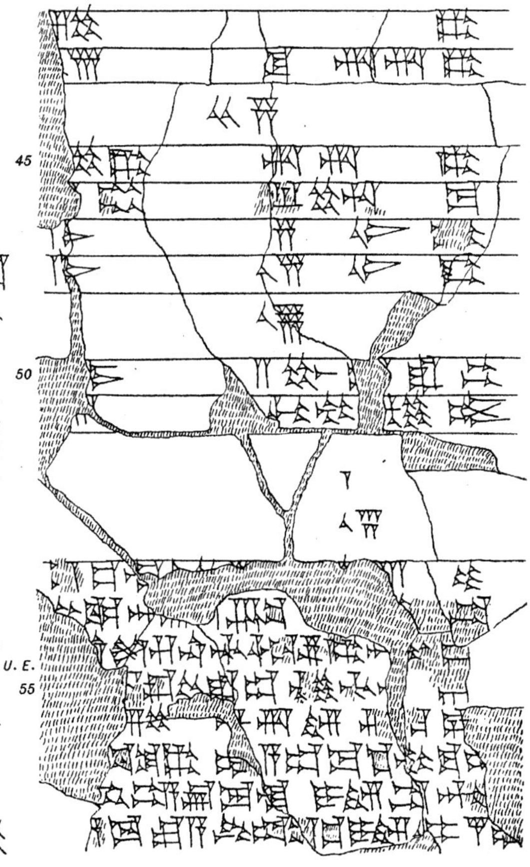

151

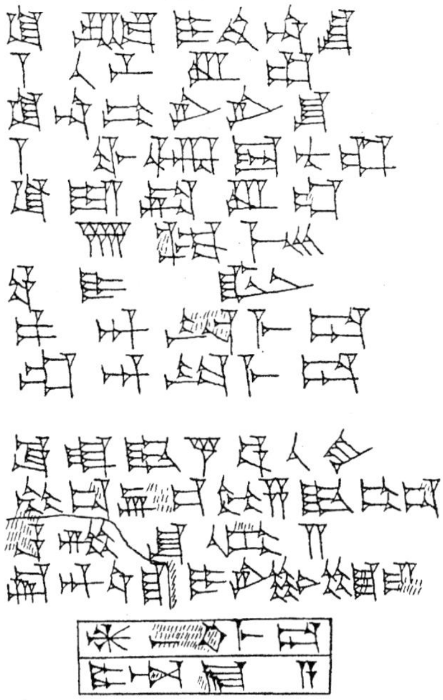

152

TABLET

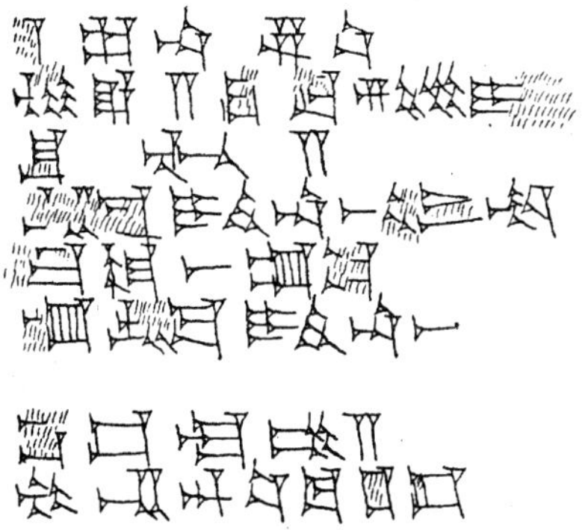

CASE

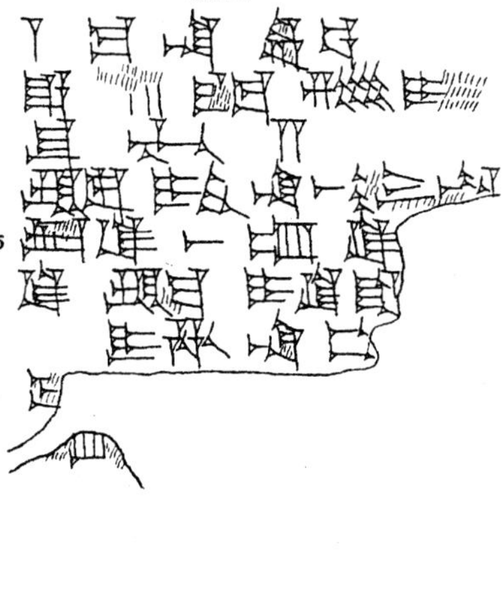

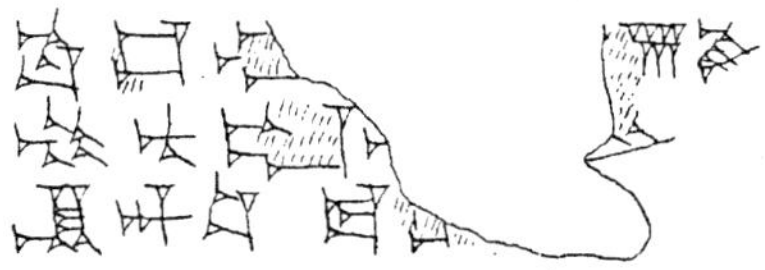

Indistinct seal impressions on case.

153

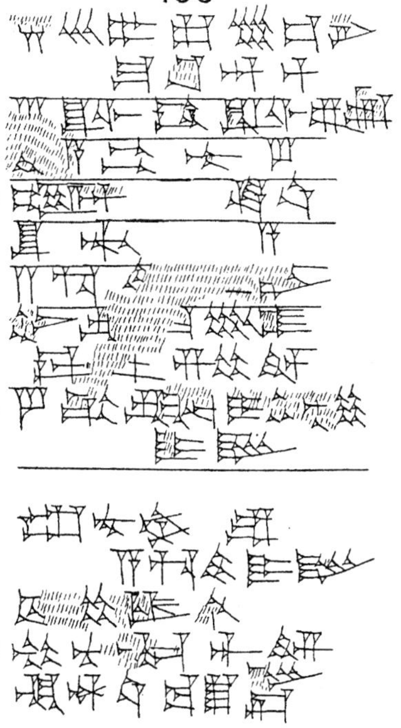

154

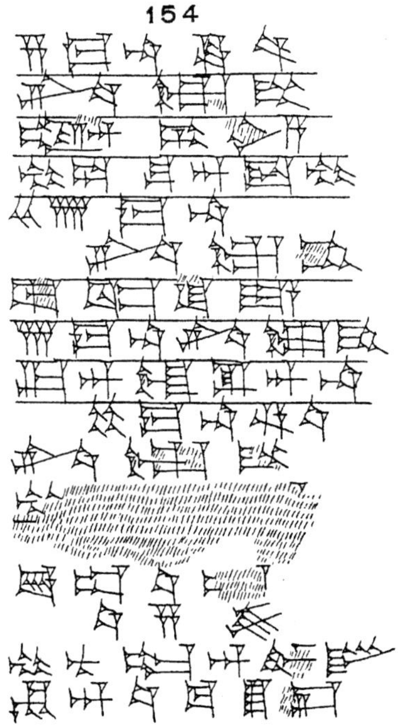

155

O.

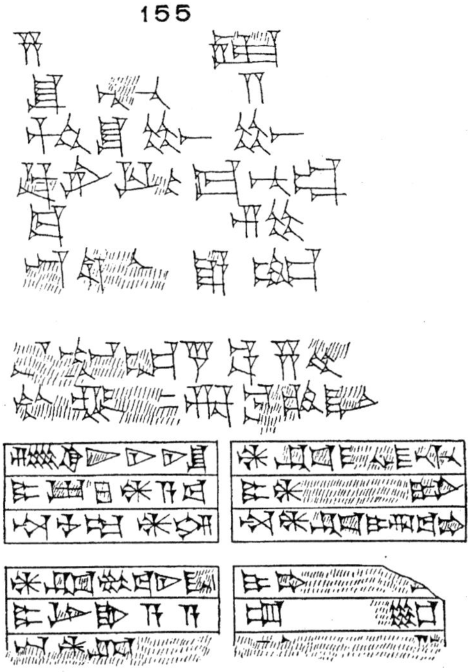

R.

156

O.

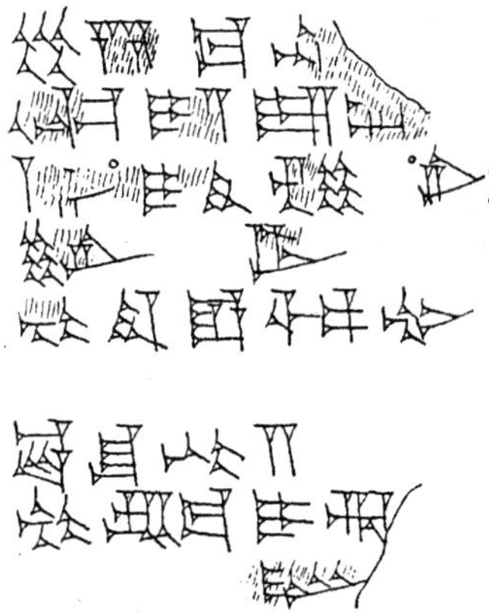

omitted by scribe.

R.

157

O.

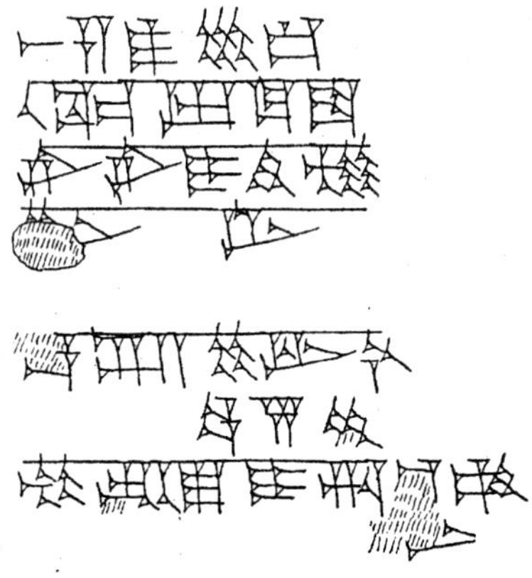

R.

158

O.

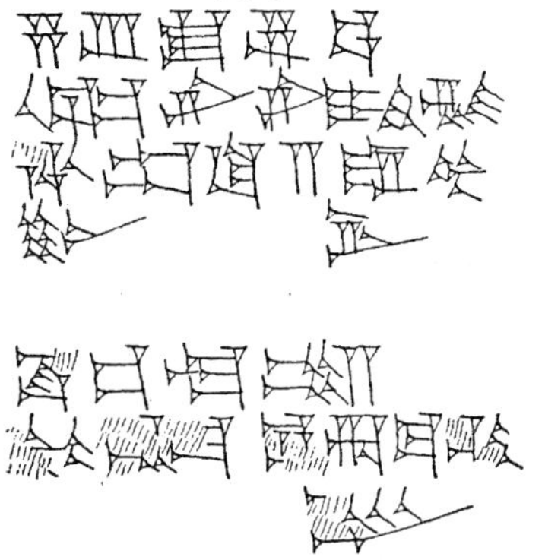

R.

159

O.

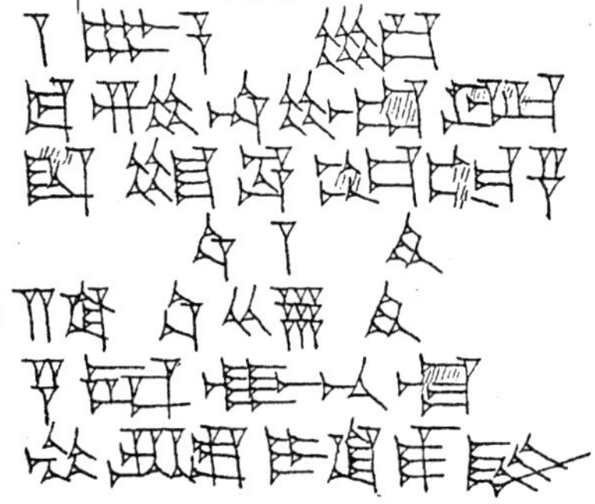

R.

160

O.

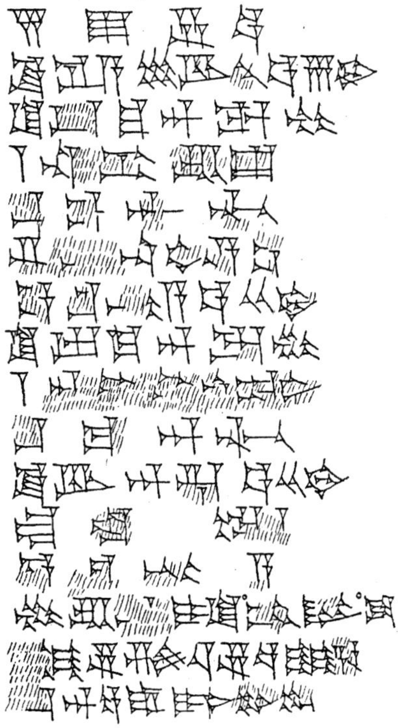

R

omitted by scribe.

U. E.

161

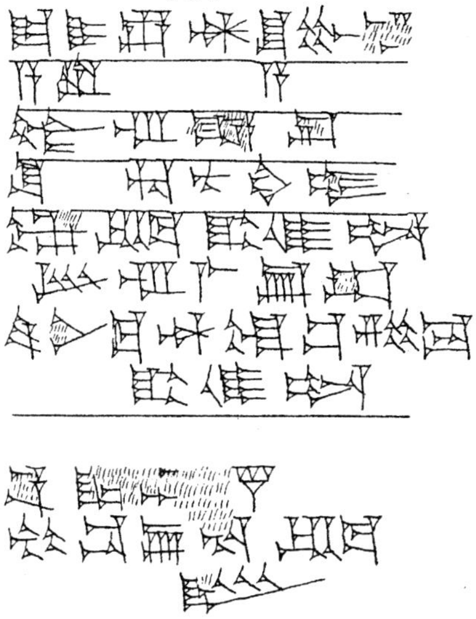

162

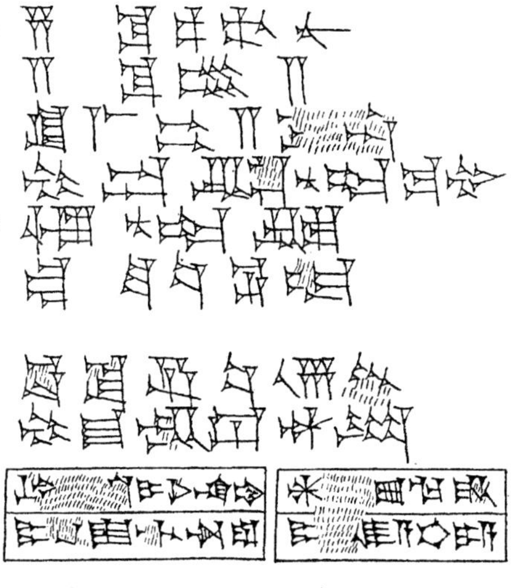

Other indistinct seal impressions.

163

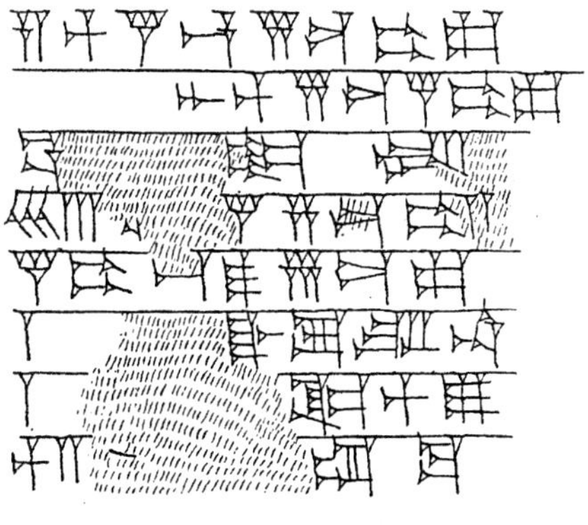

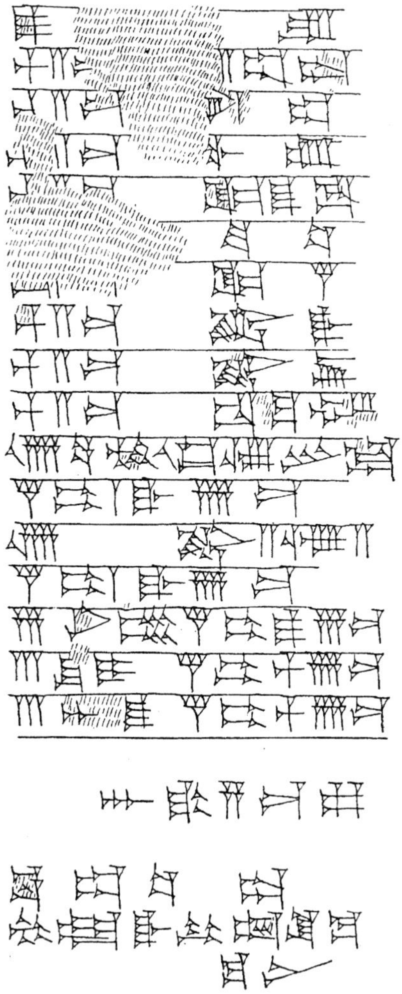

164

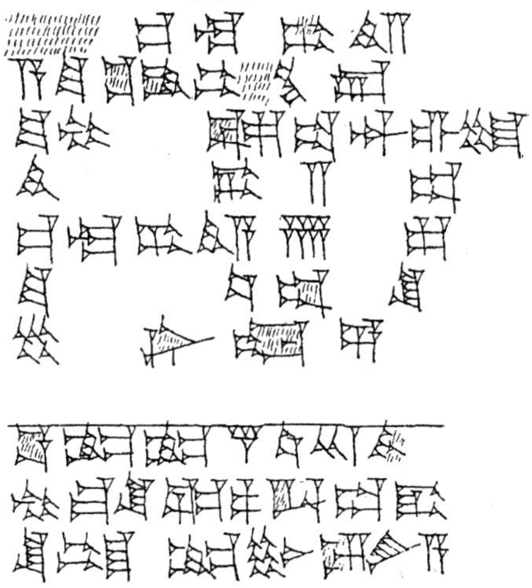

Indistinct seal impressions

165

O.

R.

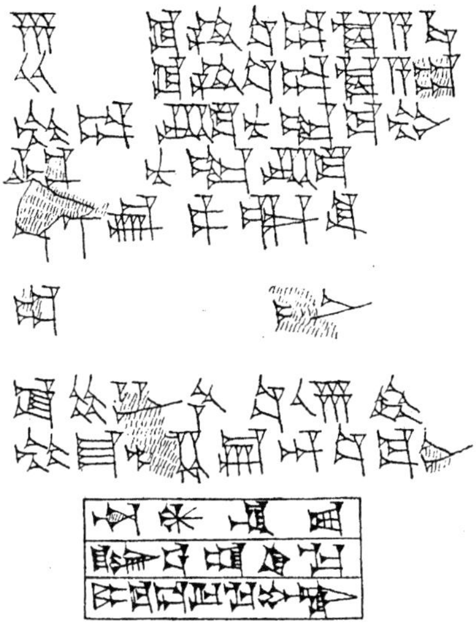

166

O.

R.

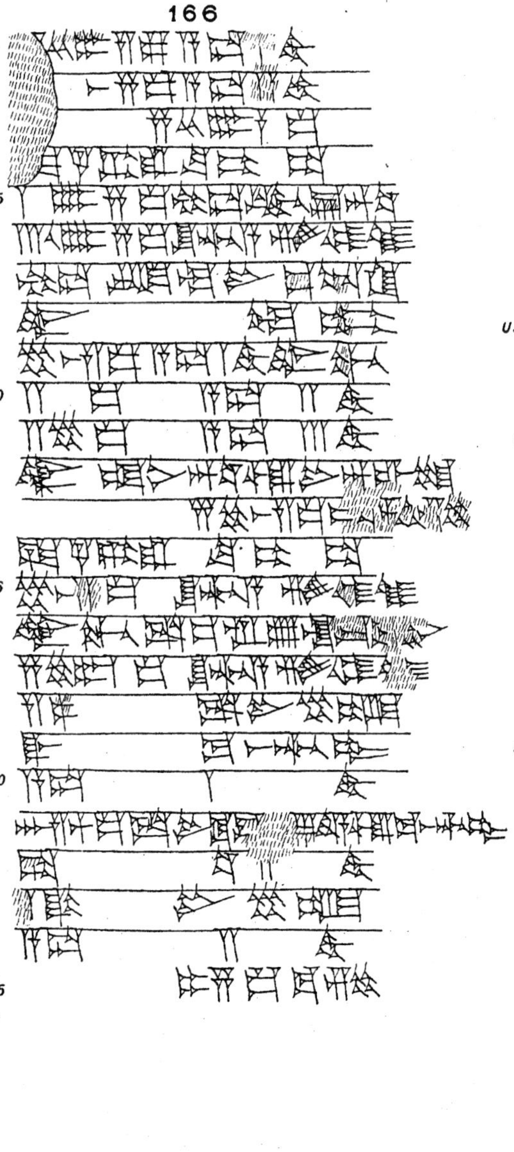

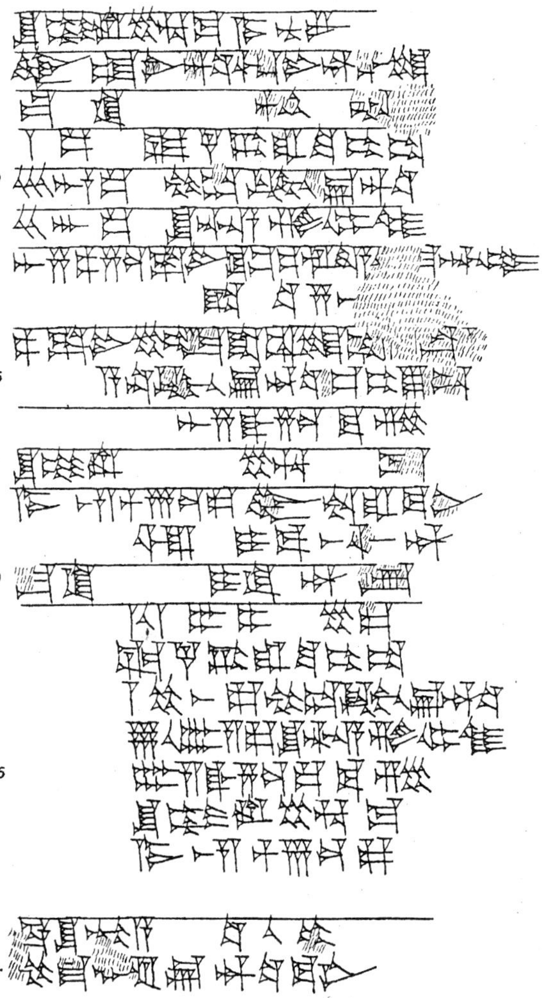

U.E.

167

O.

R.

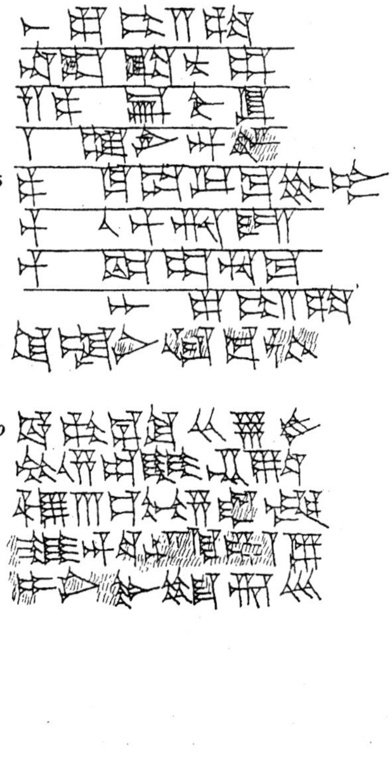

168

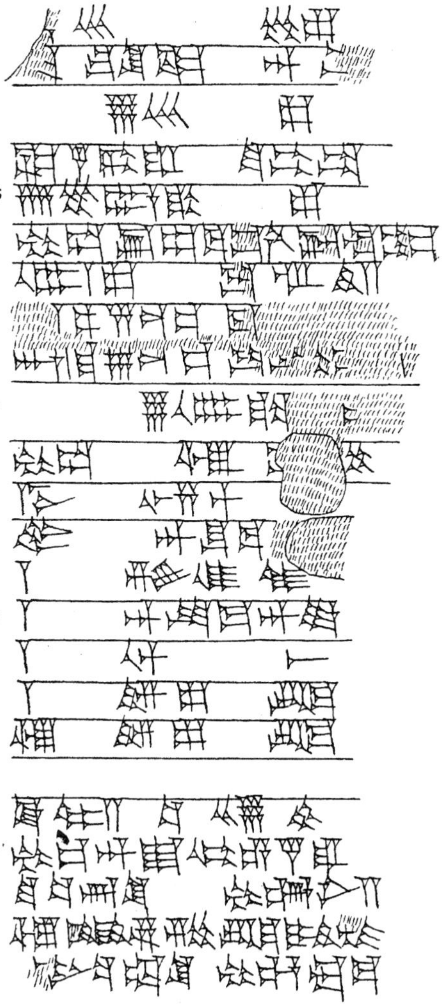

169

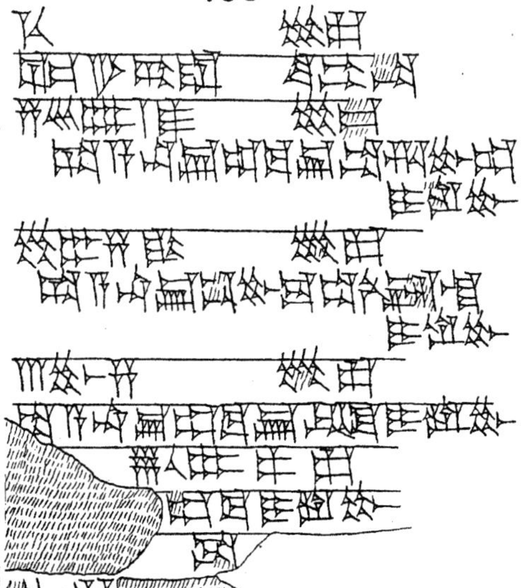

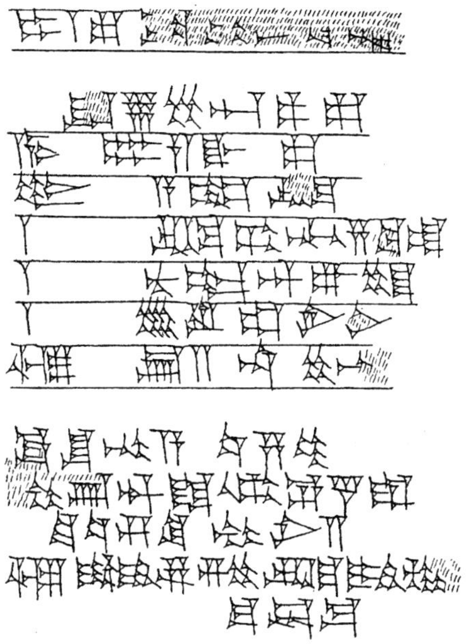

170

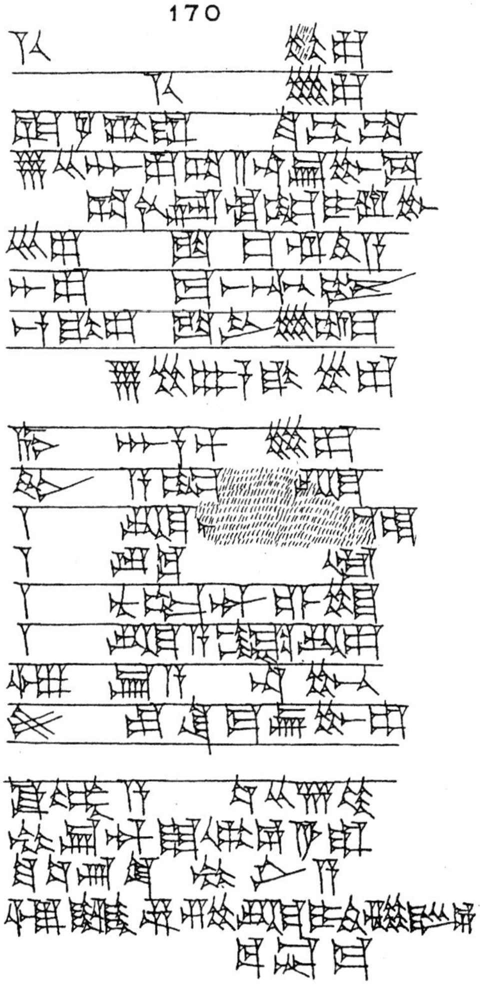

171

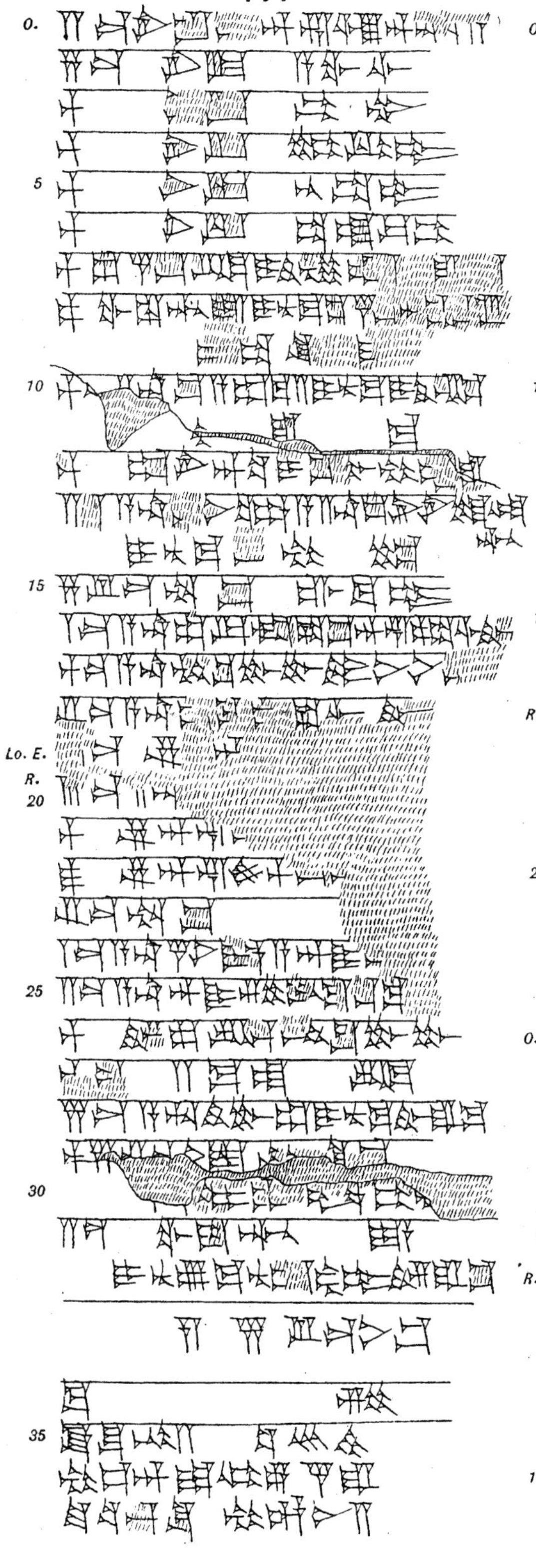

172

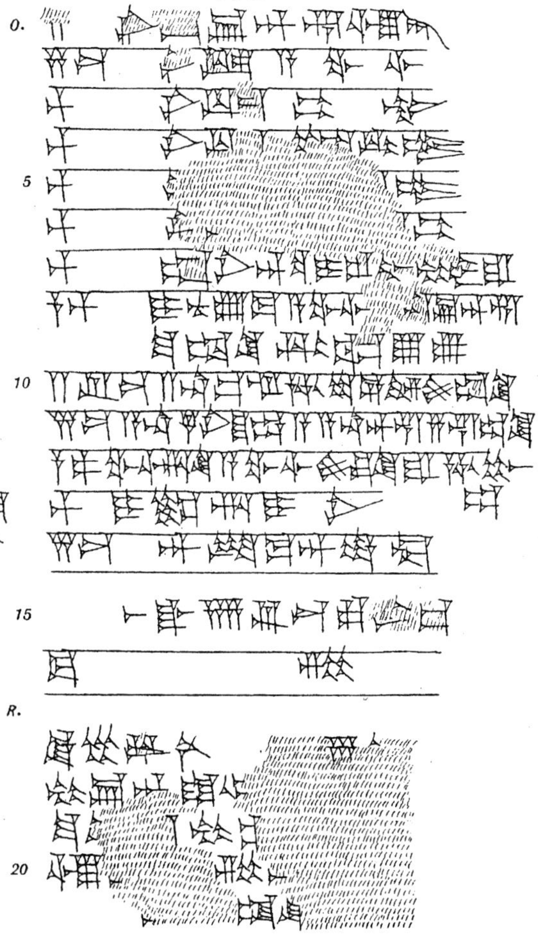

173

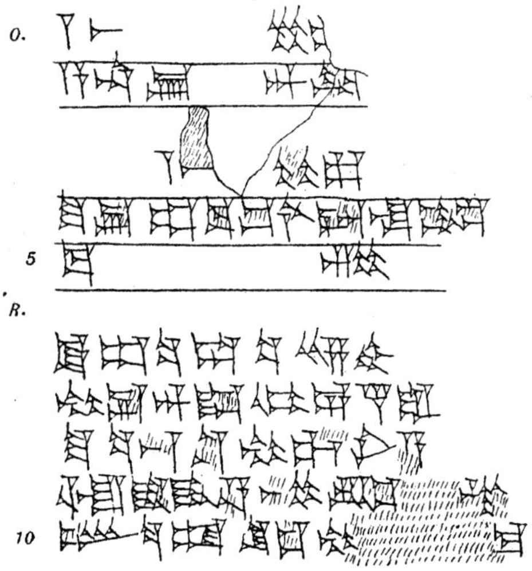

174

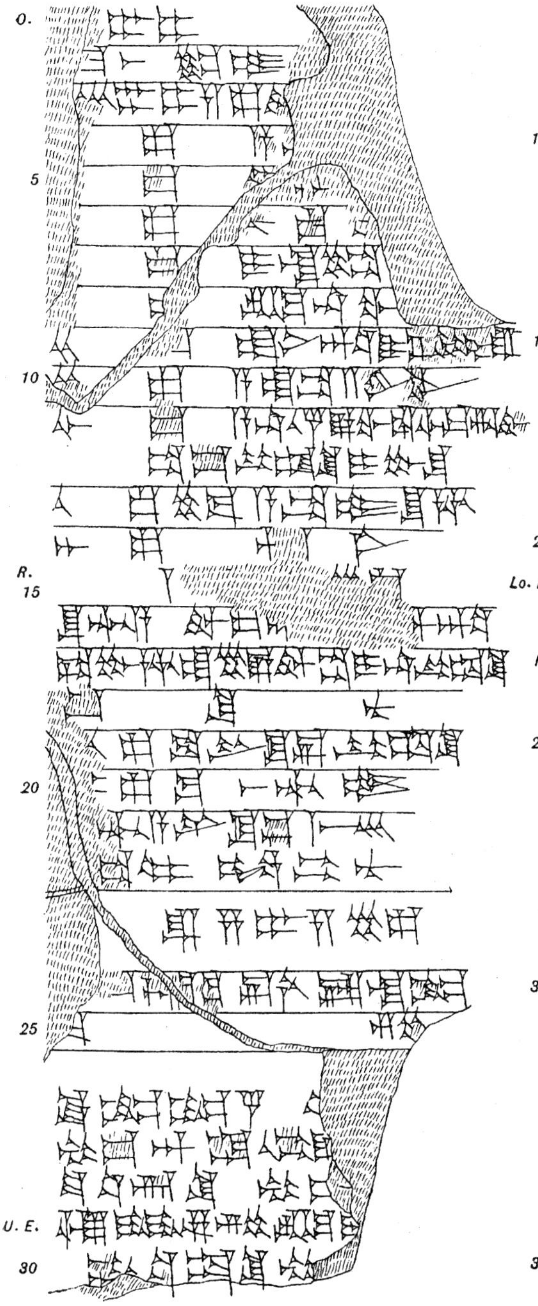

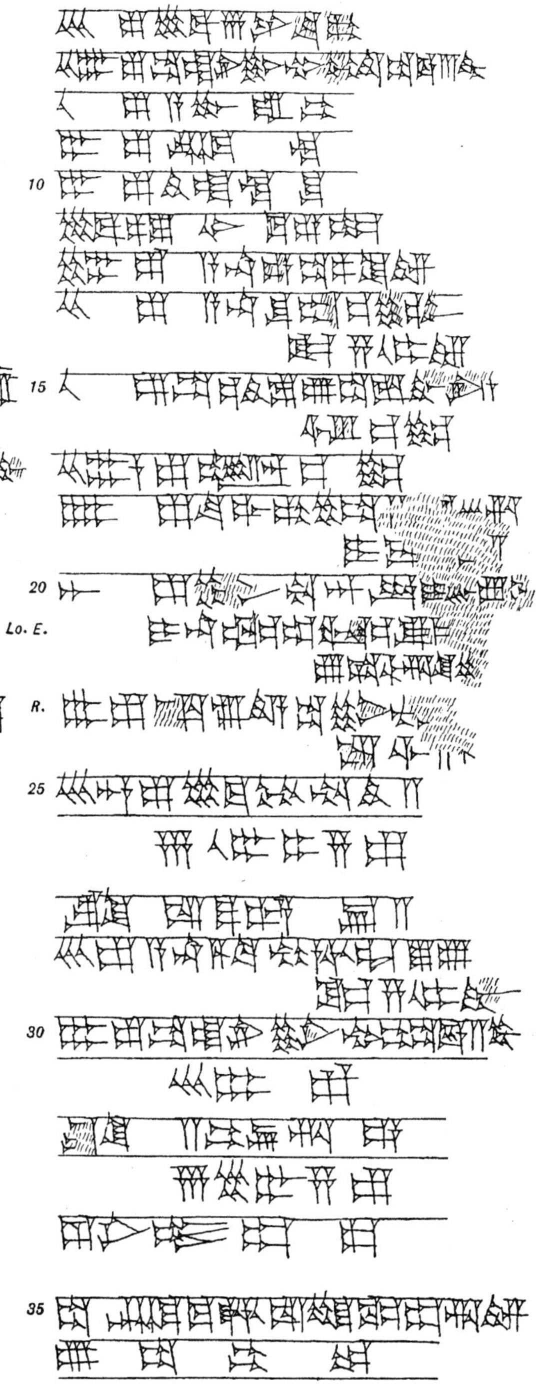

175

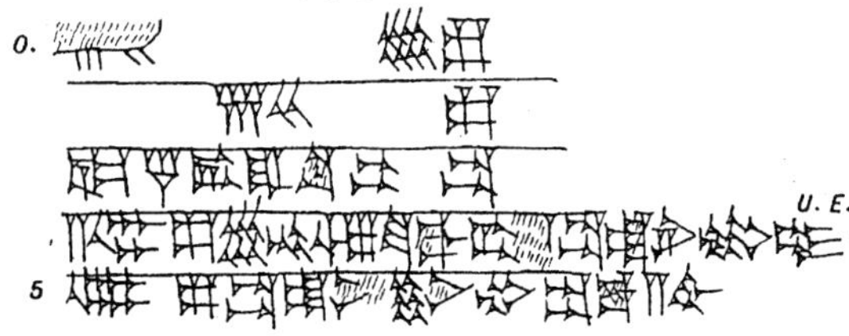

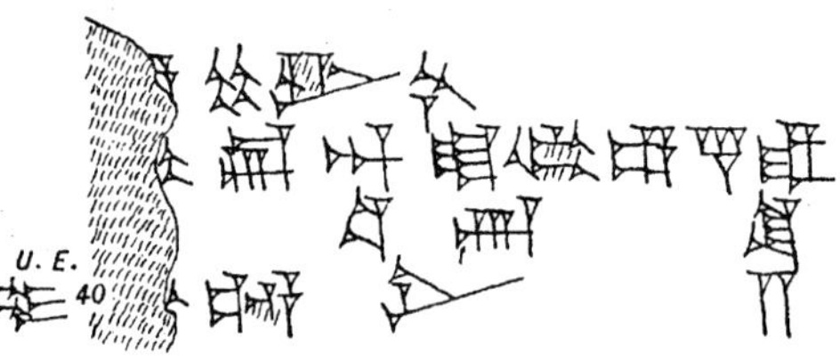

176

O. R. U.E.

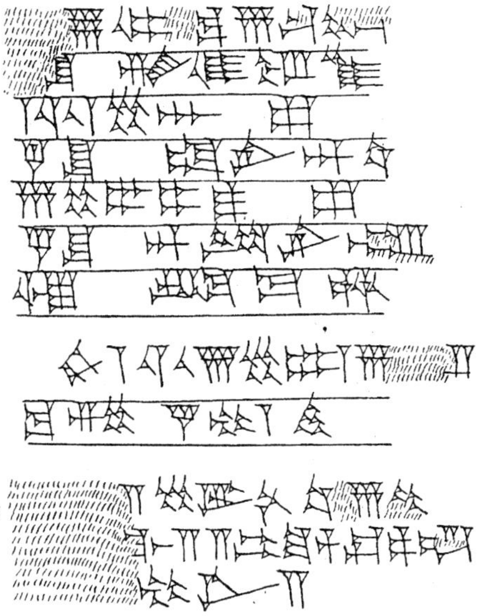

177

O. R.

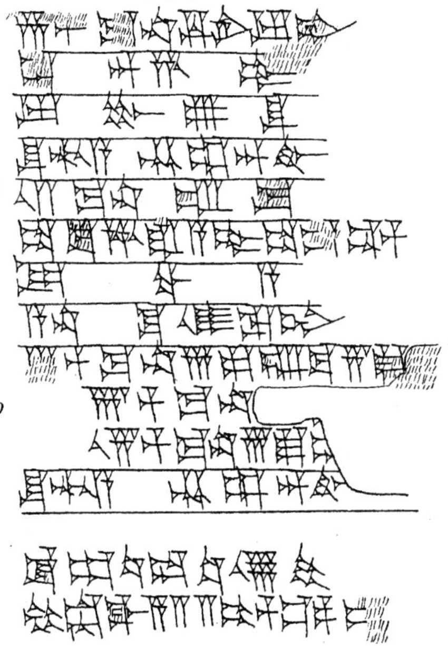

178

O. R. U.E.

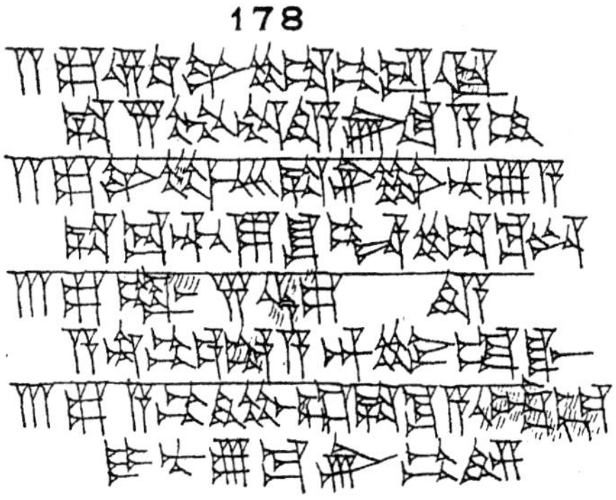

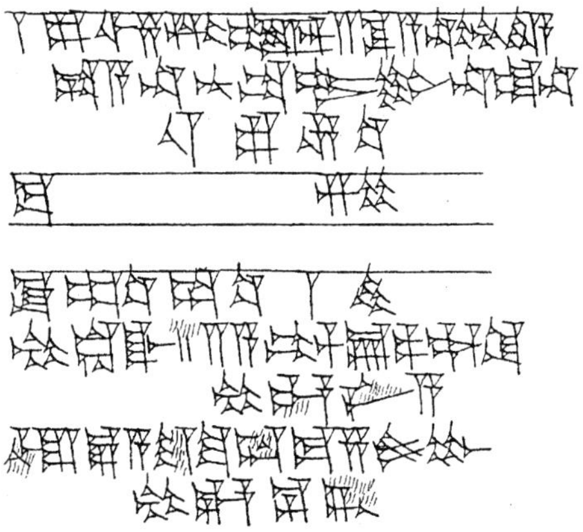

179

O. R.

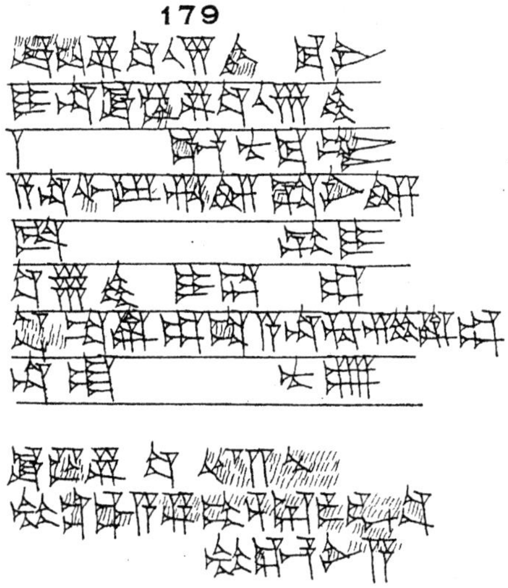

180

O. R.

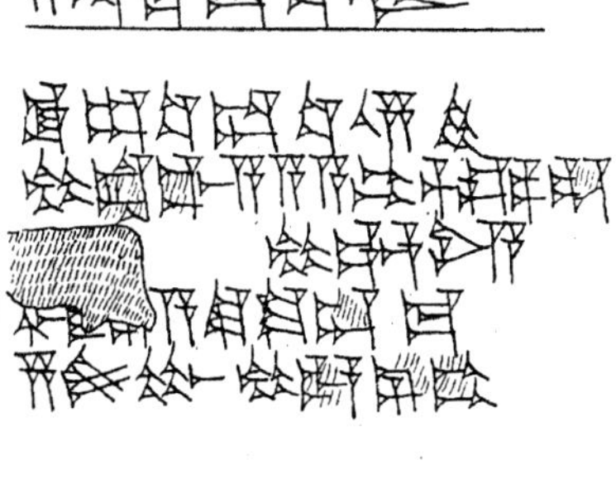

181

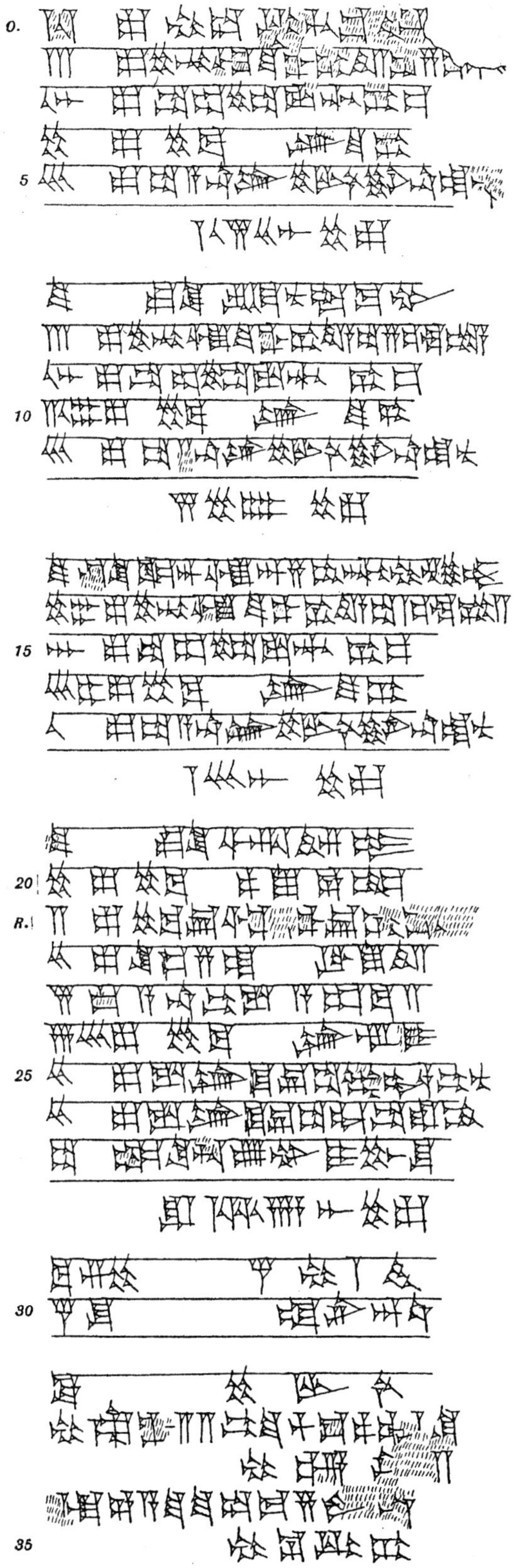

182

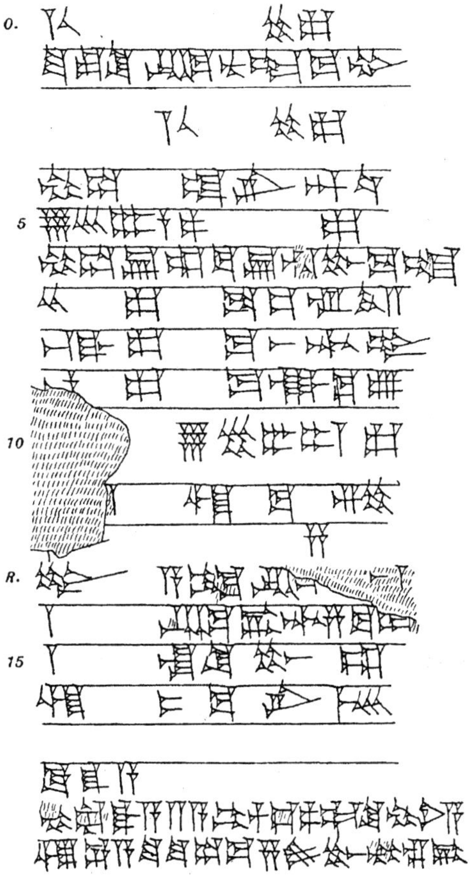

183

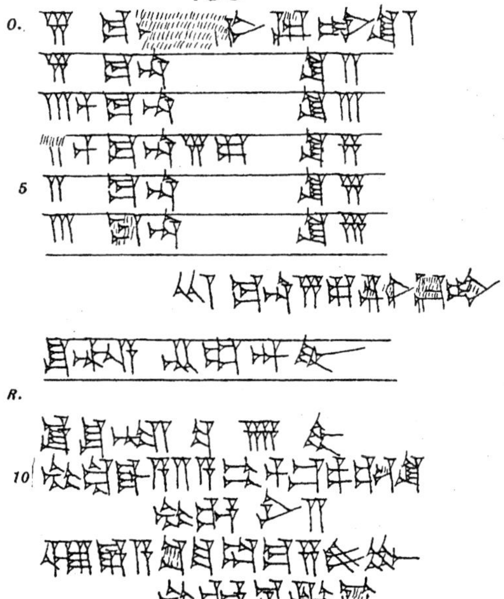

184

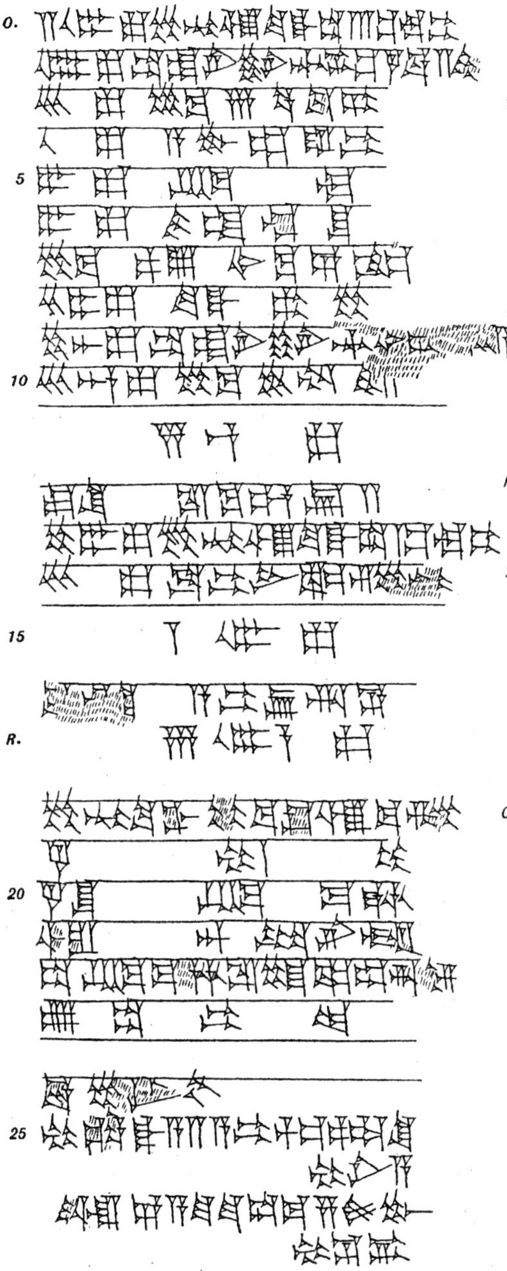

185

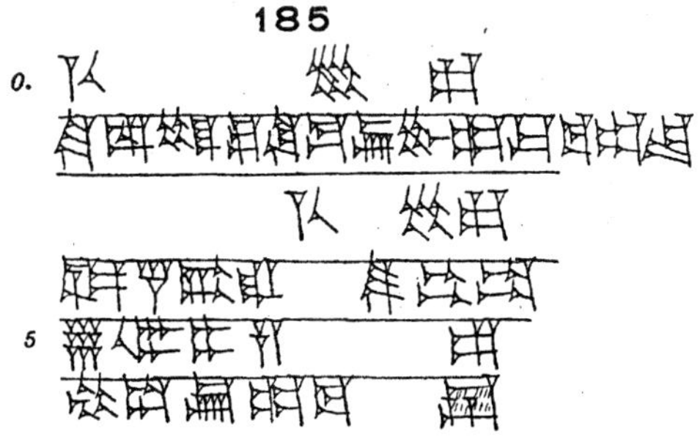

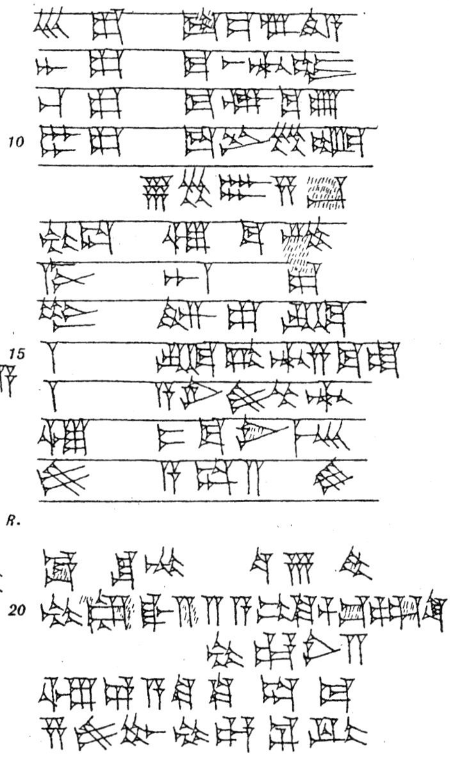

186

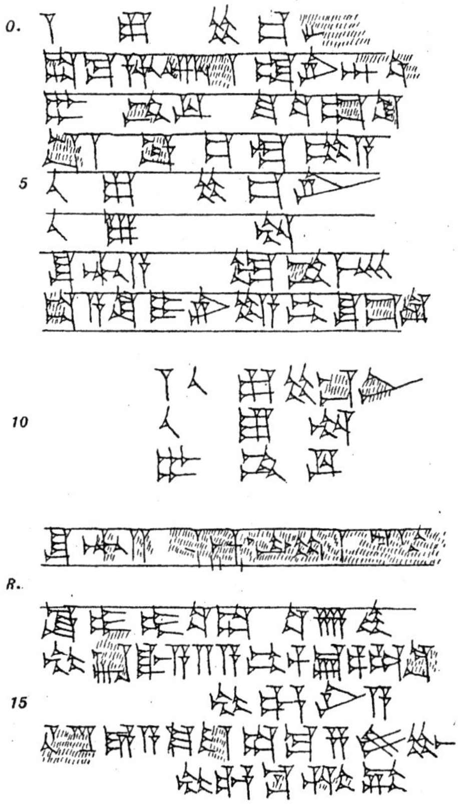

187

O.

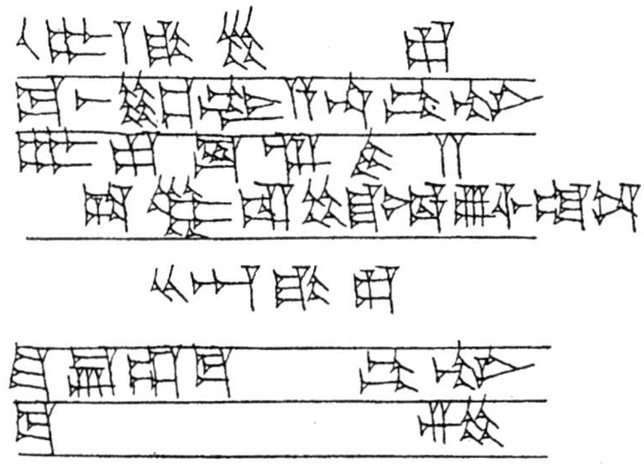

R.

188

O.

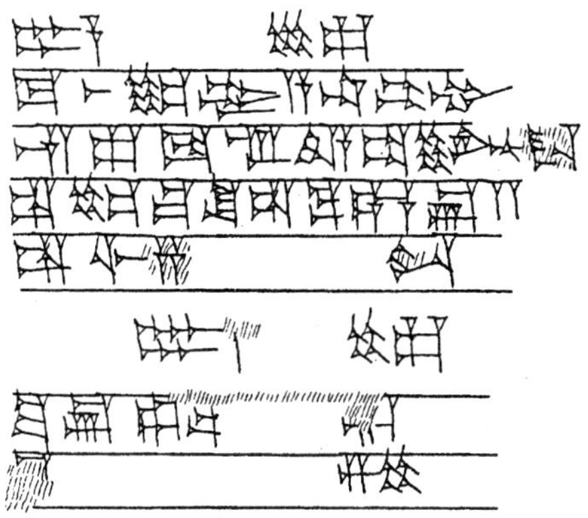

R.

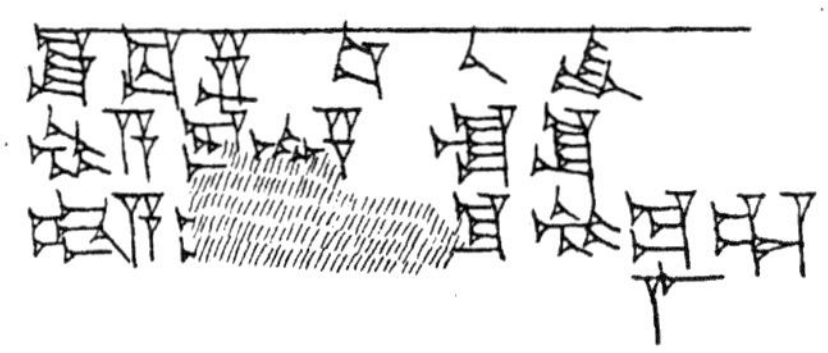

189

O.

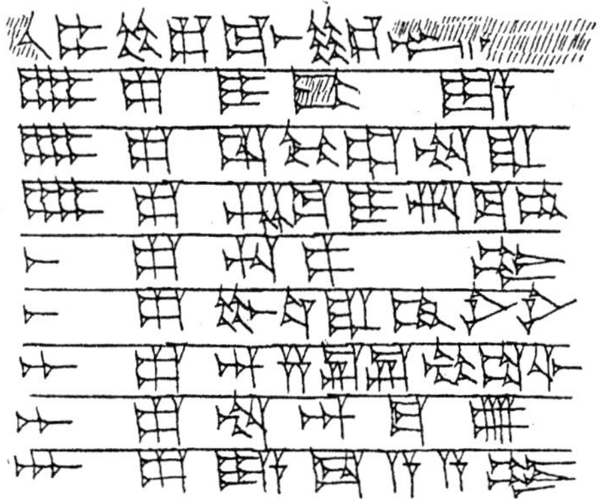

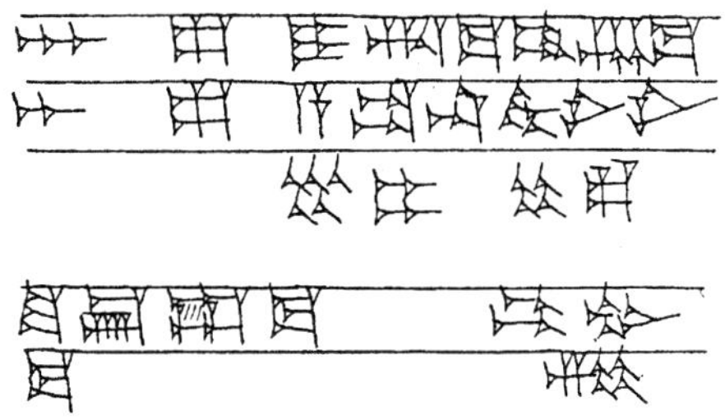

R.

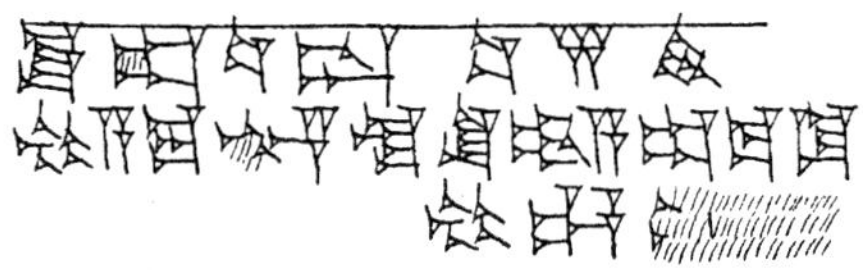

190

O.

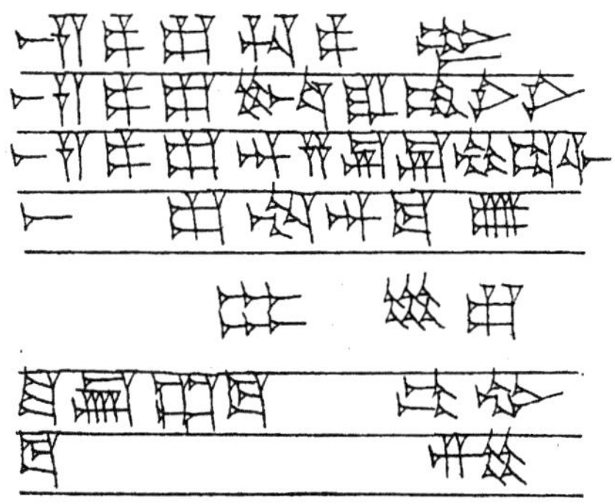

R.

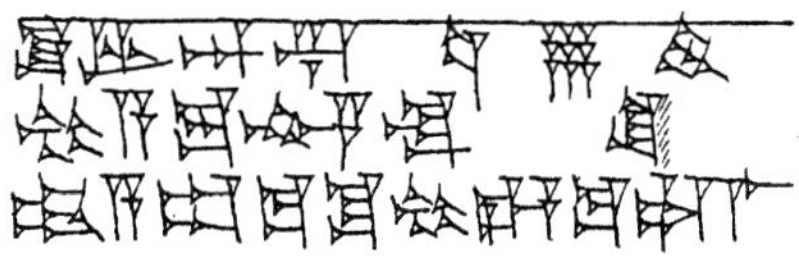

191

O.

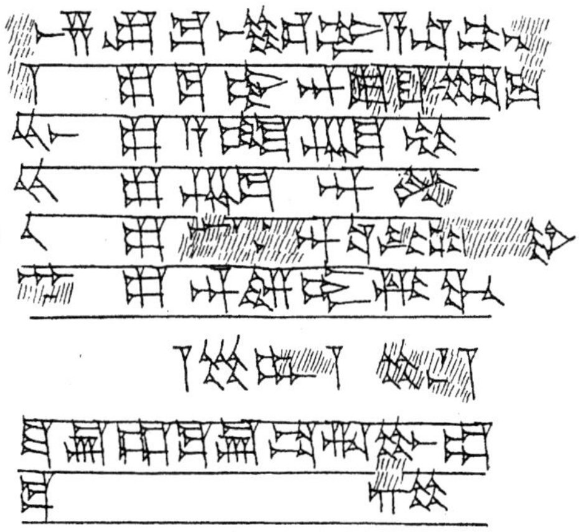

R.

192

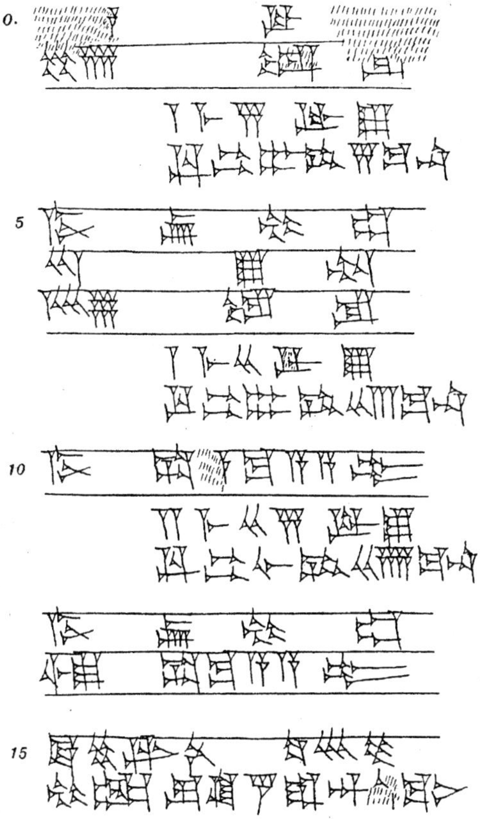

194

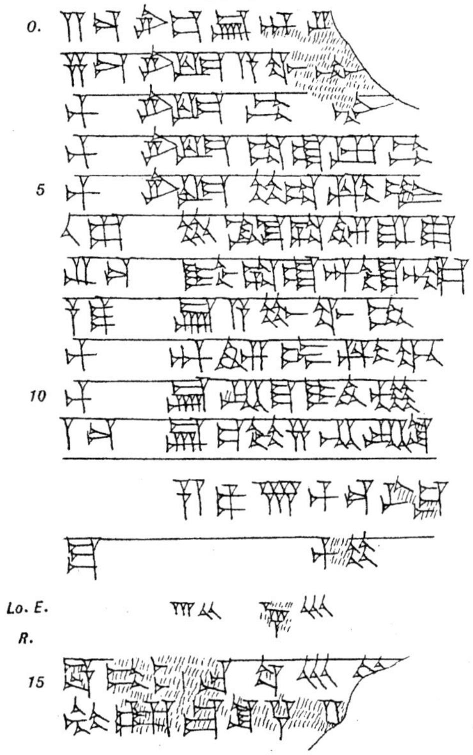

193

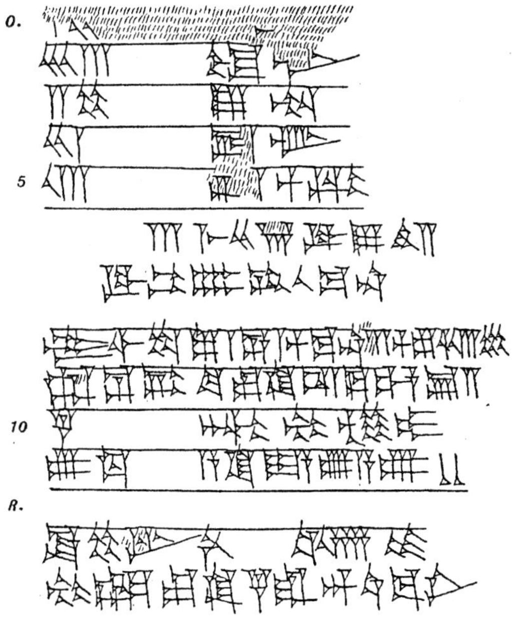

195

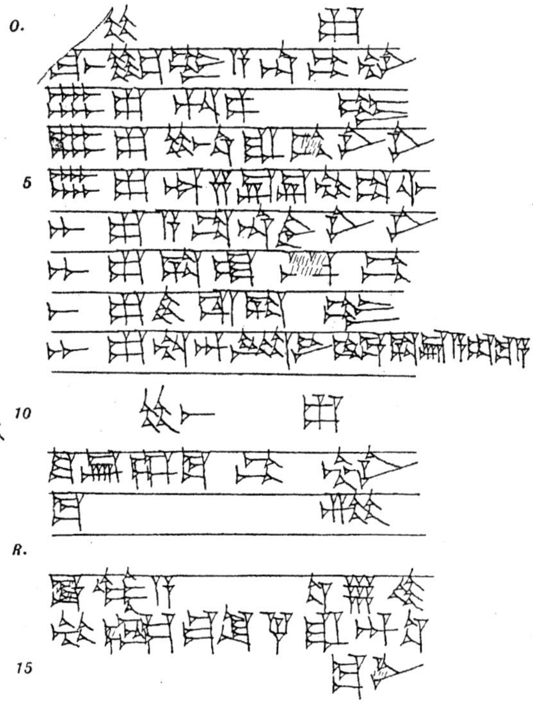

196

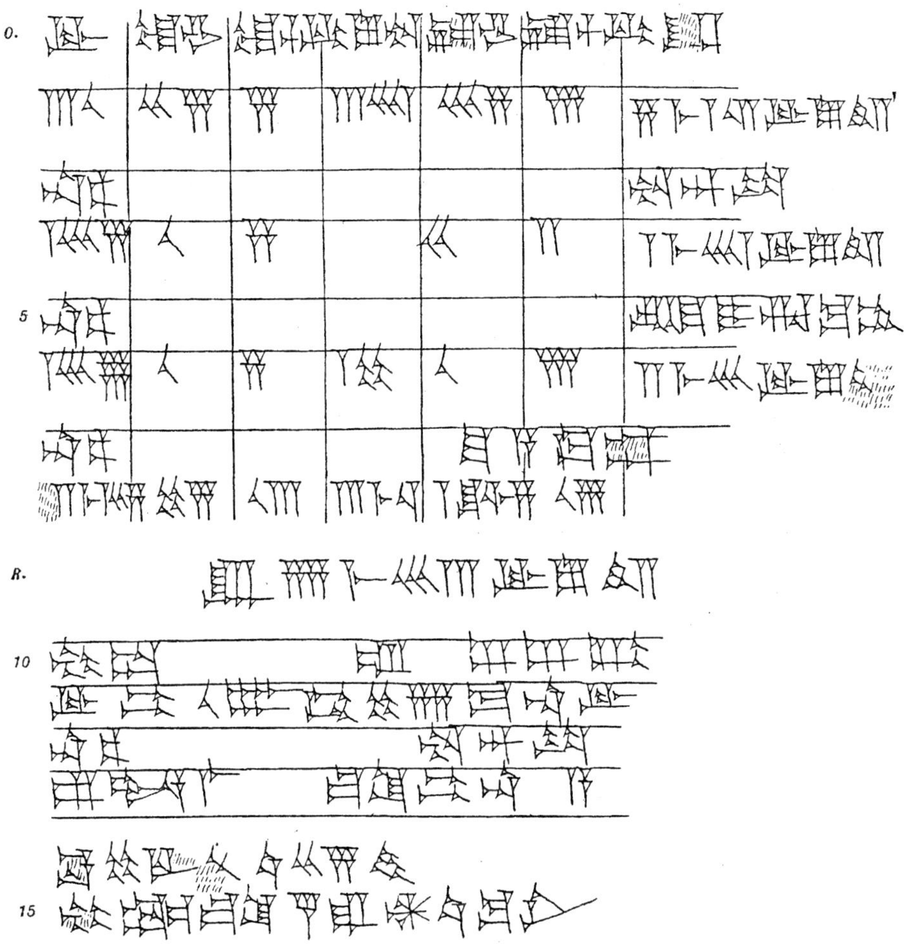

197

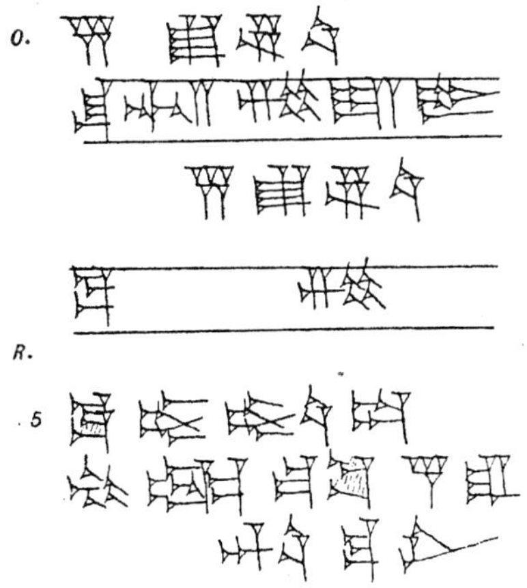

198

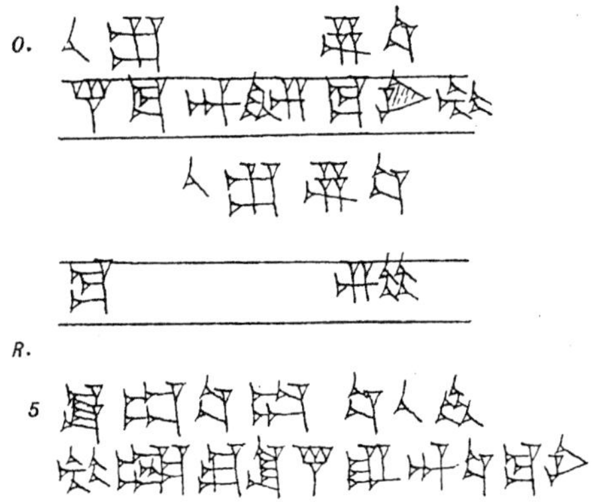

199

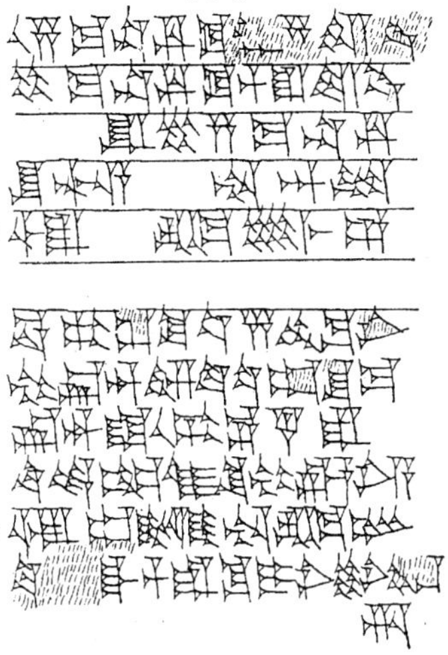

200

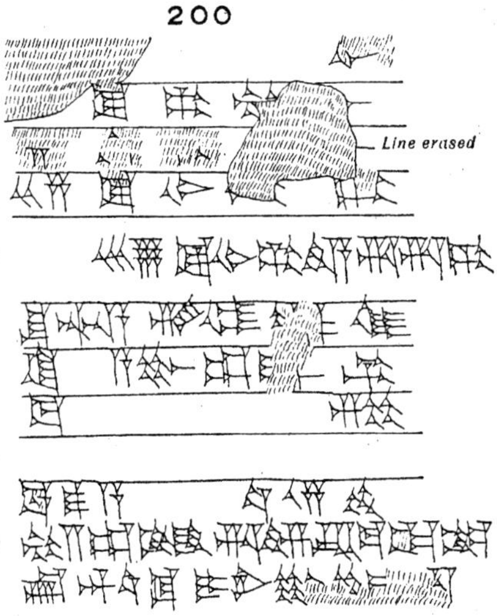

201

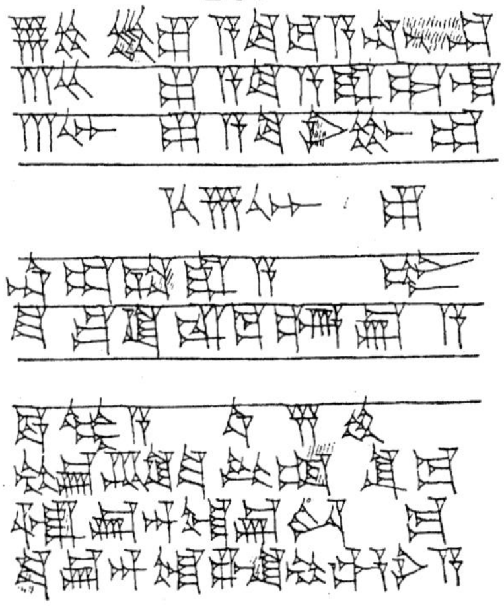

202

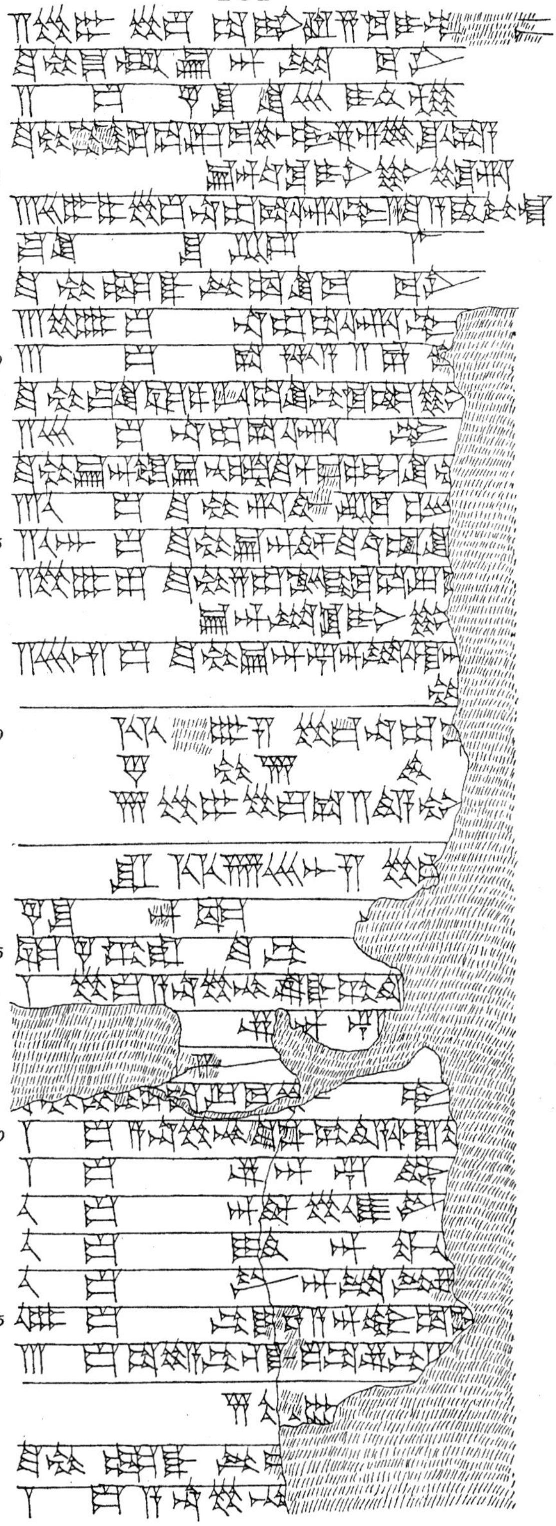

CONTINUED

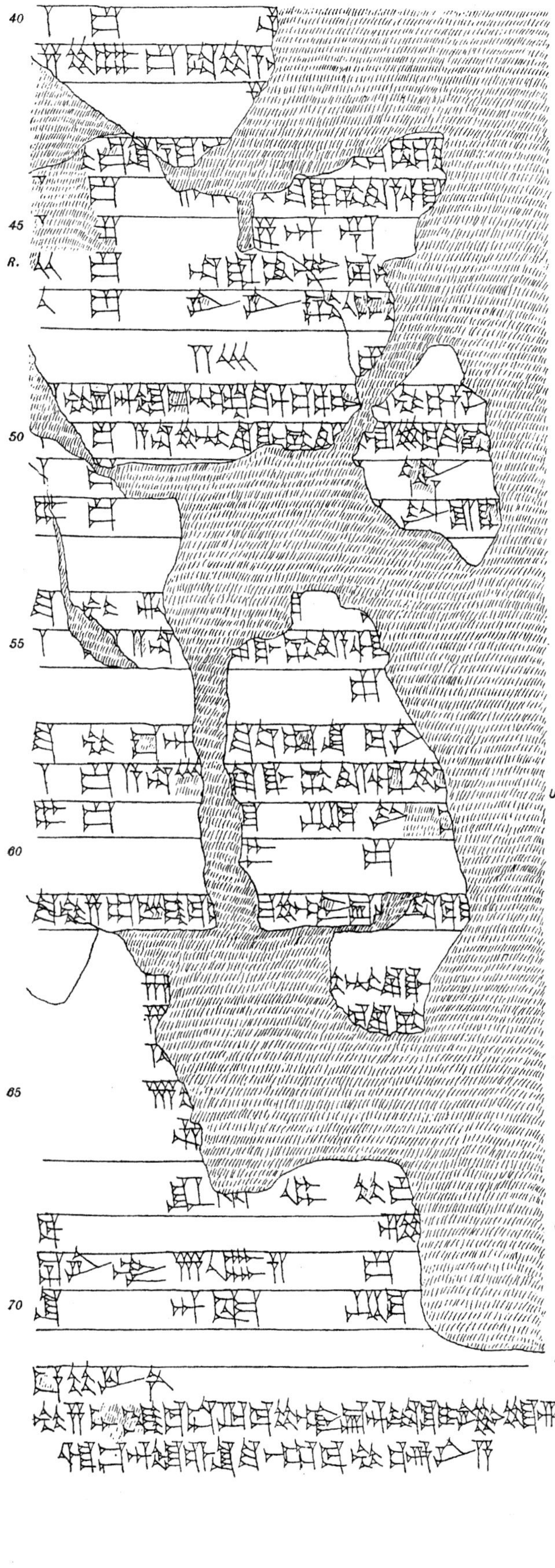

203

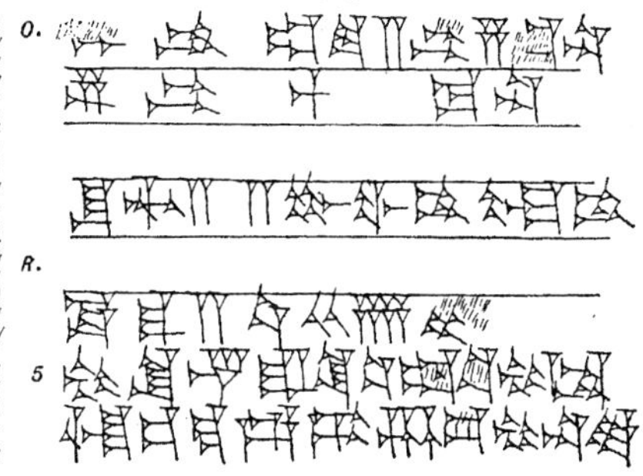

204

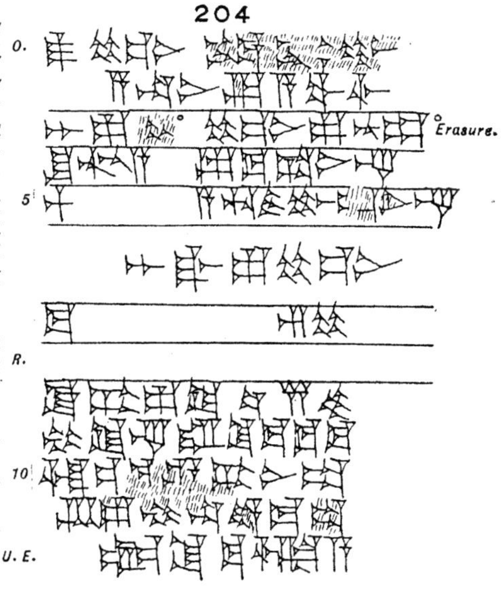

205

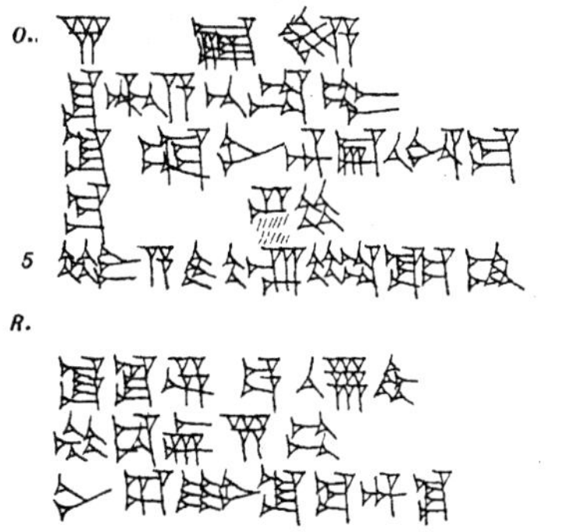

206

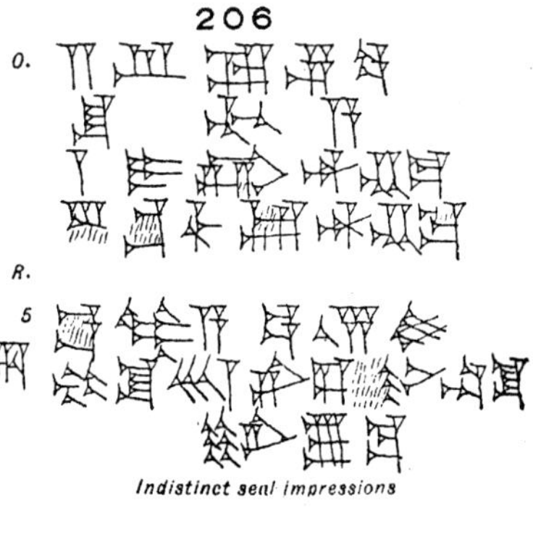

Indistinct seal impressions

OBVERSE

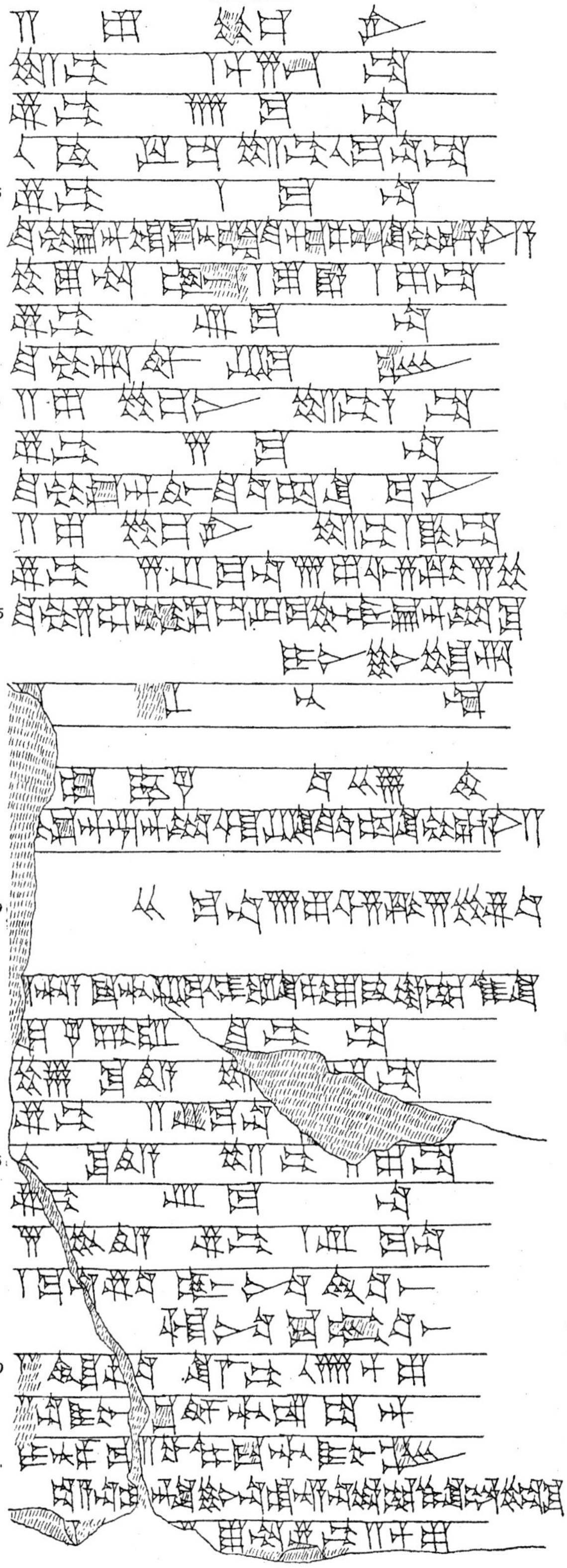

REVERSE

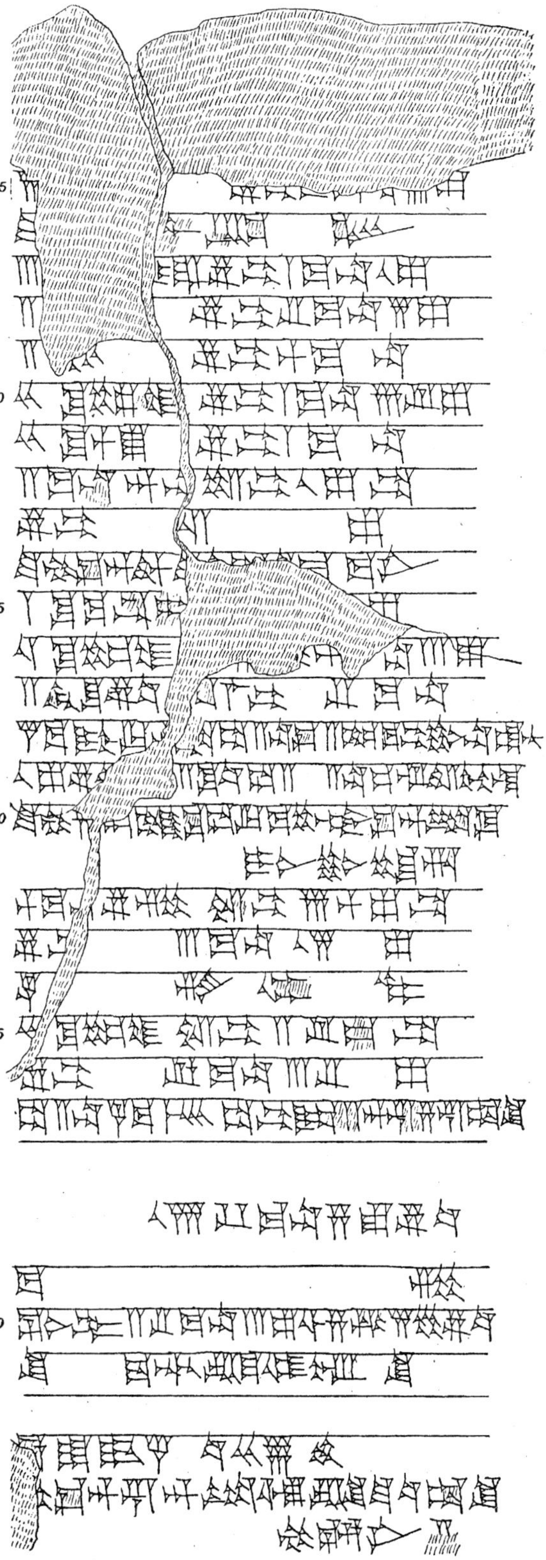

208

OBVERSE

COL I. COL II

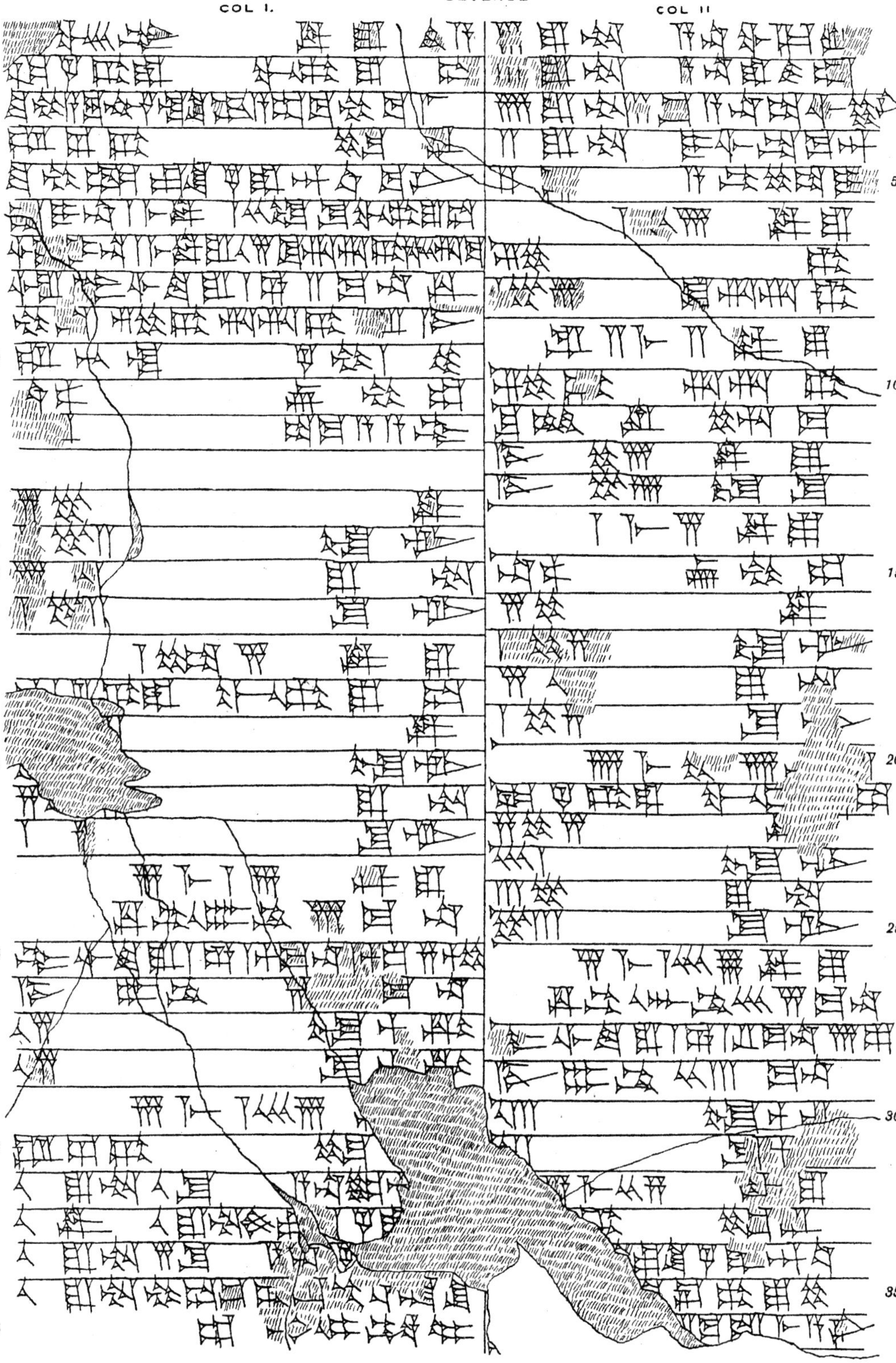

REVERSE

COL. IV. COL. III.

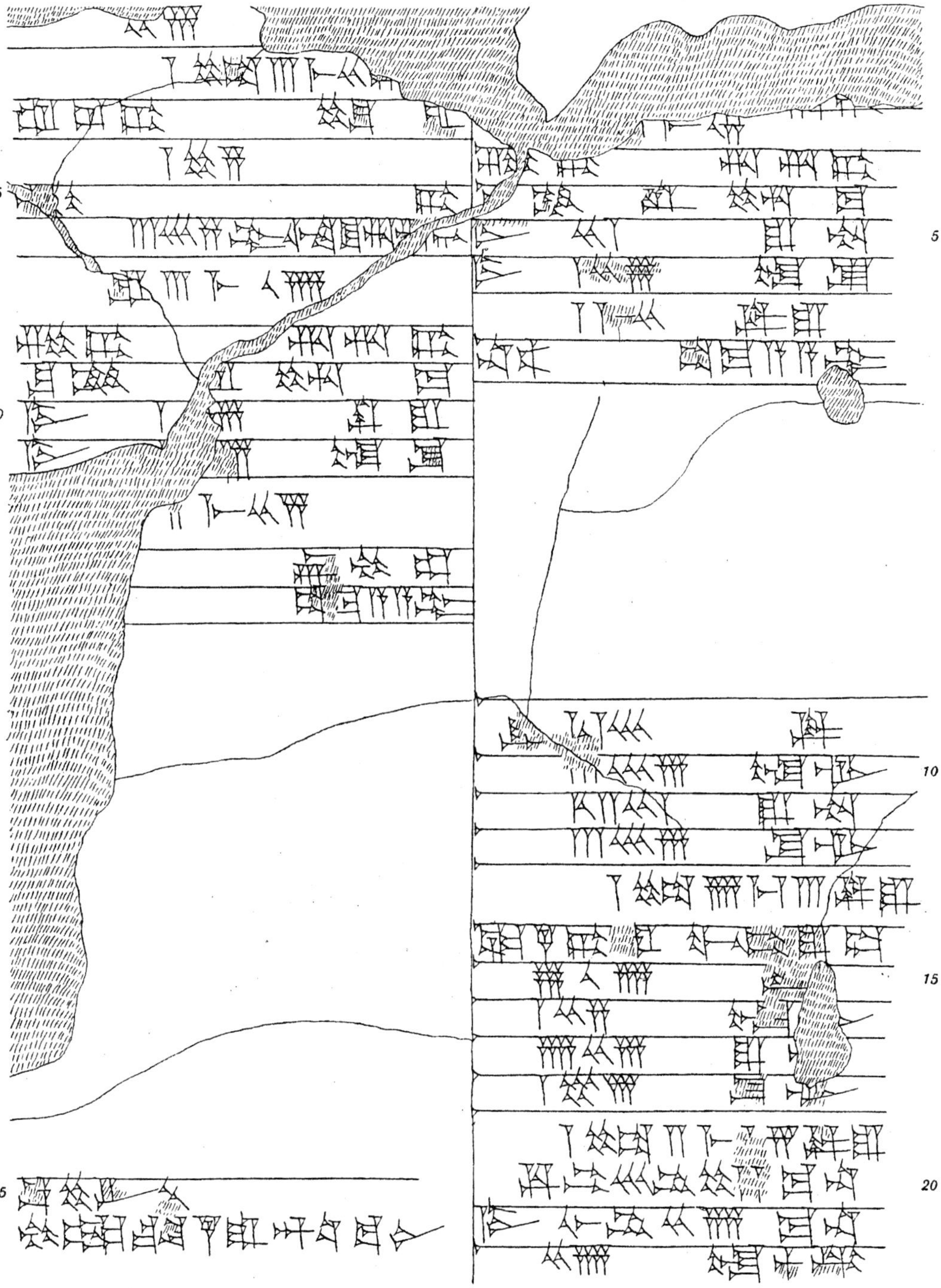

209

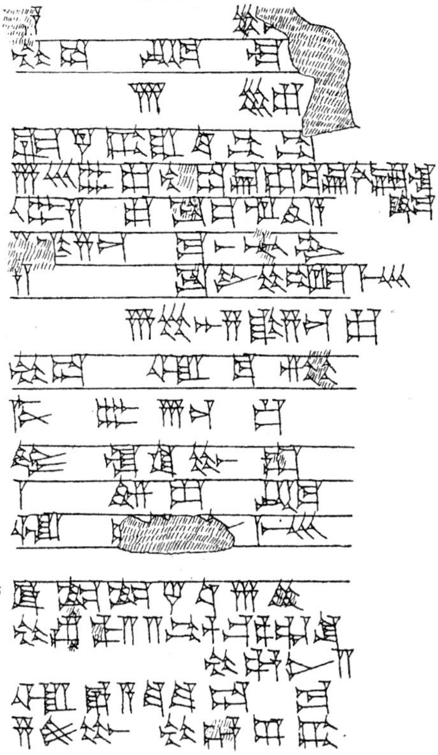

210

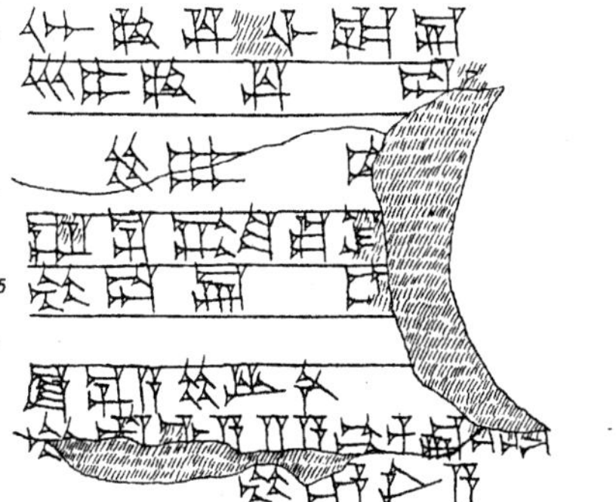

211

212

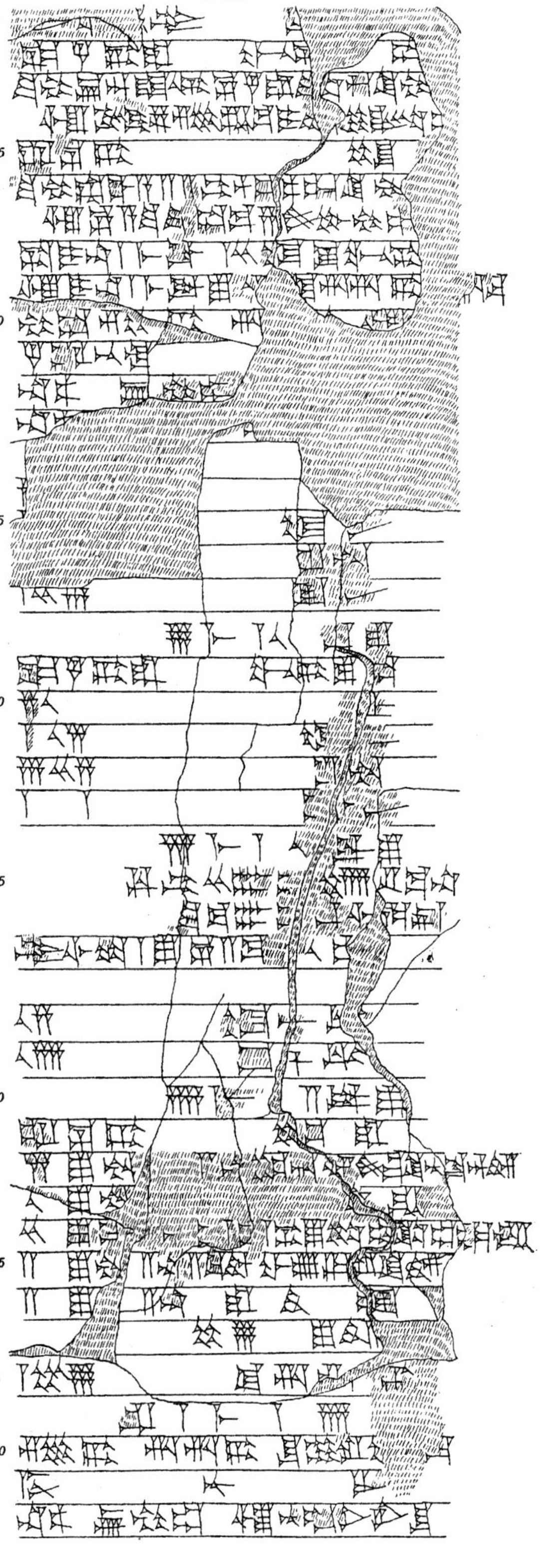

CONTINUED

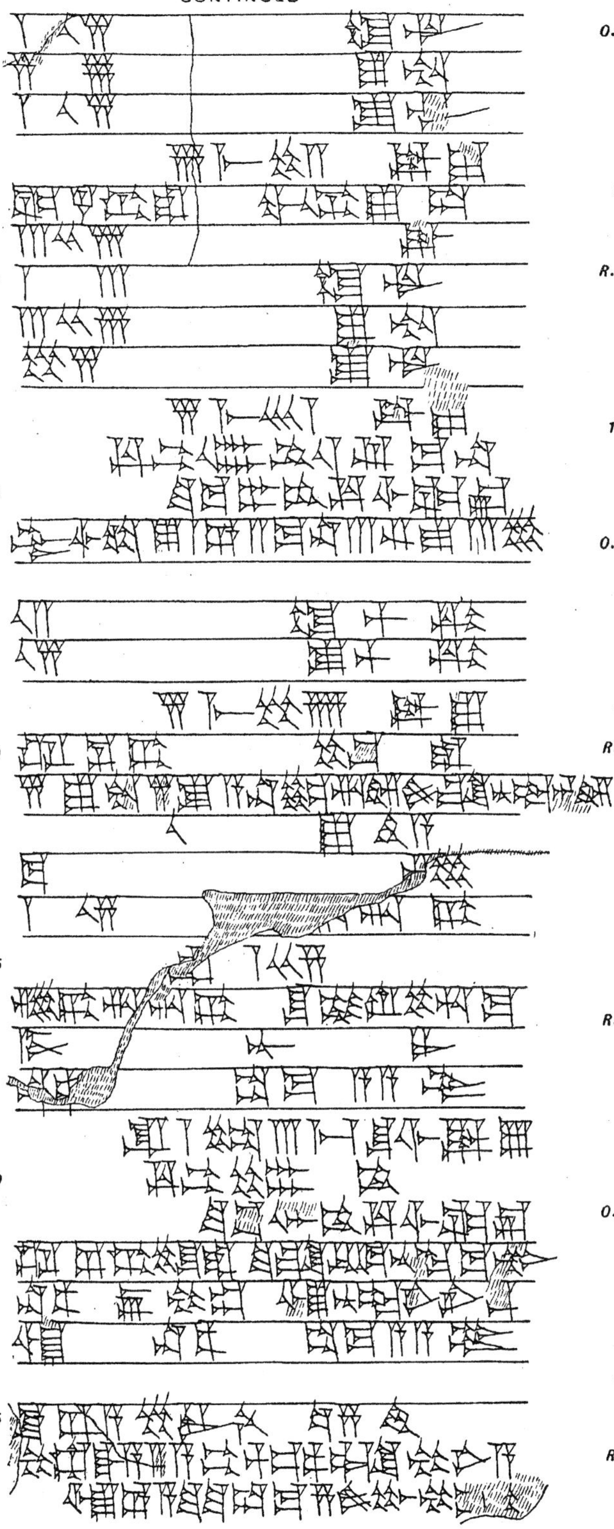

213

O. / R.

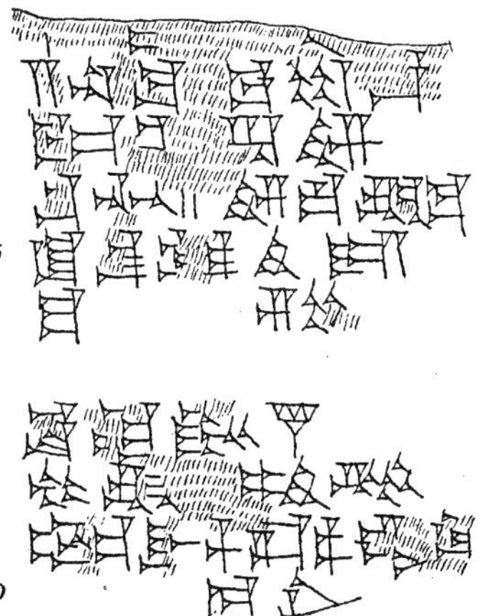

Indistinct seal impressions

214

O. / R.

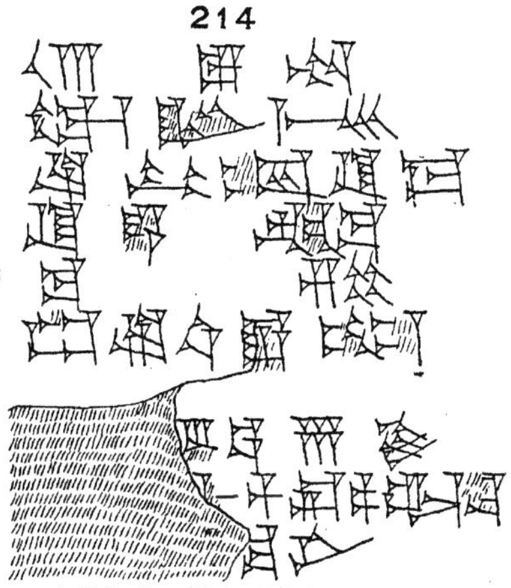

Indistinct seal impressions

215

R.

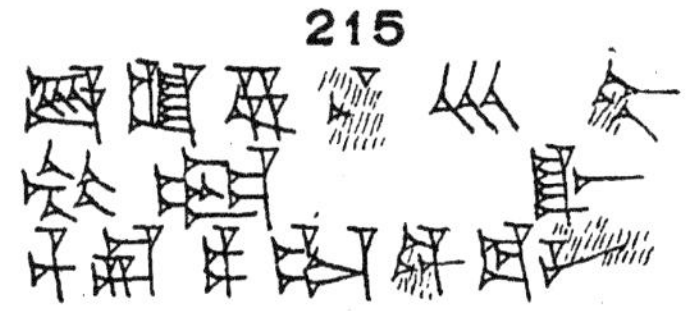

216

O. / R.

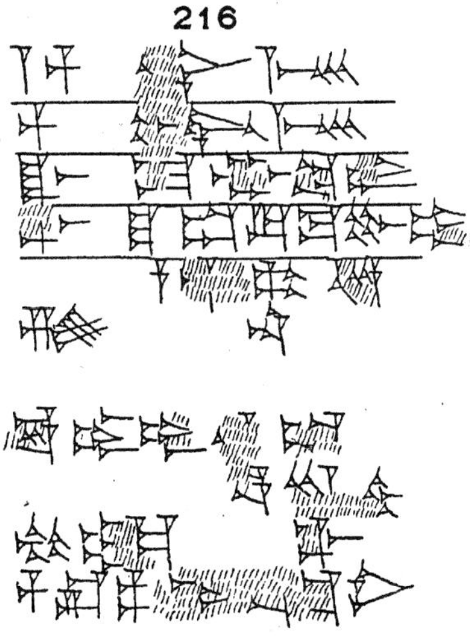

217

OBVERSE

COL I — COL II

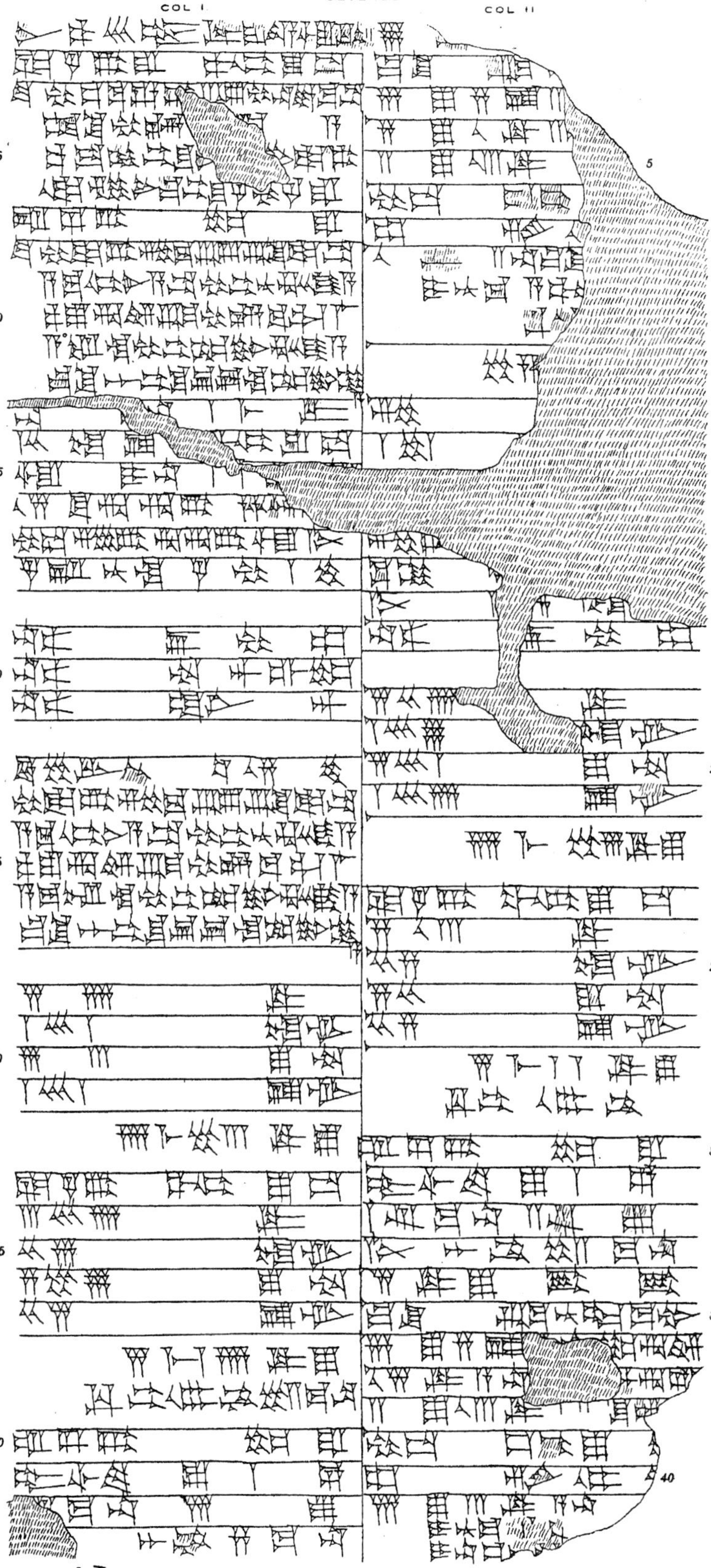

° [sign] *omitted by scribe.*

REVERSE

COL. IV. COL. III.

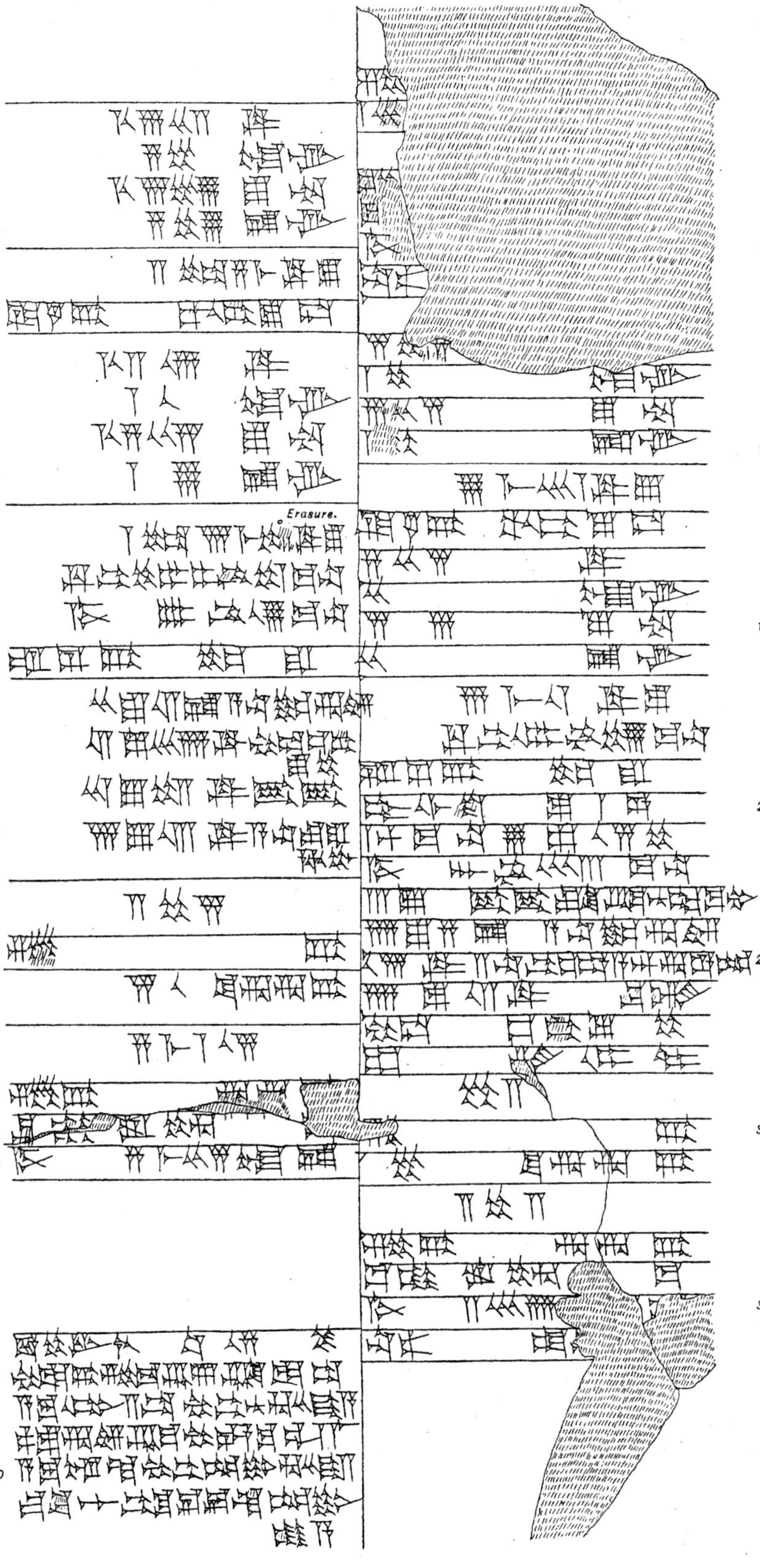

218

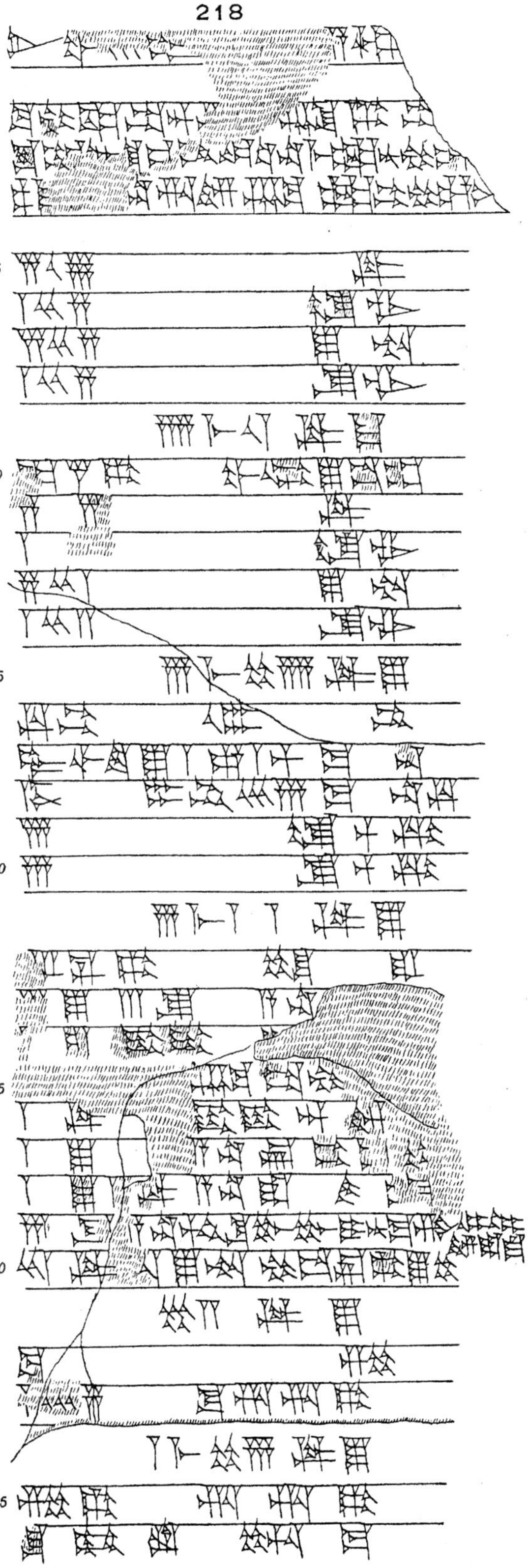

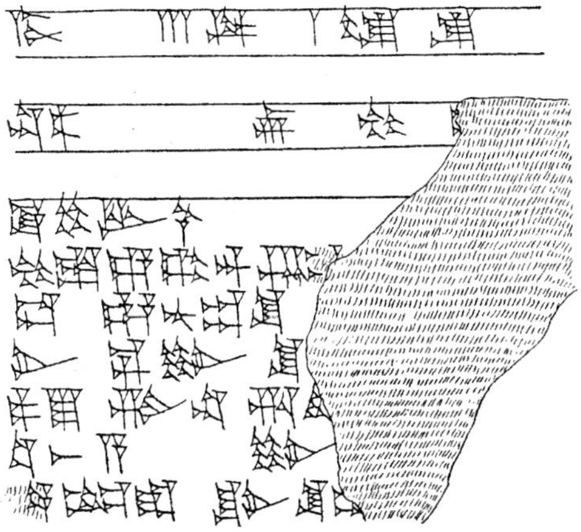

219

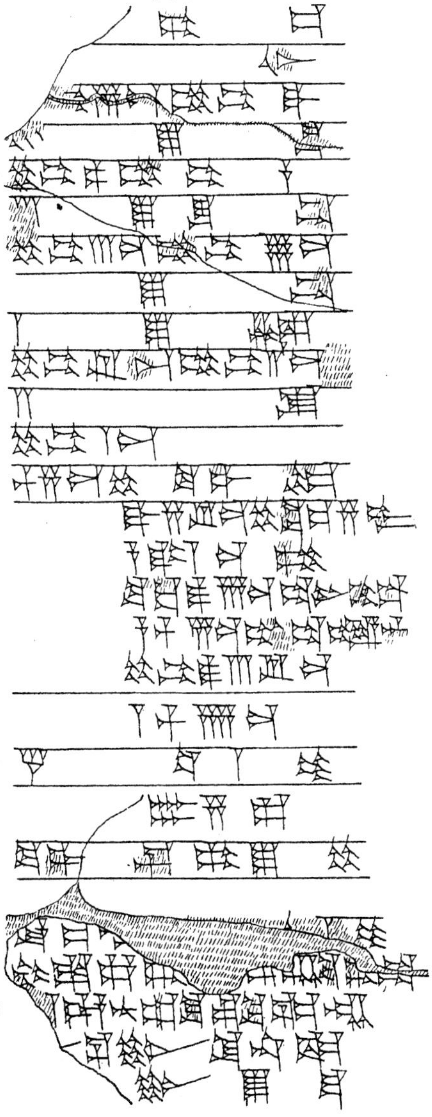

PLATE LXXXIII

220

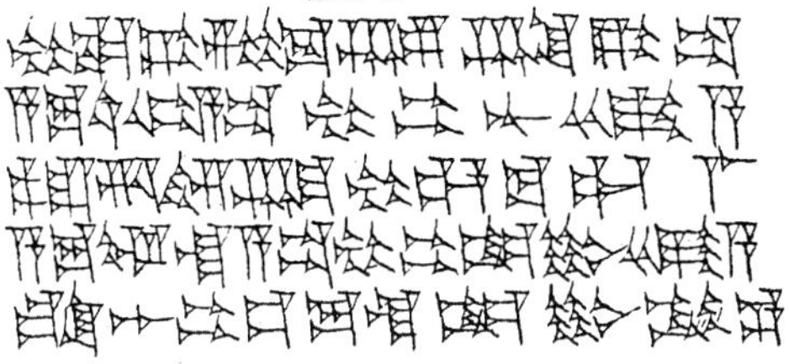

221

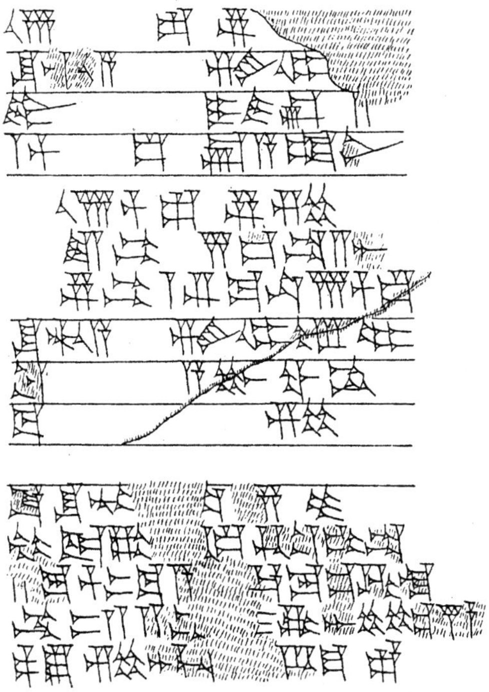

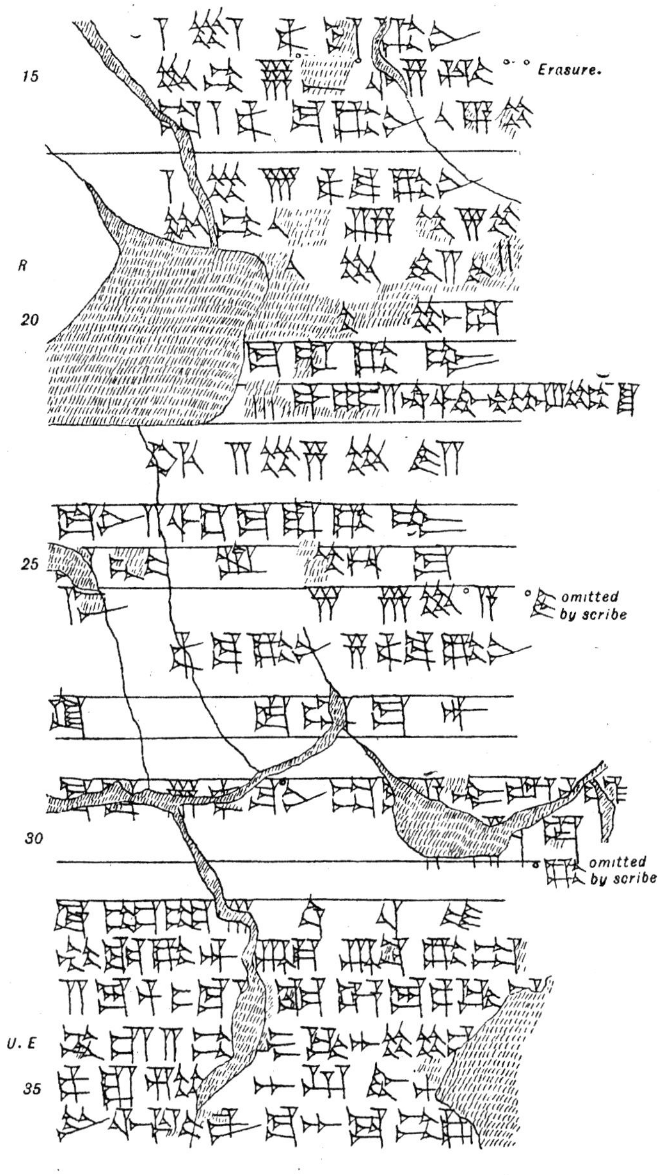

222

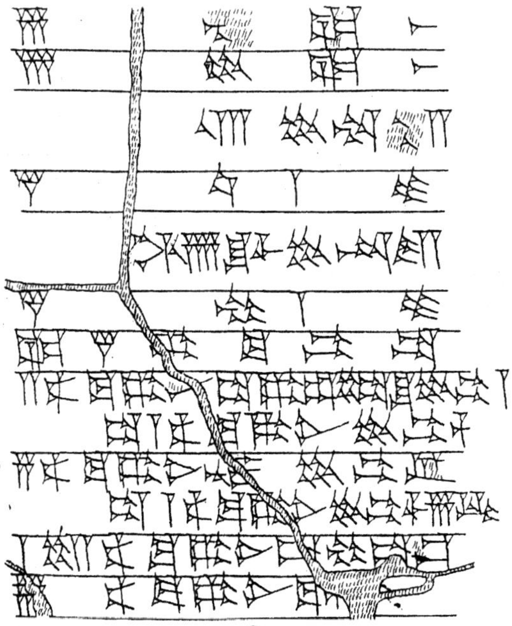

223

224

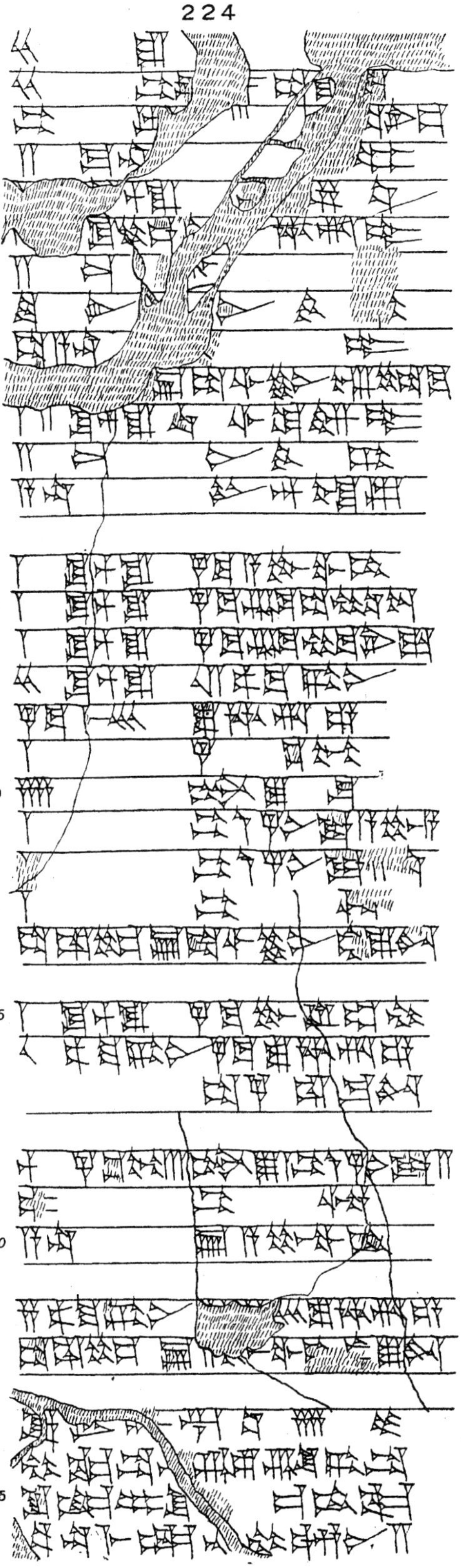

225

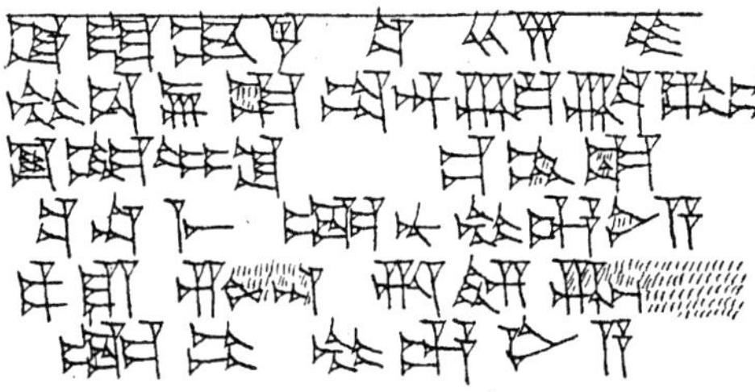

226

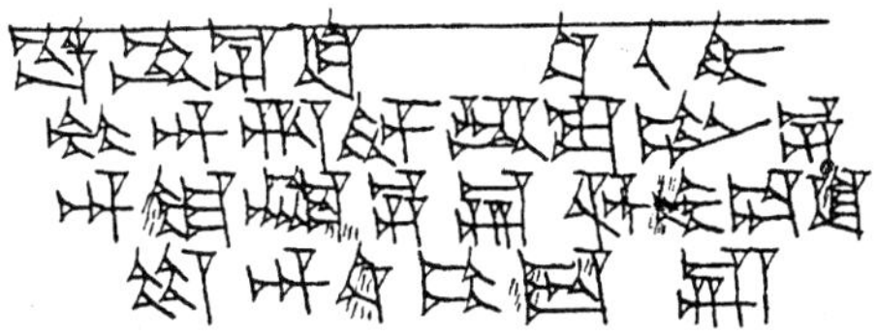

227

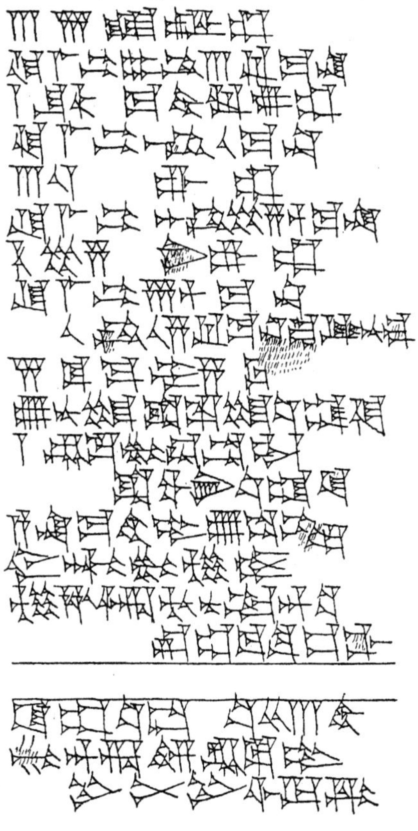

228

O.

R.

229

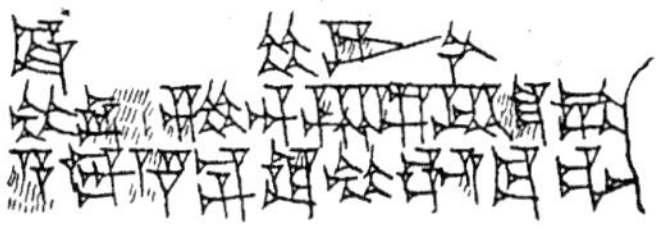

230

231

O.

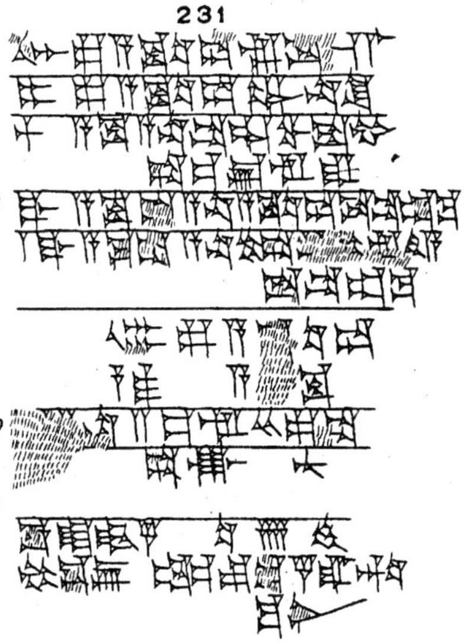

R.

232

O.

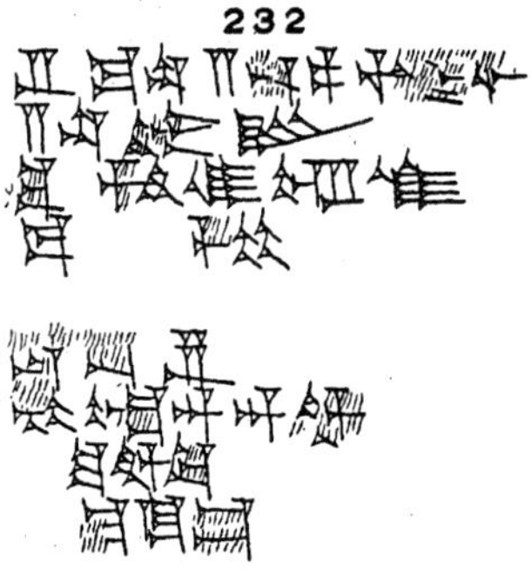

R.

Indistinct seal impressions.

233

O.

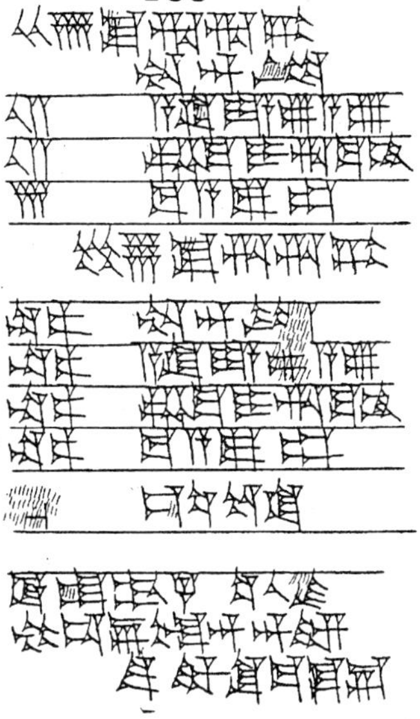

R.

234

O.

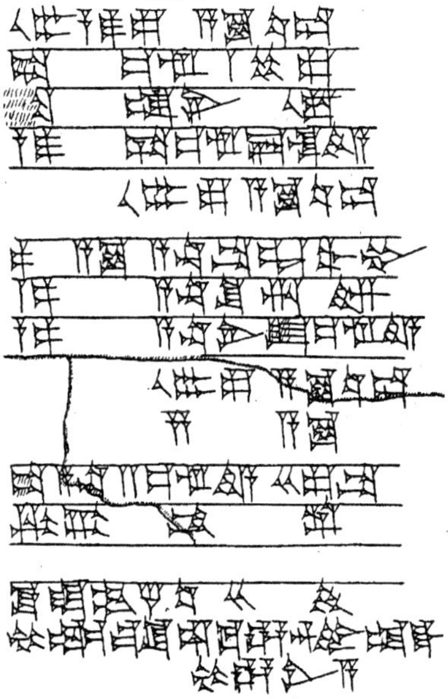

R.

235

O

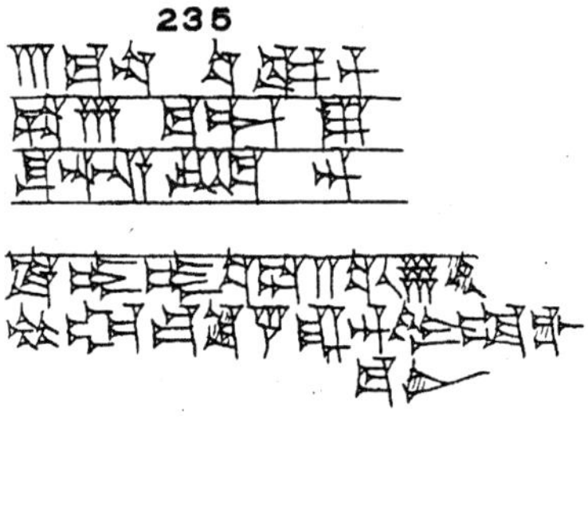

R.

236

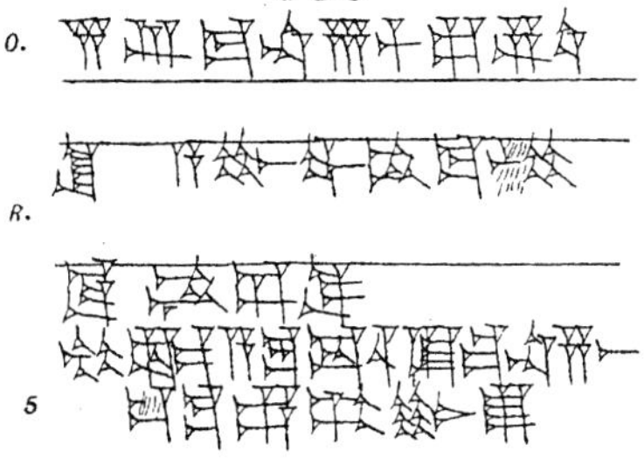

237

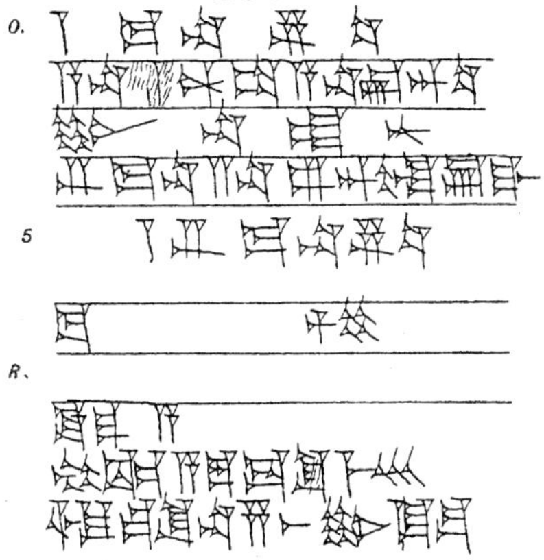

238

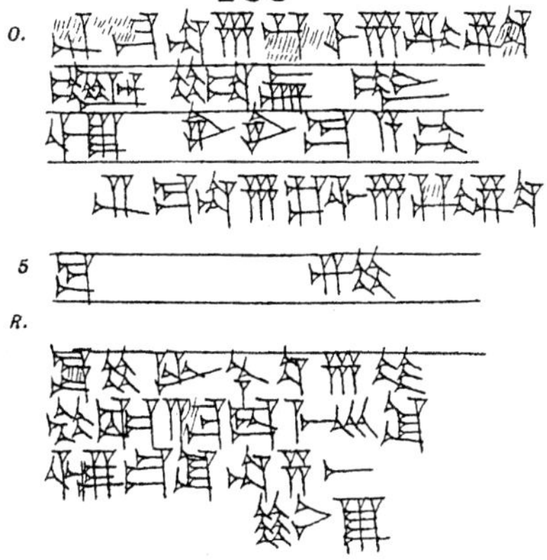

239

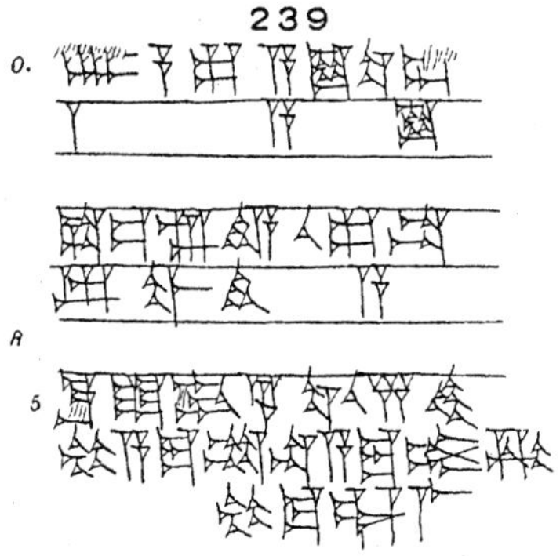

240

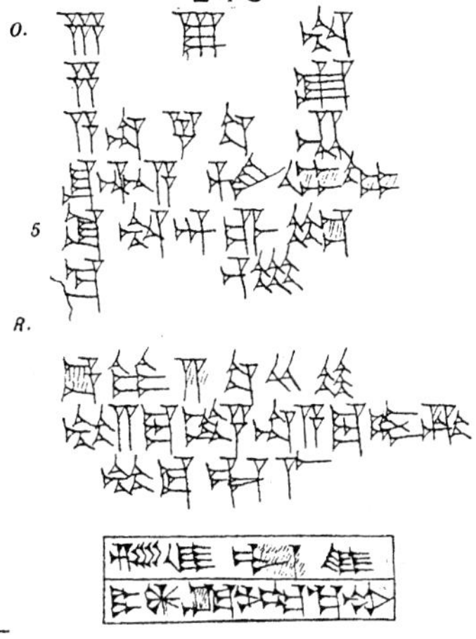

241

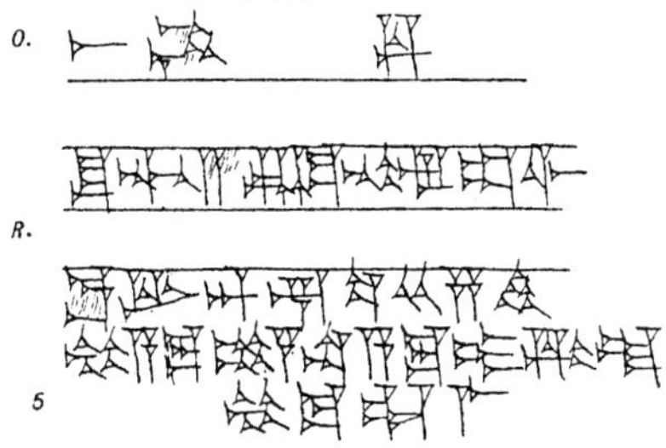

242

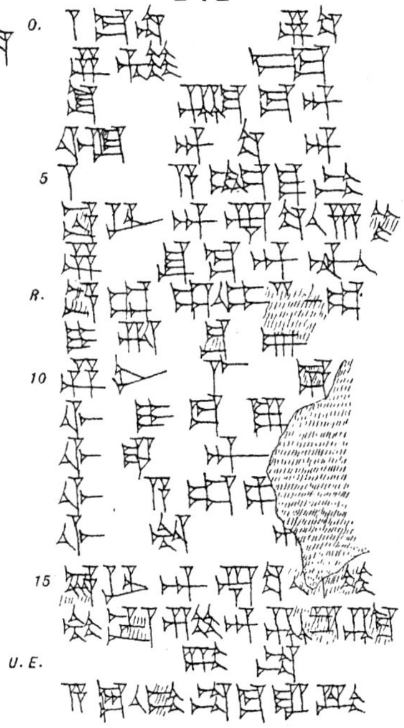

243

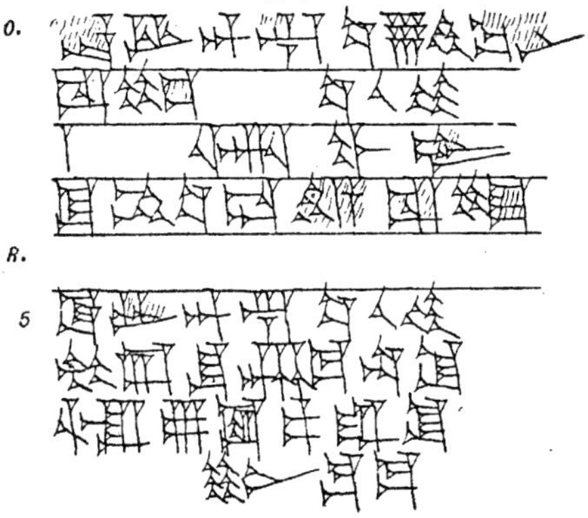

246

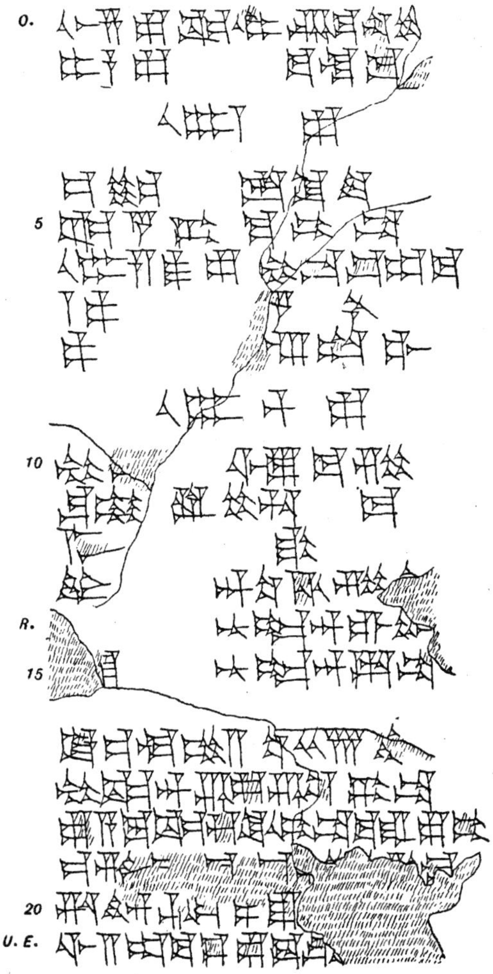

244

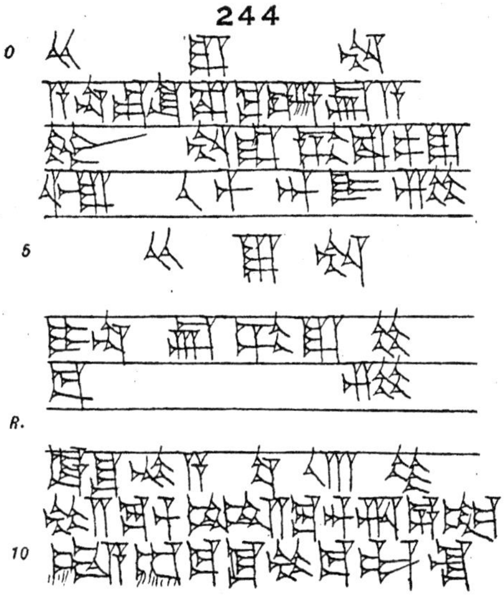

245

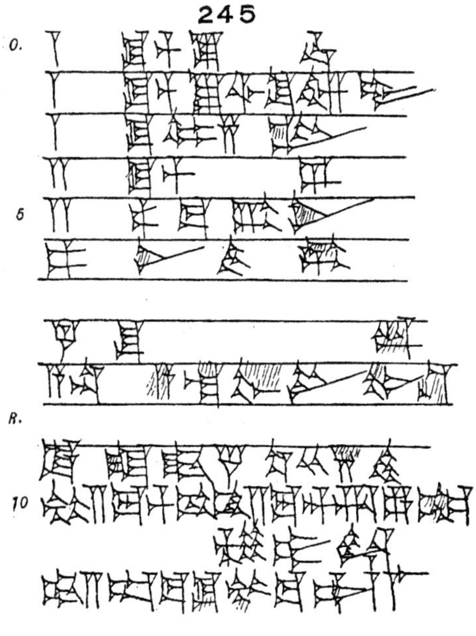

247

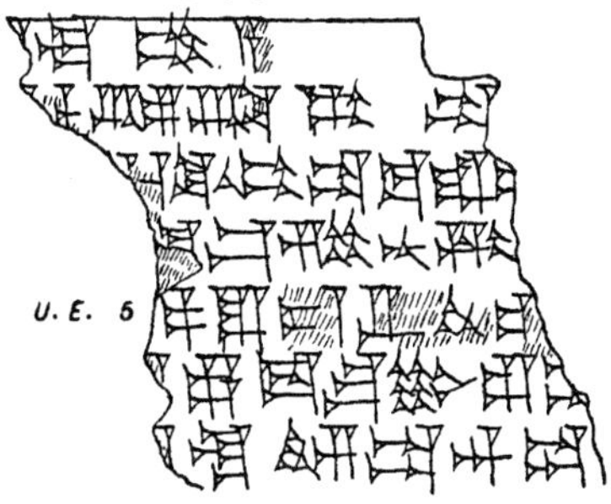

248

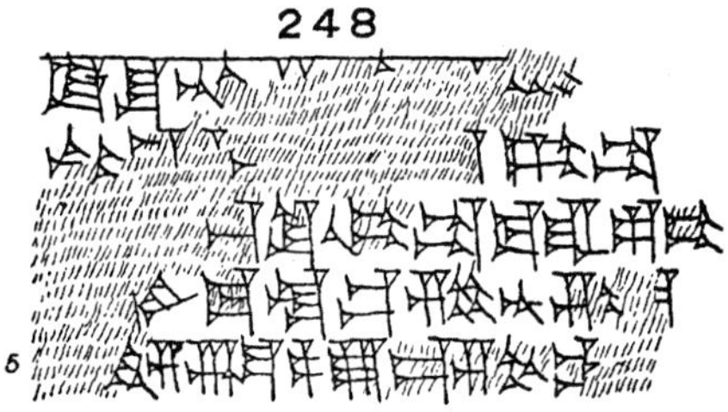

249

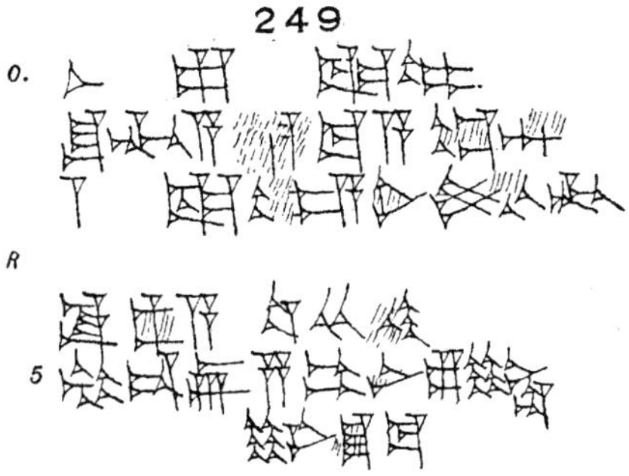

Indistinct seal impressions.

250

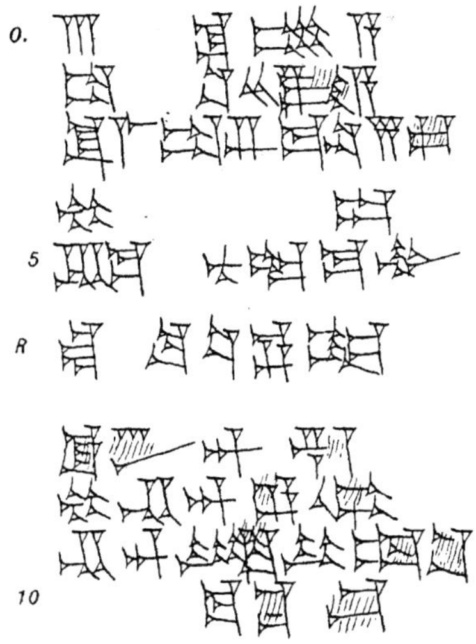

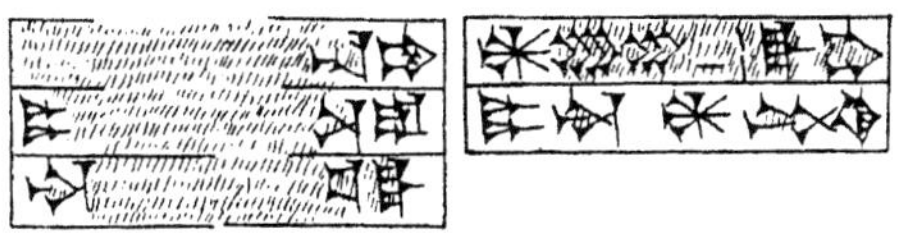

251

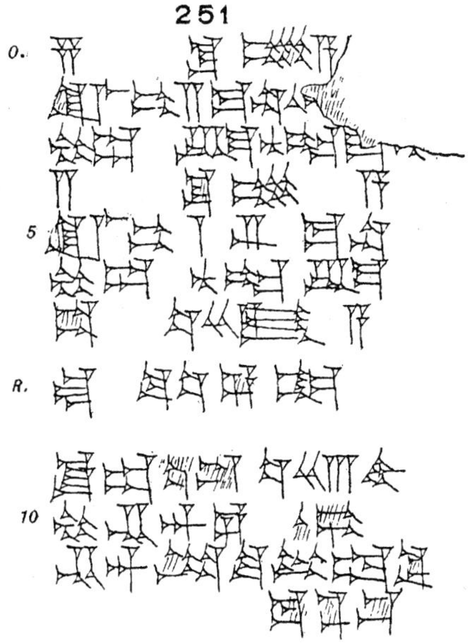

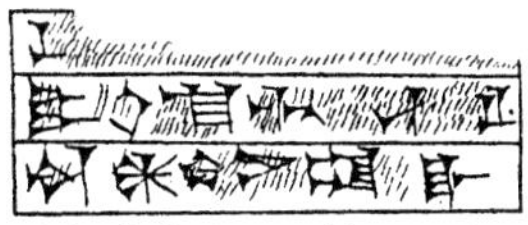

Other indistinct seal impressions.

252

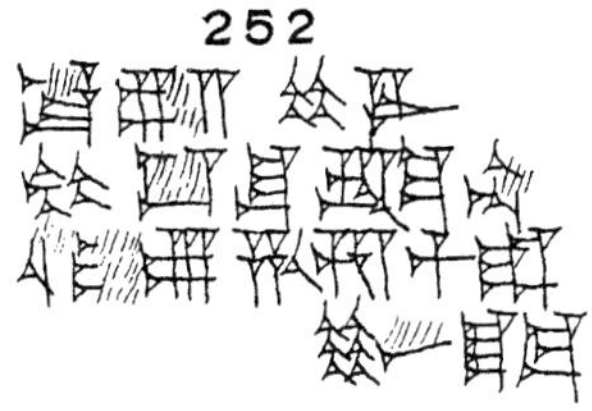

253

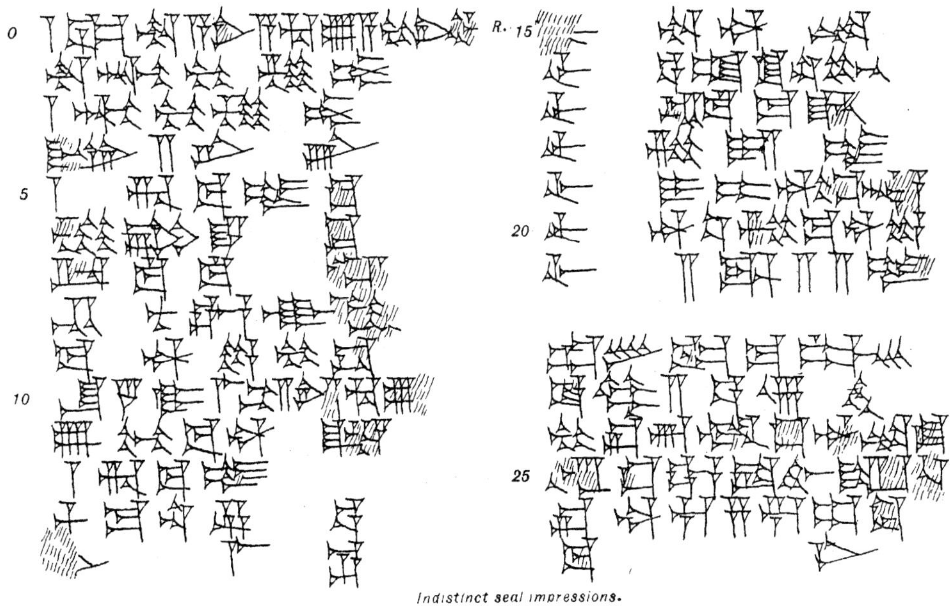

Indistinct seal impressions.